Crime On-Line

Crime On-Line

Correlates, Causes, and Context

SECOND EDITION

Edited by

Thomas J. Holt
MICHIGAN STATE UNIVERSITY

CAROLINA ACADEMIC PRESS
Durham, North Carolina

Library of Congress Cataloging-in-Publication Data

Crime on-line : correlates, causes, and context / [edited by] Thomas J. Holt. -
- 2nd ed.
    p. cm.
Includes bibliographical references and index.
ISBN 978-1-61163-105-0 (alk. paper)
1. Computer crimes. I. Holt, Thomas J., 1978-

HV6773.C763 2012
364.16'8--dc23

2012042057

CAROLINA ACADEMIC PRESS
700 Kent Street
Durham, North Carolina 27701
Telephone (919) 489-7486
Fax (919) 493-5668
www.cap-press.com

Printed in the United States of America

This work is dedicated to the contributors to this text, as well as to those young scholars whose research will steer the field of inquiry into cybercrimes and Internet-based deviance over the next decade.

Contents

Tables and Figures   xi

Acknowledgments   xv

1   Crime On-Line: Correlates, Causes, and Context
    Thomas J. Holt   3

    Defining and Measuring Cybercrime   6
    Cybercrime Framework   10
       Cyber-trespass   10
       Cyber-deception/Theft   11
       Cyber-porn and Obscenity   13
       Cyber-violence   15
    The Structure of This Book and Its Contributions   16
    References   18

2   Hacker Woodstock: Observations on an Off-line Cyber Culture
    at the Chaos Communication Camp 2011
    Patrick T. Kinkade, Michael Bachmann, and Brittany Smith-Bachmann   27

    Hacker Culture   29
    Perspectives, Procedures, and Settings   34
    Identity Assignments within a Grounded Online Culture   37
    The Emergent Grounded Hacker Culture   44
    The Vocabulary of Motives   48
    Conclusion   51
    References   53

3   The Evolution of Online Piracy: Challenge and Response
    Johnny Nhan   61

    Review of the Literature   62
    Individual Motivations and Factors Influencing Participation in Piracy
       Activities   62
    The Impact and Harm of Piracy   65

Enforcement of Piracy Laws   65
Timeline   67
    The Digital Transition: From Hard Goods to Soft Goods   67
    Website Hosting Music   68
    Peer-to-Peer: The Napster Era   69
    Peer-to-Peer: BitTorrent Era   70
    Litigation   72
    Internet Culture   74
Conclusion and Limitations   75
References   76

4 **Understanding Online Work-at-Home Scams through an Analysis of Electronic Mail and Websites**
   Sarah Turner, Heith Copes, Kent R. Kerley, and Gary Warner   81

Work-at-Home Scams   82
Online Fraud in Context   83
Data and Methodology   85
Analysis of Emails   88
Analysis of Websites   94
Discussion and Conclusions   104
References   107

5 **Internet Child Pornography: Legal Issues and Investigative Tactics**
   Marcus K. Rogers and Kathryn C. Seigfried-Spellar   109

Scope and Context   110
The COPINE Project   113
The Courts and COPINE   115
A Hypothetical Case Study   117
Criticisms of Court Image Classifications   119
Classification System for the United States   121
Technical Investigations   122
Lanning Model   123
Krone Model   124
Rogers and Seigfried-Spellar Hybrid Model   126
Case Study   130
Conclusions   136
References   137

6 **Examining Cyberstalking and Bullying: Causes, Context, and Control**
   Catherine Marcum   141

Cyberbullying   142

Prevention of Cyberbullying   145
Cyberstalking   146
Prevention of Cyberstalking   149
Emergence of Legislation   149
Addressing Free Speech Issues   151
Conclusion   152
References   153

7 **The Internet as a Tool for Terrorists: Implications for Physical
   and Virtual Worlds**
   Marjie T. Britz   159

Defining Terrorism   161
Traditional Definitions of Cyberterrorism   164
Operationalizing Cyberterrorism as a Multipurpose Tool   165
Propaganda, Information Dissemination, and Recruitment   166
The Internet as a Medium of Communication   173
Training, Research, and Facilitation   176
As an Attack Vector   179
Conclusions   183
References   184

8 **Industrial Control Systems and Cybercrime**
   Aunshul Rege   191

Industrial Control Systems   192
Industrial Control System Vulnerabilities   194
Industrial Control System Threats   196
Critical Infrastructure Cybercrime Cases   197
    Oil and Gas Infrastructure   199
    Transportation Infrastructure   199
    Sewage Infrastructure   200
    Finance and Communication Infrastructure   200
    Power Infrastructure   201
The Brief Criminological Industrial Control System Cybercrime
    Research   201
Expanding the Criminological Lines of Inquiry   205
Primary Data Collection   206
Offender Decision-Making, Crime Scripts, and Situational Crime
    Prevention   206
Simulation Studies and Agent Based Modeling   208
Trend Analysis   208
Physical Components of Industrial Control System Cyberattacks   209

Glossary   210
References   211

9 **Examining State and Local Law Enforcement Perceptions of
   Computer Crime**
   Thomas J. Holt, Adam M. Bossler, and Sarah Fitzgerald   219

   Policing Computer Crime   221
   Data   224
   Findings   225
      Demographic Composition   225
      Investigations   227
      Attitudes toward Computer Crime   229
      Perceptions of Computer Crime Offending   231
      Awareness of Technology   236
   Discussion and Conclusions   238
   References   240

Contributors   245

Index   249

Tables and Figures

Tables

4 Understanding Online Work-at-Home Scams through an Analysis
of Electronic Mail and Websites   81

   Table 1   Message Content of Work-at-Home Email   89
   Table 2   Personalization and Targeting of Work-at-Home
              Email Content   90
   Table 3   Message Legitimacy Claims in Work-at-Home Email   91
   Table 4   Financial Aspects of Work-at-Home Email   92
   Table 5   Branding and Legitimacy Work-at-Home Email   93
   Table 6   Layout of Work-at-Home Websites   94
   Table 7   Advertised Work Opportunities in Work-at-Home Websites   99
   Table 8   Testimonials and Gender in Work-at-Home Websites   100
   Table 9   Financial Matters in Work-at-Home Websites   101
   Table 10   Legitimacy of Work-at-Home Websites   103
   Table 11   Information About Work-at-Home Websites   103
   Table 12   Compete Rankings of Work-at-Home Websites   104

5 Internet Child Pornography: Legal Issues and Investigative Tactics

   Table 1.   The Suggested Canadian System for Classifying Images
              Seized in Child Pornography Related Cases   117
   Table 2   Classification System of Images Seized from Child
              Pornography Cases Suggested for the United States of
              America by Rogers and Seigfried-Spellar   124
   Table 3A   Lanning Computer Offender Typology   128
   Table 3B   Rogers Seigfried-Spellar Hybrid Model   128

8 Industrial Control Systems and Cybercrime

   Table 1   Summary of Industrial Control Systems, Vulnerabilities
              and Threats   198

Table 2   Summary of Industrial Control System Cybercrime
           Incidents   202

9 Examining State and Local Law Enforcement Perceptions
  of Computer Crime
Table 1   Size and Geographic Location of Law Enforcement Agencies 225
Table 2   The Percentage of Officers Trained for Digital Evidence
           and Computer Crime   227
Table 3   Types of Computer Crimes Investigated by State and
           Local Agencies   228
Table 4   Number of Active Cases Involving Digital Evidence or
           Computer Crime   229
Table 5   Officers' Reported Attitudes Toward Computer Crimes   230
Table 6   Perceived Severity of Computer Crimes   232
Table 7   Perceived Frequency of Computer Crimes   234
Table 8   Perceived Threat of Cyberterror Attacks from
           Multiple Nations   235
Table 9   Knowledge of Terms Related to Computer Technology
           and Computer Crime   236
Table 10   Knowledge of Terms Related to Computer Technology
           and Computer Crime   237

Figures

4 Understanding Online Work-at-Home Scams through an Analysis
  of Electronic Mail and Websites   81
Figure 1   Example of Piggybacking Website   95
Figure 2   Example of News Report Website   95
Figure 3   Reader Comments from News Report Website   96
Figure 4   Work-at-Home Website Asking for Personal Information   97
Figure 5   Work-at-Home Website Asking for Registration   97
Figure 6   Example of Work-at-Home "Regular" Website   97
Figure 7   Example of Website Asking to Make a Purchase   98
Figure 8   Example of "Other" Type of Work-at-Home Website   99
Figure 9   Image of Check Found on Work-at-Home Website   102

5 Internet Child Pornography: Legal Issues and Investigative Tactics

Figure 1   A Hypothetical Collection of Images   118
Figure 2   Directory Listing   131
Figure 3   Recycle Bin   131
Figure 4   User Accounts   132
Figure 5   Cookies Folder   132
Figure 6   Cookie Content Information   133
Figure 7   Browser History   134
Figure 8   Browser History   135

Acknowledgments

As the field of criminological research on cybercrime continues to evolve, I am grateful to the many individuals whose assistance and contributions to this edited work facilitated its creation, value, and applicability. I am very grateful to those authors whose revised chapters help document the shifts in policy and practice in the field. Also, my thanks go to those authors whose chapters are appearing in this second edition for the first time. Their research is helping to shape the field and includes several scholars whose work provides excellent insights into underexamined issues in the field. These contributions compose the intellectual core of this work, and should help define and identify new areas of research in criminology and criminal justice. As the empirical investigation of cybercrime gains greater prominence in the social sciences, my hope is that this work will provide guidance to the discipline. I must also thank the various reviewers whose feedback helped improve the quality and theoretical impact of the chapters who appear in this work. Great thanks are also due to the publishing team at Carolina Academic Press, especially Beth Hall for her assistance throughout the creation and submission of this second edition. I appreciate all of their efforts to market the book and ensure its success. Finally, I would like to thank my family and friends for all of their support throughout this process, most especially my wife Karen for all of her love and assistance.

Crime On-Line

1

Crime On-Line: Correlates, Causes, and Context

Thomas J. Holt

In 2009, Heartland Payment Systems announced that their system security had been compromised during 2008 by a small group of hackers. The company processes over 11 million credit and debit card transactions for over 250,000 business across the US. The impact of the breach was massive, as hackers were able to acquire information from 130 million credit and debit cards processed by 100,000 businesses (Verini 2010). This was the largest breach of customer data in the United States and was thought to stem from malicious software planted inside of the company's network in order to record payment data sent from retail clients (Krebs 2011). Even more disconcerting, this breach was apparently masterminded by Albert Gonzales and a few other hackers who compromised the payment systems of Marshalls department stores and its parent company, TJX, a few years prior. That compromise led to the loss of 45 million credit card records and over $1 billion dollars in customer damages (Roberts 2007). Thus, these actors were not simply hackers who were lucky enough to make one big score. Instead, they were proficient and dedicated repeat offenders who sought out high value targets in succession and made lucrative profits as a result.

The scope of these attacks is quite large and serves as an unfortunate example of the myriad criminal incidents that stem from the use of computer technology and the Internet. News reports have increased worldwide regarding the tremendous impact of computer attacks against businesses and personal web users alike (Furnell 2002; Taylor, Fritsch, Liederbach, and Holt 2010). Press coverage of viruses and malicious software indicate the risks that many computer users face from computer based attacks (Brenner 2008; Wall 2007). There is also growing evidence that technology is being used to facilitate social protests against governments on and off-line, as evident in the recent Arab Spring

(Stepanova 2011) and cyber attacks by the group Anonymous (Denning 2011). The totality of these issues emphasizes the need to understand how modern society can cope with the threats posed by the ubiquity of technology.

In fact, access to computers and high-speed Internet connectivity have dramatically changed the way people communicate and do business around the world, with far reaching consequences that affect all facets of modern life (Jewkes and Sharpe 2003). Most every critical financial, government, medical, business, and private entity is connected through the global interconnected computer networks which constitute the Internet. As a result, a massive amount of information and resources can be leveraged to benefit consumers and citizens. Businesses depend on the Internet to draw in commerce and make information available on demand. The banking and financial industries have implemented new technology enabling customers to gain electronic access to their funds and manage accounts.

The ability to utilize these resources is derived directly from low-cost, easy-to-use home computers coupled with home-based, high-speed, dedicated Internet access. In fact, there are now 2.1 billion Internet users worldwide, and 245 million of those individuals reside within the US (Central Intelligence Agency 2011). The United States has the second largest population of Internet users worldwide, behind China. Individuals between the ages of 18 and 34 now own the most technological resources and are among the heaviest Internet users in the United States (Lenhart, Purcell, Smith, and Zickuhr 2010). There are approximately18 million youth on-line every day using CMCs in various ways. For instance, 89 percent of youth send or read email while on-line, and 81 percent play on-line games (Lenhart et al. 2010). In addition, individuals between the ages of 18 and 34 comprise 49 percent of the entire population of Facebook users in the United States (socialbakers 2011).

Smart phones and tablet PCs allow users to be connected to the Internet at all times to do everything from check email to regularly update social networking profiles. Over 80 percent of adults own a cell phone, and almost one third of those are smart phones that can be used to check their email or connect to the Internet (Smith 2011). Today, youth acquire their first cell phones when they are between the ages of 12 and 13 (Lenhart 2010).

Though the growth and penetration of computer technology has many benefits, it has also spawned a range of deviant and criminal behaviors with unique challenges to law enforcement and the legal system (Wall 1998, 2001; Yar 2005). As noted in the mass compromises discussed earlier, the prevalence of networked computers and databases enables individuals to come into contact with a massive number of potential victims with little effort. In fact, one of the common forms of fraud perpetrated on-line is Nigerian email schemes, where individuals claim to be foreign princes or bankers who need assistance in moving large sums of money (Holt and Graves 2007; Newman and Clarke 2003; Wall 2004). They request information from the e-mail recipients so that they can reuse the information for identity theft or bank fraud. Criminals can send out millions of e-mails in a short amount of time to identify and solicit potential victims for fraud schemes (Grabosky et al. 2001; Holt and Graves 2007; Newman and Clarke 2003). By casting a wide net of email messages, the offenders increase the likelihood of finding a victim that will respond (Buchanan and Grant 2001; Wall 2004). Thus, email and other computer-mediated communication methods are ideal for fraudsters because even if a small percentage of individuals respond, they can still obtain a significant amount of money or information (see Holt and Graves 2007; Newman and Clarke 2003).

Virtual environments are also an ideal mechanism for attacks against nation states and large groups due the ability to effectively compromise a target with minimal physical engagement and conceal the origin of the attack (Brenner 2008; Denning 2001). An excellent example of such an attack in action is that of Stuxnet, a computer worm that was used in attacks against the Natanz uranium enrichment facilities in Iran (Clayton 2010; Kerr, Rollins, and Theohary 2010). This malicious software was designed to specifically compromise and harm computer systems called Programmable Logic Controllers (PLCs) inside of centrifuges in these plants in order to surreptitiously but systematically hinder the development of the Iranian nuclear program (Clayton 2010; Kerr et al. 2010). Recent evidence suggests that this program was created by the United States under the Bush administration and actively implemented by an executive order of President Obama because it was thought that this sort of attack would be more targeted, difficult to detect, and produce fewer civilian casualties or collateral damage than a physical strike (Sanger 2012). As a result, cyber-attacks may be an increasingly common way for nation-states to engage one another to cause harm.

In addition, computer technology affords criminals a significant degree of anonymity. Individuals can create fictitious user profiles to hide their real identities, as with hackers who create screen names or "handles" that protect their actual identity while engaging in hacking (Jordan and Taylor 1998, 765). Similarly, individuals can use a variety of technology to mask their physical location. For example, individuals who pirate music and media often utilize a technology called "torrents" as a means of reducing their likelihood of detection (see Holt and Copes 2010). Torrent programs enable individuals to download bits of a larger file, such as a complete album or discography for a musical group or motion picture, from multiple computers, making it difficult to trace the original location of where the file was found or who actually maintains the media (Holt and Copes 2010).

In light of the significant threat posed by computer and cybercrimes, there is a strong need to identify and understand the nature of on-line criminality, as well as the causes and correlates of cybercrime. Thus, this chapter will provide an overview of computer and cybercrimes, including the complexities of defining these problems and measuring the prevalence and incidence of offenses. A framework to understand and examine cybercrime is also discussed in detail to give some insight into the diverse threats on-line. Finally, the chapter concludes by outlining the chapters of this book and their contribution.

Defining and Measuring Cybercrime

In order to understand cybercrime, one must first understand the nature of the Internet, on-line environments, and crime. The emergence and ubiquity of computer technology has led criminological scholarship to engage in some debate over this issue. Specifically, Grabosky (2001) argued that crime in cyberspace is "old wine in new bottles," in that traditional forms of offending are enabled through new tools. For example, criminals can very easily engage in identity theft through *low-tech* methods, such as stealing personal information from mailboxes or during the commission of a robbery or burglary (Allison, Schuck and Lersch 2005). Offenders may also use *high-tech* methods via computers and/or the internet to obtain personal information that is seemingly unprotected by the victim (Holt and Graves 2007; Newman and Clarke 2003). Computer technology simply provides another medium by which such information can be obtained from potential victims (Grabosky 2001).

Wall (1998), however, argued that the structure and power of virtual environments can be perceived as an issue of "new wine, but no bottles" (Wall 1998, 202). Specifically, the global reach of the Internet enables a scale of connectivity unparalleled in history. People can now form virtual communities that span the globe with speed and efficiency that were previously not possible. Individuals with sexual interests that are considered outside of societal norms quickly adapted to on-line environments, where they may operate in relative anonymity without fear of shame or social stigma (Rosenmann and Safir 2006). Technology also acts as a force multiplier, in that computing power and automation allow an individual, or "single agent," to engage in crimes that would have previously involved multiple partners (Pease 2001, 24; Wall 2007). This has forced a shift in the social organization of thieving, by decreasing the need for conspirators and divisions of labor, and is leading to a "new 'improved' underworld" where criminals can obtain all manner of resources and engage in crimes (Mann and Sutton 1998, 225; Holt and Lampke 2010). Thus, our traditional models of policing and law must be restructured to adequately deal with the challenges posed by this new environment.

To that end, there is some debate over the terms used to describe crimes involving computers in some fashion. The terms "cybercrime" and "computer crime" have become nearly synonymous, although there is a difference between these two events. Cybercrime refers to crimes "in which the perpetrator uses special knowledge of cyberspace," while computer crimes occur because "the perpetrator uses special knowledge about computer technology" (Furnell 2002, 21; Wall 2001). Despite the differences in these two events, the terms cybercrime and computer crime are frequently treated as interchangeable in popular media and academic literature (Furnell 2002). This work will use the term cybercrime due to the large number of offenses that can occur in on-line environments and the overwhelming number of computers that are connected to the Internet.

It is important to note, however, that these schemes are rather vague and are not the only definitions used by the law enforcement community. The Federal Bureau of Investigation, for example, does not use the classification cybercrime, only *computer crime*, "where the computer is the victim" (Stephenson 2000, 167). The U.S. Department of Justice uses a similarly open definition: "any violation of criminal law that involved the knowledge of computer technology for its perpetration, investigation, or prosecution" (Conly 1989, 6). These terms are both rather broad and obscure. The U.K. police, however, use a more specific typology that distinguishes between "computer-assisted crimes" and "computer-focused crimes" (Furnell 2002, 22). "Computer-assisted crimes" involve computers in a supporting role in the commission of a crime, although the activity could be performed without computer assistance, while incidents called "computer-focused crimes" are a direct result of computer technology, such as hacking and viruses (Furnell 2002, 22). This typology presents a clearer explication than other current definitions and illustrates the wide variety of terms used to classify computer crimes.

One of the most comprehensive definitions applied to computer-based crimes was used by the National Institute of Justice (Stambaugh et al. 2001) in their seminal study on the capacity of state and local law enforcement to handle cybercrime. Before conducting this study, the researchers recognized the complex issues surrounding the measurement and definition of computer-based offenses. Thus, they worked in collaboration with state and local agencies to develop a definition of "electronic crime" that refers to:

fraud, theft, forgery, child pornography or exploitation, stalking, traditional white-collar crimes, privacy violations, illegal drug transactions, espionage, computer intrusions, or any other offenses that occur
in an electronic environment for the purpose of economic gain or
with the intent to destroy or otherwise inflict harm on another person or institution (Stambaugh et al. 2001, 2).

A similarly broad definition of cyberterrorism was developed, recognizing any
"premeditated, politically motivated attack against information systems, computer programs and data ... to disrupt the political, social, or physical infrastructure of the target" (Stambaugh et al. 2001, 2). The wide range of offenses
included in these definitions was meant to provide some standard to assess
computer-based crime, though it is unclear how much the definition perme-
ates agency and academic definitions of cybercrime.

Some researchers utilize a different method to define cybercrimes through
comparisons of the laws made by various countries to identify criminal activity in cyberspace. As legislation against cybercrimes has increased dramatically
over the past ten years, some agreement has developed regarding what acts are
considered illegal on-line. For instance, the Global Cyber Law Survey of 50
countries, including nations in Africa, the Americas, Asia, Europe, the Middle East, and Oceania, found 70 percent of countries with laws against computer
crimes identified seven specific acts as prohibited (Putnam and Elliott 2001,
37). These acts, considered consensus crimes (based on the agreement in many
countries that these activities are criminal), include: unauthorized access,
computer-mediated espionage, privacy violations with personal data acquisition
or use, damage or theft of computer hardware or software, illicit tampering
with files or data, computer or network sabotage including denial-of-service
attacks and worms, and the use of information systems to commit fraud, forgery, and "traditional crimes" (Putnam and Elliott 2001, 38).

While comparative law analyses provide a helpful starting point for research,
it is important to note that few nations actually define what cybercrimes are,
only what behaviors constitute them. Most industrialized countries that are
heavily dependent on computers and information networks are the most likely
to have laws against computer crimes. Emerging industrial nations are less
likely to have developed such legislation, creating safe havens where cyber criminals can operate with minimal risk of extradition (Brenner 2008; Putnam and
Elliott 2001). This disparity in codified law adds to the difficulty of defining cybercrimes in a transnational context.

The lack of a clear or universal definition for cybercrime is also related to
the significant undercounting of cybercrimes (see Holt 2003; Taylor et al. 2010).

Part of this is due to user difficulty in recognizing when cybercrimes occur. Failing computer systems and hardware can mimic criminal acts or the results of criminal activities, obfuscating the situation (Symantec 2003; Stephenson 2000). In fact, almost 25 percent of personal computers around the world that use a variety of security solutions have malicious software, such as a virus, loaded into their memory (PandaLabs 2007). Thus, many individuals are victimized despite the presence and use of antivirus software and other protective programs to defend their system against the random nature of damaging computer attacks.

There are also a range of attacks that can occur in the workplace that may go unreported to law enforcement. Many in the general public believe intrusion attempts come largely from hackers outside of computer networks (Furnell 2002). For example, one estimate of losses due to one form of external attacks called a Denial of Service attack, which keeps others from accessing web based services, was an average of $187,506 for US companies in 2011 (Ponemon Institute 2011). This relatively small figure may not reflect all attacks that occur since businesses and financial institutions may lose face by reporting compromised systems (see also Holt 2003; Furnell 2002; Nasheri 2005). As a consequence, the true number and losses attributed to external penetration is unknown, but considered to be relatively significant and substantial (Newman and Clarke 2003).

Research involving case studies of insider attacks suggest that hackers may operate within secure environments as trusted system administrators or security professionals (Cappelli, et al. 2006; Dhillon and Moores 2001; Shaw et al. 1998). The actions employees take to misuse or misappropriate resources may go unnoticed, particularly by individuals with administrative privileges (Cappelli et al. 2006; Dhillon and Moores 2001). Insiders may also surreptitiously steal information or place backdoors in programs that can be accessed to cause damage in case they are fired or mistreated (see Cappelli et al. 2006; Shaw et al. 1998). The attacks individuals engage in can be relatively simple in nature and exploit known flaws in internal systems, though some sophisticated intrusions have been documented (see Cappelli et al. 2006). In these situations, office politics and management may enable cover-ups to occur that can increase the likelihood of non-reporting (see Shaw et al. 1998).

Confusion over where to file reports or complaints also leads to undercounting. As cybercrimes can cross state, territorial, and continental boundaries, jurisdictional issues can arise. In the U.S., for example, the involvement of local or federal law enforcement is dependent upon the crime and the extent of monetary damage to the victim. Unfortunately, many local police departments do not have the tools needed to enforce laws against cybercrime,

including knowledge, forensic equipment, and personnel, decreasing the potential for resolution of these crimes (Speer 2000, 267; Stambaugh et al. 2001).
Also, if an incident report must be passed from one agency to another after
being filed, the likelihood of resolution is further reduced. When expanded to
the international level where both the perpetrator and victim are in different
nations these problems are even greater in magnitude. Questions develop as to
who is responsible for the investigation along with other issues that can negatively affect a case, such as "the number of nations involved, the presence or
absence of extreme urgency, the existence of consent and the extent to which
the data sought is protected by firewalls, passwords, or encryption" (Putnam
and Elliott 2001, 62). These complications make undercounting a considerable problem, particularly at the international level, when coupled with the
absence of computer crime laws in some countries.

An even greater obstacle facing researchers is identifying actual statistical
measures for cybercrimes. Relatively few countries produce quality data on
these offenses, regardless of their level of industrialization. For example, only
two members of the G-8, an organization of economic world powers including the U.S., Canada, France, Germany, Japan, Italy, Russia, and the U.K.,
produce centralized official cybercrime statistics: the U.K. and Japan. Despite
its role as a world superpower, the United States does not provide much data
on computer crimes from a centralized outlet (Holt 2003; Goodman 2001).
Such information is notably absent from the FBI's Uniform Crime Report and
is just beginning to appear in the National Incident Based Reporting System (see
Taylor et al. 2010). As a consequence, there is a significant dark figure of cybercrime that requires further examination in the U.S. and abroad.

Cybercrime Framework

Though there is a paucity of statistics on cybercrime, a growing body of
criminological and sociological research has improved our understanding of the
forms of cybercrime that exist. One of the most well referenced and constructed
frameworks to understand cybercrimes is Wall's (2001) four category typology of computer crime to identify the wide range of behaviors encompassed
by computer based crimes.

Cyber-trespass

The first category is cyber-trespass, encompassing the crossing of invisible,
yet salient boundaries of ownership on-line. The most notable cybercriminals

engaging in acts of trespass are computer hackers, due to their desire to penetrate computer systems that they do not own (Furnell 2002; Jordan and Taylor 1998). One of the more comprehensive research definitions identifies hackers as those individuals with a profound interest in computers and technology that have used their knowledge to access computer systems for malicious or ethical purposes alike (see Holt 2007; Schell, Dodge and Moutsatsos 2002). The need for the inclusion of ethical applications lies in the fact that the term "hacker" was originally used as a term of respect for programmers in the 1950s and '60s who had significant computer skill (Jordan and Taylor 1998; Levy 1984; Holt 2007). Many in the general public, however, associate modern hackers with costly criminal breaches of computer networks and system boundaries (Furnell 2002; Schell et al. 2002).

Hackers are also responsible for malicious software programs, or malware, that automate a variety of attacks and break into computer systems (Furnell 2002). Malware typically includes computer viruses, worms, and Trojan horse programs that alter functions within computer programs and files. These programs can disrupt e-mail and network operations, access private files, delete or corrupt files, and generally damage computer software and hardware (Taylor et al. 2010). In addition, some forms of malicious software can enable identity theft, fraud, and the loss of personal information (Britz 2004; Taylor et al. 2010). Thus, malware infection poses a significant threat to Internet users around the globe.

The dissemination of viruses across computer networks can be costly due in part to the time spent removing the programs as well as losses in personal productivity and system functions (Symantec Corporation 2003; Taylor et al. 2010). This is reflected in the dollar losses associated with malware infection, as the average cost of an infection in a US business was $126,787 in 2011 alone (Ponemon Institute 2011). Because of the interconnected nature of computer systems today, an infected system in one country can spread malicious software across the globe and cause even greater damage. The Melissa virus, for example, caused an estimated $80 million in damages around the globe (Taylor et al. 2010). Thus, cyber-trespass offenses are a significant concern for home users, businesses, and governments alike.

Cyber-deception/Theft

The second and related category within Wall's (2001) typology is cyber-deception and theft. This form of cybercrime includes all the various criminal acquisitions that may occur on-line, particularly for thefts due to trespass. The increased use of on-line banking and shopping sites also allows consumers to transmit sensitive personal and financial information over the Internet (James

2005; Newman and Clarke 2003). This information can, however, be surreptitiously obtained by criminals through different methods such as phishing (James 2005; Wall 2007). In a phishing attack, consumers are tricked into transmitting financial information into fraudulent websites, where the information is housed for later fraud (see James 2005; Wall 2007). These crimes are particularly costly for both the individual victim and financial institutions alike, as the Gartner Group estimates that phishing victims in the U.S. lost $3 billion dollars in 2007 alone (Rogers 2007).

In addition, there is an emerging marketplace on-line where computer criminals sell and buy information (Franklin et al. 2007; Honeynet Research Alliance 2003; Thomas and Martin 2006). Specifically, Internet Relay Chat, or IRC, channels and web forums operate where hackers sell significant volumes of data obtained through phishing, database compromises, and other means. Individuals in these sites sell credit card and bank accounts, pin numbers, and supporting customer information obtained from victims around the world in lots of tens or hundreds of accounts (Franklin et al. 2007; Holt and Lampke 2010; Honeynet Research Alliance 2003; Thomas and Martin 2006). Some also sell their services as hackers and offer cash out services to obtain physical money from electronic accounts (Holt and Lampke 2010). As a consequence, criminals who frequent these markets can quickly and efficiently engage in credit card fraud and identity theft without any technical knowledge or skill (Franklin et al. 2007; Holt and Lampke 2010; Honeynet Research Alliance 2003; Thomas and Martin 2006). In addition, these markets can lead individuals to be victimized multiple times without their knowledge.

Beyond theft due to computer intrusions, there are several different types of fraud that are perpetrated on-line, including electronic auction or retail-based fraud schemes, stock scams, and work-at-home plans (Grabosky and Smith 2001; Newman and Clarke 2003). One of the most prevalent and most costly forms of Internet fraud are advance fee e-mail schemes (Internet Crime Complaint Center 2009; Holt and Graves 2007; Wall 2004). These messages are often referred to as "Nigerian" or "419" scams because the e-mails often come from individuals who claim to reside in a foreign country such as Nigeria or other African nations (Buchanan and Grant 2001; Holt and Graves 2007). The sender claims to need assistance transferring a large sum of money out of their country. In return, the sender will share a portion of the sum with the individual who aids them (Holt and Graves 2007). Victims of this type of fraud often lose thousands of dollars on average and may be too embarrassed to report their experiences to law enforcement because of the often obviously false nature of the message they responded to (Buchanan and Grant 2001; Newman and Clarke 2003; Wall 2004).

Another high-profile form of cyber-theft is digital piracy, or the illegal copying of digital media, such as computer software, digital sound recordings, and digital video recordings, without the explicit permission of the copyright holder (Gopal et al. 2004). Such files can be easily downloaded from one of many internet file sharing services or web sites and commonly do not stem from a single user. IDATE (2003) has suggested that illegal file sharing accounts for over four times the amount of official sales of sound recordings worldwide. The same report suggested that peer-to-peer (P2P) file sharing accounts for between 50 and 90 percent of all broadband internet traffic in any given day, depending on the time of day.

The financial losses estimated to result from digital piracy are staggering and participation levels in this illegal activity are commonplace, particularly among college students (Hinduja 2001; 2003; Ingram and Hinduja 2008; Morris and Higgins 2009; Rob and Waldfogel 2006; Zentner 2006). For example, the Motion Picture Association of America (MPAA) reported fiscal losses upwards of $6 billion in 2005 from movie piracy in the U.S. alone. Over 40 percent of these reported losses were argued to be a result of university students in the U.S. (MPAA 2007). In addition, Siwek (2007) reported that the U.S. sound recording industry loses over twelve billion dollars annually due to piracy and another $422 million each year in tax revenue that would have been generated via corporate and personal income taxes (Siwek 2007). Taken as a whole, cyber-deception and theft encompass a wide range of activities, each with significant economic impact.

Cyber-porn and Obscenity

The third category within Wall's (2001) typology includes cyber-porn and obscenity. Sexually expressive or explicit materials are readily available across the World Wide Web, though they may not be illegal in certain areas (DiMarco 2003; Wall 2001). As a consequence, on-line pornography has become an extremely lucrative and thriving business (Edelman 2009; Lane 2000). In fact, the adoption and popularity of various forms of media, particularly VHS and DVD media, webcams, digital photography, and streaming web content is intimately tied to the pornography industry (Lane 2000). The Internet has dramatically affected the way that pornographic content is distributed, customers are targeted, and amateur stars are made. For example, estimates suggest that the on-line pornography industry earns over $3,000 per second (Gobry and Saint 2011).

The development of the Internet and computer mediated communications has also fostered the growth of a wide range of communities supportive of deviant sexual behaviors. Those whose sexual preferences are socially marginalized can identify a wide range of resources, such as newsgroups, web forums, and list serves where individuals can exchange all sorts of information almost instantaneously (DiMarco 2003). On-line spaces also allow individuals to find others who share their interests, creating supportive communities where individuals feel "they are part of a group, from which validation can be drawn, and sexual scripts exchanged" (Rosenmann and Safir 2006, 77). As a consequence, subcultures have developed in cyberspace around myriad acts of sexual deviance (DiMarco 2003; Quinn and Forsyth 2005). For example, the phenomenon of bugchasing has been identified, where HIV negative individuals seek HIV positive sex partners (Tewksbury 2003), as well as money slavery, where individuals give money to other individuals in the hopes of receiving sadistic treatment via e-mail or some other electronic medium (Durkin 2007).

The illegal sex trade has also moved to on-line spaces, such as websites and forums specifically designed for johns to discuss prostitution in cities around the globe (see Holt and Blevins 2007; Hughes 2003; Sharpe and Earle 2003; Soothill and Sanders 2005). Recent research suggests that the clients of prostitutes use the Internet to share information about their real-world experiences with all types of sex workers (Holt and Blevins 2007; Hughes 2003; Sharpe and Earle 2003). Johns reveal their motivations for paying for sex, as well as detailed accounts of their interactions with prostitutes, escorts, and other sex-workers. In addition, johns use these methods to describe and warn others about the presence of law enforcement or particularly active community groups in a given area (see Holt, Blevins, and Kuhns 2008). As a result, these on-line forums can provide insight into the nature of displacement and the methods johns use to obviate the wide range of targeted law enforcement strategies to reduce levels of street prostitution (see Scott and Dedel 2006).

One of the most publicly recognized and feared forms of cybercrime within this framework of cyber-porn and obscenity is pedophilia, where individuals seek out sexual or emotional relationships with children (Jenkins 2001). Recent media attention has focused on the behavior of pedophiles, creating a sort of panic around the number of sexual predators on-line (Berson 2003; McKenna and Bargh 2000). In fact, the number of arrests for child pornography possession has increase substantially over the last decade, with over 3,700 arrests in 2009 alone (Wolack, Finkelhor, and Mitchell 2012). Criminological research has provided significant insight into the ways pedophiles use the Internet as a means to facilitate criminal behavior (Durkin 1996, 1997; Durkin and Bryant 1999; Jenkins 2001; Quayle and Taylor 2002). For example, the Internet is a vehicle for the identification, trade, and distribution of pornographic and sexual materials, including comic books, stories, pictures, and films (Durkin 1997; Jenkins 2001; Fontana-Rosa 2001; Quayle and Taylor 2002). In addition, computer-mediated communications provide a wealth of potential victims that can be groomed for sexual contact off-line (see Wolack, Finkelhor and Mitchell 2003; Wolack, Mitchell and Finkelhor 2004).

The Internet also provides a mechanism for pedophiles to identify and talk with others through usergroups, web forums, and chatrooms (Durkin 1996, 1997; Durkin and Bryant 1999; Holt, Blevins, and Burkert 2010). These sites provide a way for pedophiles to come together to validate their sexual interests, share information about their habits, and find support for their behaviors (Durkin and Bryant 1999; Jenkins 2001). Exchanges between individuals provide information on the ways individuals become interested in relationships with children and how to justify these behaviors (Durkin and Bryant 1999; Holt et al. 2010). For example, on-line communities often use the term "child love" to refer to their attractions, rather than the more derogatory and stigmatizing word "pedophile" (Durkin 1997; Holt et al. 2010; Jenkins 2001).

Cyber-violence

The final form of crime within Wall's (2001) typology is cyber-violence, representing the distribution of a variety of injurious, hurtful, or dangerous materials on-line. For example, individuals have begun to use the Internet as a means to harass or bully others (Bocij 2004; Finn 2004; Holt and Bossler 2009). Harassment can take various forms, such as threatening or sexual messages delivered to an individual privately via e-mail, instant messaging services, or cell phone (see Bocij 2004). The emergence and popularity of social networking websites like Facebook, however, allow individuals to post threatening or hurtful content in public settings for anyone and everyone to see (see Hinduja and Patchin 2009). The victims of such harassing communications respond in a variety of ways; some view these messages to be nothing more than a nuisance, while others experience significant physical or emotional stress, including depressive symptoms and suicidal ideation (Finkelhor et al. 2000; Finn 2004; Hinduja and Patchin 2009). Estimates of on-line harassment and stalking appear to be on the rise, particularly among adolescent and young adult populations, due in part to frequent Internet use (Bocij 2004; Finn 2004; Hinduja and Patchin 2009; Holt and Bossler 2009; Jones, Mitchell, and Finkelhor 2012). For example, a recent national examination of young Internet users found that 11 percent of the sample experienced some form of harassment while on-line, which is a 50 percent increase over the last decade (Jones et al. 2012). In addition, evidence suggests that having peers who engage in cyber-crime increases an individual's risk of harassment (Hinduja and Patchin 2009; Holt and Bossler 2009). Thus, the risk of on-line violence may share similar correlates with real-world violence (Holt and Bossler 2009).

The Internet has also become an important resource for political and social movements of all types. Mainstream and alternative political and social movements have grown to depend on the Internet to broadcast their ideologies across the world. Groups have employed a range of tactics depending on the severity of the perceived injustice or wrong that have been performed (see Jordan and Taylor 2004). Often, these virtual efforts develop in tandem with real-world protests and demonstrations (see Cere 2003; Jordan and Taylor 2004). For example, the native peoples, called Zapatistas, in Chiapas, Mexico, used the Internet to post information and mobilize supporters to their cause against governmental repression (Cere 2003).

Politically driven groups have also employed hacking techniques to engage in more serious strikes against governments and political organizations (see Furnell 2002). These actions are sometimes called "hacktivism," as the "hack" or attack is used to promote an activist agenda or express an opinion (Furnell 2002, 44). Their actions may, however, violate the law and produce fear or concern among the general population (Jordan and Taylor 2004). For instance, the activist group Anonymous and its more radical offshoot LulzSec began targeting government and industry targets on-line in order to express their dissent against attempts to limit the availability of pirated media and against general corruption (Correll 2011). Their attacks ranged from Denial of Service attacks to mass compromises of sensitive information from law enforcement and industrial service providers. At the same time, various groups in support of Al-Qaeda operate web forums to distribute hacker tools and coordinate attacks. One such hacker named Younis Tsouli promoted the use of hacking tools against various targets in support of global jihad under the handle Irhabi 007, or Terrorist 007 (Denning 2011). He posted a manual titled "The Encyclopedia of Hacking the Zionist and Crusader Websites," which detailed various attack methodologies and a list of vulnerable targets on-line in order to disrupt on-line systems of Western nations (Denning 2011). Thus, there are significant risks and threats from politically motivated crimes on-line.

The Structure of This Book and Its Contributions

Taken as a whole, there is a need for a diverse body of research to understand the correlates and causes of cybercrime, as well as shifts in deviant behavior that can occur over time as a consequence of technology and the Internet (see also Holt 2007; Mann and Sutton 1998; Quinn and Forsythe 2005). The various chapters of this book discuss these issues in depth by exploring the spectrum of cybercrimes in detail. The organization of this book follows the structure of Wall's (2001) typology by focusing on cyber trespass, deception, obscenity, and violence.

In Chapter Two, Patrick Kinkade and his colleagues explore the subculture of hacking through an ethnography of attendees at a hacker conference. Computer hacking is unique in that most all offenses take place virtually, though individuals may have relationships with deviant peers in the real world and on-line. Few have explored the dynamics of hacker relationships in the real world, thus this chapter provides a much needed investigation of the way in which hackers engage one another and the way that this shapes the experience of hacking generally.

Johnny Nhan provides an overview of the legal responses to the related problem of digital piracy in Chapter Three. Specifically, this section discusses the evolution of the problem of music piracy as a form of cyber-theft over time. Not only have the tactics of pirates changed along with technological shifts, but so have the legislative and law enforcement practices to combat piracy. Thus, this paper provides a careful historical review of the difficulties inherent in combatting cybercrime and the complexities of balancing freedom of information with controls.

In Chapter Four, Sarah Turner and her colleagues consider the problem of spam-driven work-at-home fraud schemes. The authors examine this relatively common form of fraud and the way in which spam messages are structured to entice individuals to respond, from the written content of the initial email to any external websites that the sender may link to online. Their investigation demonstrates that spam distributors can easily structure messages to convince prospective recipients to respond in such a way as to increase their risk of fraud victimization.

Though hackers and data thieves generate significant public concern, they receive much less attention than the activities of pedophiles and child pornographers in on-line environments. There is significant fear over the presence of child predators in cyberspace, which has spurred a variety of social science research to understand this problem. Marcus Rogers and Kathryn Seigfried-Spellar elaborate on this issue in Chapter Five through a discussion of frameworks to understand pedophilia and child pornography users and creators. They argue that the existing typologies used to investigate and prosecute child pornography in various countries do not adequately account for the role of technology in the acquisition and use of these materials. Rogers and Seigfried-Spellar provide their own framework in this chapter and detail how it can be used to better combat this problem.

The use of technology to facilitate sexual activities and interests are also related to the most common forms of cyber-violence. Catherine Marcum details the problem of on-line harassment, bullying, and stalking in Chapter Six, with a distinct focus on the impact of these crimes among juvenile and college populations. Young people are the most likely to utilize emerging technologies to communicate and connect with others, thereby increasing their risk of exposure to unwanted sexual or aggressive content. She also considers the legislative response to these crimes and discusses how prosecutions will impact free speech and civil rights.

Marjie Britz provides a critical overview on the most problematic and nebulous form of cyberviolence in Chapter Seven: cyberterror. She notes that there is no single definition for this term, though various activities have been labeled as cyberterror. Britz provides an overview of the research literature on this issue from the social and military sciences and gives various examples of terror incidents to give context to this phenomenon.

In Chapter Eight, Aunshul Rege provides a detailed exposition of a pertinent target for both hackers and cyber-terrorists: industrial control systems. These systems are used to manage and remotely control water, power, and electrical systems, but could be easily compromised and impacted by malicious actors acting on behalf of an extremist group or nation-state. Rege gives a carefully considered examination of these systems and the ways that attackers have or may harm systems in the future.

The final chapter focuses on the capacity of state and local law enforcement agencies to respond to the various forms of cybercrime discussed throughout the book. Thomas Holt, Adam Bossler, and Sarah Fitzgerald utilize a sample of respondents from police agencies across the United States to understand the number of officers trained to investigate cybercrimes, the types of crimes reported, and officer attitudes toward these offenses and the individuals who participate in these activities. The authors argue that local law enforcement agencies have significantly increased their ability to combat cybercrime, though there are several issues that require improvement and investment.

References

Allison, Stuart F.H., Amie M. Schuck, and Kim Michelle Lersch. "Exploring the crime of identity theft: prevalence, clearance rates, and victim/offender characteristics," *Journal of Criminal Justice* 33 (2005): 19–29.

AVN Media Network. "Industry Stats," Accessed February 1, 2009. http://www.avn medianetwork.com/index.php?content_about_industrybuzz.

Berson, Ilene R. "Grooming cybervictims: The psychosocial effects of online exploitation of youth," *Journal of School Violence* 2 (2003): 5–18.

Bocij, Paul. *Cyberstalking: Harassment in the Internet age and how to protect your family.* Westport: Praeger, 2004.

Bossler, Adam M. and Thomas J. Holt. "On-line Activities, Guardianship, and Malware Infection: An Examination of Routine Activities Theory," *The International Journal of Cyber Criminology* 3 (2009): 400–420.

Brenner, Bill. Banks prepare lawsuit over TJX data breach, 2007. Accessed October 7, 2008. http://searchfinancialsecurity.techtarget.com/news/article/ 0,289 142,sid185_gci1294453,00.html.

Brenner, Susan W. *Cyberthreats: The Emerging Fault Lines of the Nation State.* New York: Oxford University Press, 2008.

Britz, Marjie T. *Computer Forensics and Cybercrime: An Introduction.* Upper Saddle River, NJ: Prentice Hall, 2004.

Buchanan, Jim, and Alex J. Grant. "Investigating and Prosecuting Nigerian Fraud," *United States Attorneys' Bulletin,* November (2001), 29–47.

Cappelli, Dawn, Andrew Moore, Timothy J. Shimeall, and Randall Trzeciak. 2006. *Common Sense Guide to Prevention and Detection of Insider Threats.* Pittsburg, PA: Carnegie Mellon Cylab, 2006. Accessed November 1, 2007. http://www.us-cert.gov/reading_room/prevent_detect_insiderthreat0504.pdf.

Central Intelligence Agency. *The World Factbook 2011.* Washington, DC: Central Intelligence Agency 2011. Accessed January 13, 2012. https:// www.cia.gov/library/publications/the-world-factbook/index.html.

Cere, Rinella. "Digital counter-cultures and the nature of electronic social and political movements." In *Dot.cons: Crime, deviance and identity on the Internet,* ed. Yvonne Jewkes, 147–163. Portland, OR: Willan Publishing, 2003.

Choi, Kyung-Schick. "Computer crime victimization and integrated theory: An empirical assessment," *International Journal of Cyber Criminology,* 2 (2008): 308–333.

Clayton, Mark. "Stuxnet malware is "weapon" out to destroy ... Iran's Bushehr Nuclear Plant." *Christian Science Monitor,* 21 September, 2010. Accessed November 11, 2011. http://www.csmonitor.com/USA/2010/0921/Stuxnet-malware-is-weapon-out-to-destroy-Iran-s-Bushehr-nuclear-plant.

Computer Security Institute. *Computer Crime and Security Survey,* 2007. (June 3, 2007) http://www.cybercrime.gov/FBI2006.pdf.

Conly, Catherine H. *Organizing for Computer Crime Investigation and Prosecution.* Washington, DC: National Institute of Justice, 1989.

Correll, Sean P. "An interview with Anonymous." *PandaLabs Blog,* 2011. Accessed April 14, 2011. http://pandalabs.pandasecurity.com/an-interview-with-anonymous/.

Denning, Dorothy E. "Activism, hacktivism, and cyberterrorism: The Internet as a tool for influencing foreign policy." In *Networks and Netwars: The Future of Terror, Crime, and Militancy,* eds. John Arquilla and David F. Ronfeldt, 239–288. Santa Monica, CA: Rand, 2001.

Denning, Dorothy E. "Cyber-conflict as an Emergent Social Problem." In *Corporate Hacking and Technology-Driven Crime: Social Dynamics and Implications*, ed. Thomas J. Holt and Bernadette Schell, 170–186. Hershey, PA: IGI-Global, 2011.

Dhillon, Gurpreet and Steve Moores. "Computer crimes: theorizing about the enemy within," *Computers and Security* 20 (2001): 715–723.

DiMarco, Heather. "The electronic cloak: secret sexual deviance in cybersociety." In *Dot.cons: Crime, Deviance, and Identity on the Internet*, ed. Yvonne Jewkes, 53–67. Portland, OR: Willan Publishing, 2003.

Durkin, Keith F. *Accounts and sexual deviance in cyberspace: The case of pedophilia.* PhD diss., Virginia Polytechnic Institute and State University, 1996.

Durkin, Keith F. "Misuse of the Internet by Pedophiles: Implications for Law Enforcement and Probation Practice," *Federal Probation* 61 (1997): 14–18.

Durkin, Keith F. "Show Me the Money: Cybershrews and On-Line Money Masochists," *Deviant Behavior* 28 (2007): 355–378.

Durkin, Keith F., and Clifton D. Bryant. "Propagandizing pederasty. A thematic analysis of the on-line exculpatory accounts of unrepentant pedophiles," *Deviant Behavior* 20 (1999): 103–127.

Edleman, Benjamin. "Red Light States: Who Buys Online Adult Entertainment?" *Journal of Economic Perspectives* 23 (2009): 209–220.

Finkelhor, David, Kimberly J. Mitchell, and Janice Wolack. *Online victimization: A report on the nation's youth.* Washington DC: National Center for Missing and Exploited Children, 2000.

Finn, Jerry. "A Survey of Online Harassment at a University Campus," *Journal of Interpersonal Violence* 19 (2004): 468–483.

Fontana-Rosa, Julio Cesar. "Legal competency in a case of pedophilia: Advertising on the Internet," *International Journal of Offender Therapy and Comparative Criminology* 45 (2001): 118–128.

Franklin, Jason, Vern Paxson, Adrian Perrig, and Stefan Savage. "An Inquiry into the nature and cause of the wealth of internet miscreants," Paper presented at *CCS07*, October 29–November 2, in Alexandria, VA, 2007.

Furnell, Steven. *Cybercrime: Vandalizing the Information Society.* Boston, MA: Addison Wesley, 2002.

Gobry, Pascal-Emmanuel and Nick Saint. "15 things you need to know about internet porn," *Business Insider* August 5, 2011. Accessed June 15, 2012. http://www.businessinsider.com/15-things-you-need-to-know-about-internet-porn-2011-8?op=1.

Goodin, Dan. TJX breach was twice as big as admitted, banks say. *The Register*, 2007. Accessed October 20, 2008. http://www.theregister.co.uk/2007/10/24/ tjx_breach_estimate_grows/.

Goodman, Marc. "Making computer crime count," *FBI Law Enforcement Bulletin* 70 (2001): 10–17.

Gopal, Ram, G. L. Sanders, Sudip Bhattacharjee, Manish K Agrawal, and Suzanne C. Wagner. "A Behavioral Model of Digital Music Piracy," *Journal of Organizational Computing*& *Electronic Commerce* 14 (2004): 89–105.

Grabosky, Peter N. "Virtual criminality: Old wine in new bottles?" *Social and Legal Studies* 10 (2001): 243–249.

Grabosky Peter N. and Russell Smith. "Telecommunication fraud in the digital age: The convergence of technologies." In *Crime and the Internet*, ed. David Wall, 29–43. New York: Routledge, 2001.

Grabosky, Peter N., Russell G. Smith, and Gillian Dempsey. *Electronic Theft: Unlawful acquisition in cyberspace.* Cambridge, England: Cambridge University Press, 2001.

Hinduja, Sameer. "Correlates of Internet software piracy," *Journal of Contemporary Criminal Justice* 17 (2001): 369–382.

Hinduja, Sameer. "Trends and Patterns among Software Pirates," *Ethics and Information* Technology 5 (2003): 49–61.

Hinduja, Sameer, and Justin W. Patchin. *Bullying beyond the schoolyard: Preventing and responding to cyberbullying.* New York: Corwin Press, 2009.

Holt, Thomas J. Examining a transnational problem: An analysis of computer crime victimization in eight countries from 1999 to 2001. *International Journal of Comparative and Applied Criminal Justice* 27 (2003): 199–220.

Holt, Thomas J. "Subcultural evolution? Examining the influence of on-and off-line experiences on deviant subcultures," *Deviant Behavior* 28 (2007) 171–198.

Holt, Thomas J., and Kristie R. Blevins. "Examining sex work from the client's perspective: Assessing johns using online data," *Deviant Behavior* 28 (2007): 333–354.

Holt, Thomas J., Kristie R. Blevins, and Natasha Burkert. "Considering the pedophile subculture online," *Sexual Abuse*, 22 (2010): 3–24.

Holt, Thomas J., Kristie R. Blevins, and Joseph B. Kuhns. "Examining the Displacement Practices of Johns with On-line Data," *Journal of Criminal Justice* 36 (2008): 522–528.

Holt, Thomas J., and Adam M. Bossler. "Examining the Applicability of Lifestyle-Routine Activities Theory for Cybercrime Victimization," *Deviant Behavior* 30 (2009): 1–25.

Holt, Thomas J. and Heith Copes. "Transferring Subcultural Knowledge On-line: Practices and Beliefs of Persistent Digital Pirates," *Deviant Behavior* 31 (2010): 31–61.

Holt, Thomas J. and Danielle C. Graves. "A Qualitative Analysis of Advanced Fee Fraud Schemes," *The International Journal of Cyber-Criminology* 1 (2007): 137–154.

Holt, Thomas J. and Eric Lampke. "Exploring stolen data markets on-line: Products and market forces," *Criminal Justice Studies* 23 (2010): 33–50.

Honeynet Research Alliance. "Profile: Automated Credit Card Fraud," *Know Your Enemy Paper* series, 2003. Accessed July 20, 2008. http://www.honey net.org/ papers/profiles/cc-fraud.pdf.

Hughes, Donna M. "Prostitution Online," *Journal of Trauma Practice* 2 (2003): 115–131.

IDATE. *Taking Advantage of Peer-to-Peer: What Is at Stake for the Content Industry?* San Diego, CA: IDATE, 2003 Accessed January 7, 2009. http://www.idate.fr/an/_qdn/an-03/ IF282/index_a.htm.

Ingram, Jason R. and Sameer Hinduja. "Neutralizing music piracy: An empirical examination," *Deviant Behavior* 29 (2008): 334–366.

Internet Crime Complaint Center. *IC3 2008 Internet Crime Report.* Accessed March 24, 2009. http://www.ic3.gov/media/annualreport/2008_IC3 Report.pdf.

James, Lance. *Phishing Exposed.* Rockland: Syngress, 2005.

Jenkins, Paul. *Beyond tolerance: Child pornography on the Internet.* New York: New York University Press, 2001.

Jewkes, Yvonne, and Keith Sharpe. "Crime, deviance and the disembodied self: transcending the dangers of corporeality," In *Dot.cons: Crime, deviance and identity on the* Internet, ed. Yvonne Jewkes, 1–14. Portland, OR: Willan Publishing, 2003.

Jones, Linda, Kimberly Mitchell, and David Finkelhor. "Trends in youth Internet victimizations: Findings from three youth Internet safety surveys, 2000-2010," *Journal of Adolescent Health* 50 (2012): 179–186.

Jordan, Tim and Paul Taylor. "A Sociology of Hackers," *The Sociological Review* 46 (1998): 757–80.

Jordan, Tim and Paul Taylor. *Hacktivism and Cyberwars: Rebels With a Cause.* New York: Routledge, 2004.

Kerr, Paul K., John Rollins, and Catherine A. Theohary. *The Stuxnet Computer Worm: Harbinger of an Emerging Warfare Capability.* Washington D.C.; Congressional Research Service, 2010.

Krebs, Brian. "Are Megabreaches Out? E-thefts Downsized in 2010," *Krebs on Security, 2011.* Accessed June 1, 2012. http://krebsonsecurity.com/tag/heartland-payment-systems/.

Lane, Frederick S. *Obscene Profits: The Entrepreneurs of Pornography in the Cyber Age.* New York: Routledge, 2000.

Lenhart, Amanda. *Is the age at which teens get cell phones getting younger?* Washington D.C.; Pew Internet and American Life Project, 2010. Accessed March 11, 2011. http://pewinternet.org/Commentary/2010/December/ Is-the-age-at-which-kids-get-cell-phones-getting-younger.aspx.

Lenhart, Amanda, Kristen Purcell, Aaron Smith, and Kathryn Zickuhr. *Social Media and Young Adults.* Washington D.C.: Pew Internet and American Life Project, 2010. Accessed January 10, 2011. http://www.pewinternet.org/ Reports/2010/Social-Media-and-Young-Adults.aspx.

Levy, Steven. *Hackers: Heroes of the Computer Revolution.* New York: Dell, 1984

Mann, David, and Mike Sutton. "Netcrime: More Change in the Organization of Thieving," *British Journal of Criminology* 38 (1998): 201–229.

McKenna, Katelyn Y. A., and John A. Bargh. "Plan 9 from cyberspace: The implications of the Internet for personality and social psychology," *Personality and Social Psychology Review* 4 (2000): 57–75.

McQuade, Sam. *Understanding and managing cyber crime.* Boston: Pearson/ Allyn and Bacon, 2006.

MENA Business Reports. *Hacktivism: Pro-Islamic hacker groups joining forces globally.* Accessed April 30, 2004. http://web.lexis-nexis.com/universe/ document?_m=a8bea342a9f56689f3986fa946c79f76&_docnum=3&wchp =dGLbVtbzSkVA&_md5=87f67b999724f1f411e93cee5da58d7f.

Morris, Robert G. and George E. Higgins. "Neutralizing potential and self-reported digital piracy: A multitheoretical exploration among college students," *Criminal Justice Review,* 34 (2009): 173–197.

Motion Picture Association of America. *2005 Piracy fact sheet,* 2007. Accessed December 12, 2007. http://www.mpaa.org/researchStatistics.asp.

Nasheri, Hedieh. *Economic espionage and industrial spying.* Cambridge Publishing, 2005.

Newman, Grame and Ronald Clarke. *Superhighway robbery: Preventing e-commerce crime.* Cullompton: Willan Press, 2003.

PandaLabs *Malware infections in protected systems.* PandaLabs, 2007. Accessed November 1, 2007. http://research.pandasecurity.com/blogs/images/ wp_pb_malware_infections_in_protected_systems.pdf.

Pease, Ken. "Crime Futures and foresight: Challenging criminal behavior in the information age." In *Crime and the Internet,* ed. David Wall, 18–28. New York: Routledge, 2001.

Ponemon Institute. *Second Annual Cost of Cyber Crime Study. Benchmark Study of U.S. Companies.* Traverse City, MI: Ponemon Institute LLC, 2011. (May 12, 2012), http://www.arcsight.com/collateral/whitepapers/2011_Cost_of_ Cyber_Crime_Study_August.pdf.

Putnam, Tonya L., and David D. Elliott. "International responses to cyber crime." In *The Transnational Dimension of Cyber Crime and Terrorism*, eds. Abraham D. Sofaer and Seymour E. Goodman, 35–68. Stanford: Hoover Institution Press, 2001.

Quayle, Ethel, and Max Taylor. "Child pornography and the Internet: Perpetuating a cycle of abuse," *Deviant Behavior* 23 (2002): 331–361.

Quinn, James F., and Craig J. Forsyth. "Describing sexual behavior in the era of the internet: A typology for empirical research," *Deviant Behavior* 26 (2005): 191–207.

Rob, Rafael, and Joel Waldfogel. "Piracy on the high C's: Music downloading, sales displacement, and social welfare in a sample of college students," *Journal of Law and Economics* 49 (2006): 29–62.

Roberts, Paul F. "Retailer TJX reports massive data breach: Credit, debit data stolen. Extent of breach still unknown," *InfoWorld*, June 4, 2007. Accessed October 1, 2007. http://www.infoworld.com/d/security-central/ retailer-tjx-reports-massive-data-breach-953.

Rogers, Jack. "Gartner: Victims of online phishing up nearly 40 percent in 2007," *SC Magazine*, 2007. Accessed January 20, 2008. http://www.sc-magazineus.com/ Gartner-Victims-of-online-phishing-up-nearly-40-percent-in-2007/article/ 99768.

Rosenmann, Amir, and Marylin P. Safir. "Forced online: Pushed Factors of Internet Sexuality: A Preliminary Study of Paraphilic Empowerment," *Journal of Homosexuality* 51 (2006): 71–92.

Sanger, David E. *Confront and Conceal: Obama's secret wars and surprising use of American power.* New York: Crown Publishing, 2012.

Schell, Bernadette H., John L. Dodge, with Steve S. Moutsatsos. *The Hacking of America: Who's Doing it, Why, and How.* Westport, CT: Quorum Books, 2002.

Scott, Michael S., and Kelly Dedel. "Street prostitution." *Problem Oriented Policing Guide Series (2).* Washington D.C.: Office of Community Oriented Policing Services, U.S. Department of Justice, 2006.

Sharpe, Keith, and Sarah Earle. "Cyberpunters and cyberwhores: prostitution on the Internet." In *Dot Cons. Crime, Deviance and Identity on the Internet*, ed. Yvonne Jewkes, 36–52. Portland, OR: Willan Publishing, 2003.

Shaw, Eric, Keven G. Ruby, and Jerrold M. Post. "The Insider Threat to Information Systems: The Psychology of the Dangerous Insider," *Security Awareness Bulletin* 2, (1998).

Siwek, Stephen E. 2007. *The true cost of sound recording piracy to the U.S. economy.* Intellectual Property Institute, 2007. Accessed January 9, 2009. http:// www.ipi.org/ipi%5CIPIPublications.nsf/ PublicationLookupFullText/ 5C2EE3D2107A4C228625733E0053A1F4.

Smith, Aaron. *Smartphone Adoption and Usage.* Washington DC: Pew Internet and American Life Project, 2011. Accessed January 1, 2012. http://pewinternet.org/Reports/2011/Smartphones.aspx.

Socialbakers. *United States Facebook Statistics,* 2011. Accessed December 15, 2011. http://www.socialbakers.com/facebook-statistics/united-states.

Soothhill, Keith, and Teela Sanders. "The geographical mobility, preferences and pleasures of prolific punters: A demonstration study of the activities of prostitutes' clients." *Sociological Research On-Line* 10 (2005). http://www.socresonline.org.uk/10/1/soothill.html.

Speer, David L. Redefining borders: The challenges of cybercrime. *Crime, Law, and Social Change* 34 (2000): 259–273.

Stambaugh, Hollis, David S. Beaupre, David J. Icove, Richard Baker, Wayne Cassady, Wayne P. Williams. *Electronic crime needs assessment for state and local law enforcement.* Washington, DC: National Institute of Justice. NCJ 186276, 2001.

Stepanova, Ekaterina. *The role of information communications technology in the "Arab Spring": Implications beyond the region.* PONARS Eurasia Policy Memo No. 159, 2011. Accessed October 5, 2011. http://www.gwu.edu/~ieresgwu/assets/docs/ponars/pepm_159.pdf.

Stephenson, Peter. *Investigating Computer-Related Crime.* Boca Raton: CRC Press, 2000.

Symantec Corporation. *Symantec Internet security threat report.* 2003. Accessed October 3, 2005. http://enterprisesecurity.symantec.com/content/knowledgelibrary.cfm?EID=0.

Taylor, Robert W., Eric J. Fritsch, John Liederbach, and Thomas J. Holt. *Digital Crime and Digital Terrorism, 2nd Edition.* Upper Saddle River, NJ: Pearson Prentice Hall, 2010.

Tewksbury, Richard. "Bareback sex and the quest for HIV: Assessing the relationship in Internet personal advertisements of men who have sex with men," *Deviant Behavior* 24 (2003): 467–482.

Thomas, Richard and Jerry Martin. "The underground economy: Priceless," *:login* 31 (2006): 7–16.

Verini, James. "The Great Cyberheist," *The New York Times.* November 14, 2010. Retrieved November 15, 2010. http://www.nytimes.com/2010/11/14/magazine/14Hacker-t.html?_r=1.

Wall, David S. "Catching Cybercriminals: Policing the Internet. International review of law," *Computers & Technology* 12 (1998): 201–218.

Wall, David S. "Cybercrimes and the Internet." In *Crime and the Internet,* ed. David S. Wall, 1–17. New York: Routledge, 2001.

Wall, David S. "Digital realism and the governance of spam as cybercrime," *European Journal on Criminal Policy and Research* 10 (2004): 309–335.

Wall, David S. *Cybercrime: The transformation of crime in the information age.* Cambridge: Polity Press 2007.

Wolack, Janice, David Finkelhor, and Kimberly Mitchell. *Internet sex crimes against minors: The response of law enforcement.* Alexandria VA: National Center for Missing and Exploited Children, 2003.

Wolack, Janice, David Finkelhor, and Kimberly Mitchell. "Internet-initiated sex crimes against minors: Implications for prevention based on findings from a national study," *Journal of Adolescent Health* 35 (2004): 424.

Wolack, Janice, David Finkelhor, and Kimberly Mitchell. *Trends in law enforcement responses to technology-facilitated child sexual exploitation crimes: The Third National Juvenile Online Victimization Study (NJOV-3).* Durham, NH: Crimes against Children Research Center, 2012.

Wolack, Janice, Kimberly Mitchell, and David Finkelhor. *Internet Sex Crimes Against Minors: The Response of Law Enforcement.* Washington, DC: Office of Juvenile Justice and Delinquency Prevention, 2003.

Yar, Majid. "The novelty of 'cybercrime': An assessment in light of routine activity theory," *European Journal of Criminology* 2 (2005): 407–427.

Zentner, Alejandro. "Measuring the effect of file sharing on music purchases," *Journal of Law and Economics* 49 (2006): 63–90.

2

Hacker Woodstock: Observations on an Off-line Cyber Culture at the Chaos Communication Camp 2011

Patrick T. Kinkade, Michael Bachmann, and Brittany Smith-Bachmann

When describing broad-based cultural patterns of expression, sociologists generally assume that identity is anchored to space. As Stone (1962, 87–89) suggests, cultural identity is associated with the process of becoming socially situated in place. Possessing such an identity implies the individual has a cultural referent and is tied to a tangible locale. Such locales range from geographically specific metropolitan places (see Simmel [1903] 1951) to the more emergent spaces individuals demarcate for specific encounters (Goffman 1963, 88–99). No matter how the spaces become established, most sociologists assume that identities endure as long as anchored places remain stable (Sennet 1977; Fine 1989; Putnam 2000).

Assuming that identity emerges in a stable space does not ignore the notion of time in relation to the development of cultural patterns. Any form of identity activation or maintenance connects processes of how "individuals locate themselves" in regard to temporal (e.g., duration and frequency) or spatial (e.g., establishment and neighborhood) dimensions (Williams 2006, 174; Oldenberg 1989). Specific types of status, such as "regular" or "temporary," hinge on the ability to manage an identity in conjunction with both spatial and temporal boundaries (Fox 1987; Fine 1987, 2002; Katovich and Hardesty 1985; Katovich and Reese 1987). However, as ethereal statuses become more prominent in online communities that exhibit less pronounced tempo-spatial boundaries (see Bachmann 2010; Blevins and Holt 2009; Burkhalter 1999; Nhan and Bachmann 2010; Wilson and Atkinson 2005), endurance of identity outside of time and independent of specific locales becomes increasingly emphasized (see Karp, Stone, and Yoels 1991, 25–27). Whereas identities explicitly linked to locales (e.g., regulars in a neighborhood bar) become anchored in particular traditions in those places, identities associated with temporality pertain more to ongoing accomplishments than to an established tradition of co-presence in any specific place (see Katovich and Reese 1987; Riesman, Glazer, and Denney 1961).

The shift from space to time in establishing identification coincides with the creation of more ethereal cultures, whose patterns of identification are not necessarily bound to strict correlations between time and space. Fox (1987, 345–348), for instance, maintained that the authenticity of "an anti-establishment style" favored by youth subcultures (e.g., punks) had more to do with commitment to the style over time, regardless of place. Indeed, as other recent ethnographies on dance, music, and Internet cultures have observed (see Doane 2006; Williams 2006), overt attention to space on the part of participants (e.g., "making the scene to be seen") as opposed to time (being seen and recognized as part of that(sub)culture anywhere), raises questions about one's authentic commitment to the regular status of one's identity— casting such an individual as a poseur or pretender (Fox 1987). It is easy to pose as a regular while situated in a place where such identities are expected, but it shows true commitment to an identity to stand apart from the expected and in places where such cultural patterns are not the norm.

In the following, we wish to expand on the proposition that as any particular culture becomes more ethereal, authentic regular identification becomes less anchored to measured time and literal space and more grounded in particular accomplishments beyond spatial and temporal markers. Whereas traditional ethnographers have bounded conceptions of authentic regulars to explicit spaces (e.g., bars, restaurants, dance halls) and as part of an overt and anchored culture, regular status has also been linked to ongoing activities that emerge in various social milieus. For example, Kinkade and Katovich (2008) analyzed involvement in gatherings of card players and found that as regularity became more tied to temporality, player accomplishments associated with the game itself gained importance in defining identity. In this case, communities and regularities that were once spatially defined became more ethereal and transitions in the roles and motives of the participants were a result.

In the current research, analysis and observation of an evolution of culture working in the opposite direction will be described. Hacker culture, as documented in this participant-observant ethnographic study, by its nature highly transcendent of time and space constraints, became spatially and temporally confined during the Chaos Communication Camp 2011 and its typical existence in virtual cyberspace became challenged and adapted to a more traditional, social community structure. The primary focus of this interactionist study centers on the exchanges and cultures that emerged when hackers[1] met in person. Its ethnographic approach complements previous research based on mostly quantitative data collected at hacker conferences (see Bachmann 2008, 2010, 2011; Bachmann and Corzine 2010; Holt 2007, 2009, 2010; Holt and Kilger 2008; Schell and Dodge 2002; Schell and Melnychuk 2010).

Hacker Culture

So far, the chapter has referred to "hacker culture" as if a single subculture of all hackers existed today. That is simply not the case. While the term hacker culture—for reasons of text accessibility—will continue to be used throughout the chapter, the reader should be alerted to the fact that an understanding of such a culture as an overarching category under which all hackers can be subsumed would be a gross oversimplification. Rather than being a part of one unifying subculture, individual hackers and hacker groups vary widely in their understanding of what it means to "hack" or what exactly a "hacker" is (see also Bachmann 2008, 2009, 2010; Furnell2002; Holt 2007, 2010). Moreover, both terms are fiercely contested between different types of hackers. Hackers, typically sharing an emphasis on independence and individuality, usually subscribe to their own, personal definition of these terms, thereby creating almost as many variations in understandings of these two terms as there are "hackers." Rather than aligning under the umbrella of one unifying hacker culture, hackers create "a rich and diverse culture consisting of justifications, highly specialized skills, information-sharing networks, norms, status hierarchies, language, and unifying symbolic meanings" (Turgeman-Goldschmidt 2008, 382; see also Meyer and Thomas 1990).

To complicate matters even further, commonplace discourses within the general public and the mainstream media, largely ignorant of the important differences that exist between various types of hackers, continue to perpetu-

---

1. The term "hacker" is highly contested and the difficulties involved in providing an accurate definition are detailed in the next section on hacker culture. The following sections provide a more detailed description of how the term hacker is understood in this chapter than any one abbreviated dictionary-type definition could. The controversies surrounding such a definition and the dimensions along which they arise have to be elaborated for a better understanding of why no universally agreed-on academic definition of the term "hacker" exists to date.

ate an oversimplified understanding of a hacker as a person who commits crimes on the Internet or through the means of computer technology. Needless to say that in the eyes of many hackers who have no criminal intentions and do not commit any crimes, this stigmatization is a glaring misrepresentation. In an attempt to shed some light on the contested etymology and usage of the terms, the following section provides a brief overview over the most widespread understandings of what it means to hack or be a hacker and delineates some of the more common factions of hackers (see Bachmann 2008, 2011; Bachmann and Corzine 2010; Holt 2007; Schell and Holt 2009; Thomas 2003; Turgeman-Goldschmidt 2008; Voiskounsky and Smyslova 2003; Yar 2006 for a more detailed description). Such an introduction is necessary for a contextualization and an understanding of the specific hacker camp observations presented in this chapter (see also Holt 2007; Jordan and Taylor 1998; Meyer 1989; or Taylor 1999 for further discussions of general subcultural norms and groups within broader hacker culture).

Since its first appearance in the Yiddish language, where it was used to describe an unskilled person who would use an axe to make furniture (Schell and Martin 2004), the term "hacker" has substantially changed form. After many intervening years with changing meanings, it eventually resurfaced in the context of computer technology during the 1960s. It was reintroduced as a neologism into the specialized and confined language of computer technicians and programming experts. It was used as a positive label for programmers who were particularly skilled in developing highly efficient, creative, and compact programs and algorithms. "Hacker" enthusiasts, however, were also united in their passion for technological innovations and in their playful and individualistic quest to satisfy their intellectual curiosity. "Hacker" in this understanding denotes someone who is an accomplished designer of computer software or hardware, a superb technician who possesses a high degree of skill and competence and directs much of his efforts to improving computer technology or, especially in the days prior to the TCP/IP based Internet, to exploring the technical aspects of telephone switching and communication systems. Respectively, then, "hacking" can refer to the continuous improvement of computer program codes and algorithms, of software applications and hardware components (Bachmann 2008). It was hackers who first realized the true potential of computers and their applications. All early contributors to the advancement and expansion of computer technology, all innovators who developed new computer-based solutions to a multitude of problems, all entrepreneurs who pioneered and fostered the "computer revolution" (Naughton 2000, 313), and all those who paved the way for today's omnipresent Internet, were considered prototypical hackers in this original understanding of the term (Levy 1984).

The original hacker community formed a subculture shaped by ideals and moral concepts tied to the zeitgeist of the time. As with many other sub- and counter-culture movements, the early hacking community was, in part, characterized by a fundamental distrust of governmental and military monopolies of power, and authority in general. Early hackers defied corporate domination of culture and rejected traditional and conservative values, norms, and lifestyles (Kovacich 1999). Instead, they genuinely adhered to the enlightenment ideals of human emancipation and self-fulfillment through rational thought (Yar 2006). They advocated the freedom of information and an intellectualist approach to politics, and promoted the idea that knowledge should be accessible to everyone without restriction or intervention (Thomas 2003). Many members of the early hacking community were idealists who advocated the use of computer technology for the higher goals of intellectual discovery, aesthetic expression, and for improving the overall quality of life for all (Schrutzki 1989). Today, hacker programming and other activities that support these views are oftentimes referred to as "hacktivism" within the general subculture to emphasize their political nature (Jordan and Taylor 2004; Taylor 2004).

While their exploratory quests for new information and data frequently included unauthorized accesses to remote computer systems, traditional hackers undertook such accesses without criminal intent. Instead, they were carried out to investigate and better understand the intricacies of different system setups, to utilize existing computing resources, to detect security breaches and weaknesses, and to ultimately enhance computer protections (Levy 1984). The vast majority of members of the original hacker community adhered to the "Hacker Ethic," a set of rules that was introduced by Steven Levy (1984) to describe the values of the hackers at the MIT Artificial Intelligence Laboratory. The main principles of this Hacker Ethic are that: 1) access to computers and anything that might teach something about how the world works should be unlimited and total; 2) all information should be free; 3) authority should be mistrusted and decentralization promoted; 4) hackers should be judged solely by their hacking, not ascribed criteria such as degrees, age, race, or position (hence the characterization of the hacking community as a strong meritocracy); 5) art and beauty can be created on a computer; and, 6) computers can change life for the better (Levy 1984). One important implication of this Ethic is that any form of damage to remote computer systems, be it intentional or as a result of incompetence, is principally objectionable and contemptible.

Unfortunately, the original positive meanings of the terms "hackers" and "hacking" became gradually substituted with negative connotations in the 1980s and 1990s. The increasingly mission-critical nature of computer networks for many industries and the expanding popularity of electronic financial transactions began to interest many unsavory people with less-than-noble intentions. For many at this juncture in time, breaking into computer systems was not done in an attempt to understand them or make them more secure, but to abuse, disrupt, sabotage, and exploit private information. Angered by what appeared to be tarnishing the hacking community, traditional hackers reacted to this development by introducing the new label "crackers" for unethical and menacing hackers and from whom they attempted to distinguish themselves. The term is derived from the activity of cracking, or breaking into, a safe and it refers to people who breach (or crack) security measures on a computer system, a network, or an application with the intent to damage or exploit the target or to steal information from it. Hackers who engage in these kinds of malicious activities, on the other hand, largely reject the label "crackers" because cracking typically involves programming software applications specifically designed to discover and exploit weaknesses. In their logic, the ability to create programs that are able to circumvent or breach defensive security measures is proof of their ability to write superior code. Hence, they prefer to refer to themselves as hackers. In the context of this debate, it should also be noted that the rejection of generalizing labels is a common and widespread part of the larger hacker culture. Most hackers simply reject having any labels assigned to them.

The fiercely contested battle over these two labels created considerable linguistic confusion and is not the only controversial cultural differentiation in the hacker community. Similar to the distinction that exists between "hackers" and "crackers," is the classic and somewhat antiquated differentiation (Holt and Kilger 2008) between "white hat" and "black hat" hackers. "White hat" denotes hackers who abide by the Hacker Ethic and hold its rules in highest regard, whereas "black hat" hackers do not commit themselves to the same ethical standards. Other designations within the community include "grey hats," oftentimes used to describe hackers who resort to illicit means to achieve what they see as worthy or ethical goals. Over time, the color spectrum of different "hats" has expanded further. For instance, "penetration testers," individuals employed by an outside computer security firm to probe a system prior to its launch to look for weaknesses, are also being called "blue hats." The expansion of the color of hats is, at least to some extent, also indicative of the decline of these classic distinctions within the community because similar to colors, there are simply too many types of different hackers to justify any classification in over-generalizing "hat" terms.

Other social identities for hackers include "elites," "script kiddies," and "noobies." Elites are the most skilled hackers and their exploits will circulate among the general community. An association with elite groups also typically confers credibility on the member. On the other end of the spectrum are script kiddies: unskilled dilettantes who break in using pre-packaged, automated tools written by others to carry out hacking attacks. Finally, a noobie refers to someone who is simply new to hacking and who has almost no knowledge of the workings of computer-technology (see also the taxonomies developed by Chiesa, Ducci and Ciappi 2008 or Rogers 2006).

While the majority of the masses of unskilled script kiddies who merely download and execute preconfigured attack applications and routines can adequately be subsumed under the label of black hat hackers (Twist 2003), the contested nature of the terms "hacker" and "hacking" within the scene is important to bear in mind when studying hackers. Studies that do not distinguish between white hat penetration testers and criminal black hat hackers will inevitably introduce a bias that produces distorted and inaccurate perceptions.

Notwithstanding the resistance to the criminal label within the traditional hacker community, large parts of the general public are either unaware or ignorant of the distinctions between hackers and crackers, white hats and black hats and the rest. Similarly, mainstream media outlets generally do not subscribe to these distinctions. Instead, they subsume any type of hacking activity under the currently predominant definition as an inherently negative, criminal activity (Taylor 2000). They usually also equate hackers with cybercriminals, merely because this is how the vast majority of people outside of the community understand hacking and hackers (Twist 2003; Yar 2006). The distorted picture of hackers is partly a result of the circumstance that only very few people have direct personal contacts to actual hackers in their social networks. Without direct personal experience, a majority of people derive their knowledge about hackers from representations in popular fiction and the media. Thus, the definitions of what constitute a hacker and hacking activities are not only deeply contested within the hacking community, but also between the general public and hackers, to whom the criminal label is universally applied. While many black hat hackers accept or embrace this label, self-proclaimed white hat hackers consider themselves misrepresented by it and continue to challenge and reject the label.

Both the various contested meanings of the terms "hacker" and "hacking" and the perceptions of hackers in the general public are important elements that must be taken into consideration in a scientific study of hackers. The disputed nature of the two terms implies that researchers must gather a specific understanding of what exactly the terms "hacker" and "hacking" mean to the study subjects before attempting to collect any observations regarding the motivations to attend the camp or the roles assumed at the camp with any accuracy. The common perception of hackers, on the other hand, has to be considered because it exerts an influence on the self-perception of hackers. More importantly, it is also the broader background against which a more accurate, scientific understanding of hackers is to be established.

Perspectives, Procedures, and Settings

The Chaos Communication Camp is an international open-air meeting of hackers that takes place every four years and is organized by the Germany-based hacker organization "Chaos Computer Club." The Chaos Computer Club, the largest European hacker organization, with over 4,000 members currently, describes itself as "a galactic community of life forms, independent of age, sex, race or societal orientation, which strives across borders for freedom of information, concerns itself with the risks and consequences technology has on society and individuals, and advances technological development" (Chaos Computer Club 2009).[2] Politically, the club advocates traditional hacker ideals such as governmental transparency, freedom of information, and freedom to communicate as a fundamental human right. The club also supports initiatives for free universal access to computers and technological infrastructure and undertakes active "hacktivist"[3] efforts to realize them.

The Chaos Computer Club was founded in 1981 by Herwart Holland-Moritz (alias "Dr. Wau") and other "Komputerfrieks" who realized that information technology would play a prominent role in societal evolution and as a structural support for personal freedom. The club is widely known for its many publications of large-scale security flaws and risks but also demonstrates an

---

2. The original text on the CCC Website reads "Der Chaos Computer Club ist eine galaktische Gemeinschaft von Lebewesen, unabhängig von Alter, Geschlecht und Abstammung sowie gesellschaftlicher Stellung, die sich grenzüberschreitend für Informationsfreiheit einsetzt und mit den Auswirkungen von Technologien auf die Gesellschaft sowie das einzelne Lebewesen beschäftigt und das Wissen um diese Entwicklung fördert." It has been translated from German to English for this chapter.

3. The term "hacktivism," a portmanteau of "hack" and "activism," refers to the use of legal and illegal digital tools to foster political agendas and ideals. Website defacements, redirects, and virtual sit-ins, to name but a few methods, are commonly used as online equivalents to traditional activism or civil disobedience. They are intended to protest some, oftentimes established and conservative, political agendas and designed to promote other, more progressive and liberal ideals. Many hacktivists manipulate electronic information to promote idealistic agendas centered on principals such as the protest of economic inequality or the promotion of free speech, free dissemination of information, or universal human rights.

interest in "cyber-aesthetics." For instance, it is responsible for several interactive light installations dubbed "Project Blinkenlights" that turn large buildings in Germany and around the world into giant computer screens (Blinkenlights 2012). Aside from Project Blinkenlights and the Chaos Communication Camp, the club organizes various other campaigns and events, among them the annual Chaos Communication Congress, another prominent meeting of the international hacker scene that provides a point of interaction on technical, political, and ethical issues concerning cyber-technology.

The quadrennial Chaos Communication Camp (CCC) provides a popular forum "for hackers and associated life-forms" for the dissemination of information concerning technical and societal issues tied to cyber-technology, such as privacy, freedom of information, and data security (Chaos Communication Camp 2011a). Talks of various sizes and durations are held in (in)formal areas around the camp. Participants camp at the site of the conference and experience the associated primitive accommodations but also enjoy the luxuries of a fast Internet connection and plentiful power supplies. The present chapter summarizes the participant observations collected at the CCC 2011, which was themed "Project Flow Control" and took place from August 10th to 14th in Finowfurt, a small town near Berlin, Germany. While the time spent in discussion was not formally tracked, it is estimated that between the three investigators approximately 20 hours a day was spent engaged in conversations with other camp participants concerning issues tied to hacking culture. Although the number of participants the investigators spoke with exceeds those that were recorded, a total of 23 interviews were transcribed for potential inclusion in this project (see Lofland and Lofland 1995). All interviewees were white and, with only one exception, male between the ages of 18 to 64 (most were in their 20s to 30s), a composition that closely mirrored the overall sociodemgraphic composition of the campsite.

While generating and collecting data, Snow and Anderson's (1993 24) ethnographic strategy, the "buddy researcher," or, in this case, the "fellow camper" who adapted to and adopted the conference scene, was employed. The main benefit of the establishment as camp participants was that the researchers were recognized by the others as less- to non-disruptive (see Adler and Adler 1987, 35–40; Wolcott 1995, 100). All three researchers did maintain some role distance in regard to extracurricular camp activities to establish boundaries between their identities as researchers and their commitment to the life of the social group. While regarding themselves as strangers and detached from the group consciousness, the researchers demonstrated competence and bravado while in discussion to fit the general mood of camp interaction and to gain better rapport in the hacking community.

Of particular relevance, the campers with whom the three researchers interacted most frequently demonstrated understanding and ease with the duality of the researchers' roles within the camping community. While at the camp, other participants joked with the researchers about their hacking (in)competence, often chiding and challenging them as they would any other computer expert. Such chiding efforts were probably actions motivated by social control processes linked to communicating and establishing status differences between the campers and researchers.

However, most of the campers also knew the researchers as social scientists. When this identity was emphasized, interactions changed noticeably. Other campers ceased making light of the researchers' lack of expertise and showed a good deal of deference toward their identities as university professors. In this context, it has to be noted that in Europe generally and Germany specifically, the status of university professor is one that is accorded even more status than in the United States. Clearly, the deference accorded the researchers was localized to their role as social scientists rather than hackers.

As with most participant observers, the researchers confronted the problem of maintaining co-presence within the group, establishing responsive but non-committal relations with other campers, and projecting ongoing futures with others in specific regard to their hacker roles (see Hessler 1992, 207–221 for a general discussion of these processes). After securing formal admittance to the camp, the researchers worked at informal acceptance into the core group of "regulars" at each given camp site (see Glaser and Strauss 1967; Katovich and Reese 1987; Miller 2000; Ragin 1994, 98–101; Wolcott 1995, 91–95). In the course of gaining acceptance, the researchers observed ongoing interactions at the scenes, interviewed others, and later made written field notes of statements and observations while away from other campers (see Emerson, Fretz, and Shaw 1995; Lofland and Lofland 1995, 89–98). Grounded theory methods (Glaser and Strauss 1965, 1967, 1968; Strauss and Glaser 1970), a specific set of inductive strategies used to synthesize general and systematic propositions from the constant comparing of unfolding observations from both the camp environment and the interviews, were utilized to analyze interview data and observations.

In conducting the analysis, the researchers followed the guidelines put forth by Strauss and Corbin (1990) to 1) periodically reexamine the collected data and the information contained in it, 2) maintain an attitude of skepticism, and 3) to rigorously follow systematic data collection and analysis procedures so as to produce valid and reliable observations and conclusions. Efforts were made to take control of the data by actively avoiding influences of preconceived concepts and hypotheses. Instead, early emerging themes and questions from camp observations and interviews were utilized to direct subsequent data collections. Careful attention was given to coding procedures, the pivotal link between observations and developing patterns and explanations. Rather than relying on line-by-line coding procedures, the researchers predominantly employed focused coding techniques to identify reappearing conceptual codes in their notes (Charmaz 2001).

The researchers made no attempt to conceal their professorial identities to anyone at the camp. In fact, during the observation period they made known their interest in writing an academic paper on the topic of hacking and solicited personal information from participants through questions specifically directed at the subject. Still, the three maintained low profiles as researchers. The researchers and fellow campers agreed to treat all potential analysis as a silent understanding, creating a cooperative pretense awareness in the course of maintaining identities as duelists (see Glaser and Strauss 1964). Such pretense afforded the researchers the luxury of being openly observant and curious about camper activity without causing any noticeable behavioral reactivity in the community.

Identity Assignments within a Grounded Online Culture

Identity assignments consist of various social adjustments related to how participants perceive each other, indicate perceptions, and validate (or contradict) such perceptions (see Stone 1962). Sociologists generally conceive of such assignments as bound to stable tempo-spatial anchors, which do appear in the context of the CCC. One key assignment, for instance, was indicated by the personalized nicknames called "handles"[4] given to "tag" individual characteristics manifest by a particular camper. Attendees continually proffered unique nicknames to each other during discourse. These handles may have also been used as cyber-identities or avatars in other circumstances within the hacker culture, oftentimes for functional reasons (e.g., indication of particular skills, hiding of true identities, or ability to switch between aliases in different contexts; see also Bechar-Israeli 1995; Kilger 2005; Thomas 2003). While

---

4. "Handles" in the context of computer hacking refers to online pseudonyms intended to mask the user's real identity, while at the same time allowing for the formation of an online identity. Actions performed under one handle can be attributed to one user, while at the same time allowing the real person behind the keyboard to remain anonymous. The term originated in the era of CB radio (Citizen's Band radio), where it was used for the same purposes.

such identities marked campers within the general scene, they did not serve to ground any camper in a literal place over an equally specified duration. The authors, heretofore known by their ascribed hacker monikers "War-machine," "Crash," and "Wabbit" adopted their own "handles" for their participant-observation research. It should be noted that all pseudonyms used in this text (beyond War-machine, Crash, and Wabbit) are fictitious but were re-termed to capture, when possible, the sense of the Web or camp name used or given.

In effect, ascription of identities in the CCC symbolized a more rarified acceptance into a community without reference to obdurate boundaries (see Fine and Kleinman 1979). For instance, while specific groups set up dedicated areas called "villages" (e.g., Bitcoin sofa, Freedom-not-fear, H x^2, or W00tstock) in the larger campground to focus on particular themes, interests, projects, languages, or topics, no individual entering into the camp had a "special spot." Also unlike typical spatial and temporal communities in which nicknames make reference to either other places or times (e.g., barroom regulars often have nicknames such as "Tex" or "Smitty" associated with their home states or occupations, a time specific activity) the CCC seemed filled with monikers relevant to emergent acts and arcane descriptions. Name tags such as "Poet," "Slither," and "Raider," for example, were relatively common. These tie signs, understood by those within the collective, emphasized accomplishment or interest rather than temporal or spatial awareness (Goffman 1974; Thomas 2003). The ethereal nature of the CCC community apparently changed the type of emphasis given in personal signifiers.

Some identities resemble adaptations, bridging a gap between what has occurred (and what people understand as having occurred) and what will occur (Sykes 1958). As Thorton (1995) noted in his study of club cultures, indications of belonging to any subculture involve making sense of ambiguous spaces at many different moments in time, none of which are entirely predictable. Such adaptations, then, define the parameters of behaviors in relation to ambiguous circumstances, or involve establishment of identification across time and spaces that lack specified anchors (see Katovich and Hardesty 1987; Schutz 1944; Simmel 1950).

Campers, of course, recognize established time and space boundaries and, as do regulars in any context, reconstruct and re-establish their identities within an ongoing social world. In reference to such stable markers, Katovich and Reese (1987) provided one direct application of how habitués in neighborhood bars divided drinkers into five temporal types of participants including *regulars, irregular regulars, regular irregulars, neutrals and non-regulars*. The researchers noted that in the context of the CCC, two of these temporal categories, *regulars* and *irregular regulars*, represented an ongoing commitment to community organization. This is distinctly different to the ethereal hacker culture where regularity is tied to experience in hacking as opposed to temporal commitment to the camp. "Elites," "noobies," and "script kiddies," for example, are all tied to the general hacker culture by competencies developed through time, not the time commitment itself.

Group regulars at the CCC controlled the action rates at the camp and made a point to emphasize that any sort of identification of regularity involved considerations beyond specific place and time. As one regular said:

> I haven't been to a lot of these camps but these guys still rely on me.
> I tell them when to drink and what project we are going to tie into.

Similar to the tangible tempo-spatial culture defined within barrooms, CCC regulars also moderated the acceptance of new members to the group, often ascribing a camp name to the neophyte and reveling in the use of the unique hacker lexicon. For example, Crash, who clearly was unskilled in relation to computers and ungrounded in hacker culture, derived his handle from that fact and was called a "virgin." On many occasions regulars suggested that his naïvité might lead to his subjugation by more competent camp participants. Furthermore, it became readily apparent that any demonstration of cultural ignorance of either the ascribed names of the other campers or of the "techno-speak" of the camp further distinguished and isolated the non-regular from those in the know and maintained the boundaries between insiders and outsiders.

Regulars also expected each other to enforce the informal codes that define the camp's symbolic significance and profile. Regulars enforced the routine actions within the camp and grounded the community as a shared collective where the insiders ruled and outsiders were left to react to the regulars' expectations. As one regular suggested in relation to the expected communalism of the camp:

> If you are not going to share you're gonna be outside looking in and
> left on your own when you want something from us.

Many irregular regulars actively maintained their voice in groups of regulars and their established shared histories with ongoing regulars (i.e., regulars remember them as having been around and they have experience interfacing with regulars). However, the irregular regulars have become pegged as those who have "moved on." Typically, they seem to have accepted life positions (families and employment) and simply do not have the time for hacking as they once did. While absent, current regulars continue to validate the erstwhile regularity of irregular regulars, articulating memories of their past presence. As one regular suggested about one such irregular regular:

> Yeah … Slither used to be here all the time but then he got married
> and his life intruded on all the fun …

The aforementioned identities do involve standard time markers in this traditional ethereal culture, but more importantly, they also represent strategic
validation patterns of behaviors designed to allow regulars to attend to new-
comers independent of literal tempo-spatial anchors. Such identities signify
the capacity to exploit, tutor, avoid, or accept those new to the scene and to
also organize the community. While these identities allow for an understanding of the regulation and construction of long- and short-term relationships
and camp organization, they do not explain how regulars or irregular regulars choose to participate in the culture of the camp. In this vein, six prototypical
profiles of attendees were identified that together allow for a better understanding of the specific nature of grounded hacker communal involvement
(see Mills 1940 for a discussion on typologies in qualitative research and Holt
2007 for a discussion of typological dimensions within hacker culture).

1) Artists. Artists view the hack or the manipulation of technology primarily as an aesthetic expression. As with other artists whose medium is paint, lyrics,
or stanzas, the art will be a personal expression that can be evaluated from the
perspective of the creator but which is also routinely ascribed value by the
viewing public. The value of electronic or technology-based artistry was often
commented on by campers. Some felt it was best to judge "the art" by the technical merits of its execution. The difficulty of its execution or the eloquence of
its technological application was at least partially the key to its artistic value.
Others thought to judge the work as one would commonly judge visual art,
through its aesthetics. Several of the campers, for example, created light shows
that could be enjoyed by passers-by or those localized to the production. Others incorporated sound with compressed or manipulated electronic music to
be enjoyed for their artistry and public presentations. Still others provided a
graphic presentation or transient architectural display in tent construction to
give demonstration of their artistic intent.

Whether through a technical demonstration or a traditional aesthetic, artists
at the camp clearly identified themselves as such and reveled in the viewing of
their work. As one camp artist put it:

> I want to show this to the camp … these guys can appreciate what it
> took to do this and it is a thing of beauty.

2) Dorks. This self-ascribed and self-effacing identify clearly places hacking
and hackers into larger networks and communities that are tied together by
other related interests, and it also feeds the aforementioned popular cultural

stereotypes of hacker identities and what they do away from their computers. The term also works to establish a micro-community within the larger hacker collective that serves to create insulation from any ascribed diminution about dorks that is overlaid by pure hackers. Dorks revel in other worlds of fandom that are often tied to popular culture. These may include television shows, movies, card games, comic books, and role play. They stand out in the hacking community because they typically assign a stronger emphasis on popular culture icons than do other members of the community, an emphasis that sometimes even exceeds their interest in technology.

While hacking and computer technologies may be the focus of their current discourse, the other affiliations and vocabularies are not far from their conversation or shared experience. Whether expressed in dialogue, activity, or dress, other "dork" affiliations are displayed and integrated into the camp community. For example, t-shirts adorned with references to the popular movie and television franchises "Star Trek" and "Star Wars" were commonplace on the scene. Other dorks expressed the fetish-like sexual dimension technology entails for them, for instance by wearing t-shirts imprinted with "Penetration Expert," a double play on sexual performance and "penetration testing" (i.e., legal hacking activities under contract). Several tents had campers engaged in active LAN gaming sessions of various types, and ubiquitous references to super heroes were rife throughout the camp. When asked about his participation at the CCC, one self-proclaimed dork answered:

> This is part of my routine ... I go to other conferences for other specific things (a comic book conference was later specified) but I go to them all (other conferences he attends) to talk about the things I love with guys who also love them. I used to get shit about this in high school but here it is generally cool ... I mean there are still a few assholes ... but not as many.

3) *Professionals.* Contrary to what the identity suggests, most professionals attended the camp to indulge themselves more than to take away intellectually, aesthetically, or communally. These individuals are characterized by their career positions dealing with computers, software design, Internet development or security. They have professional and personal standing that goes beyond what would be considered the norm for many of the participants in the CCC. They attend the CCC as a distraction that might be justified to peers or family as professional development or concern. The informal recreations of the camp, however, seem to be the most significant attraction to this particular group. Drinking, drug use and boisterous talking are far more common to the activity regime of the professional than attending talks, workshops or col-

laborating on projects. They are not attributed any special status by the gathered community but neither do they seem to desire any. Much like the Japanese "suitmen" who work diligently and conservatively all week only to drink with reckless abandon on the weekend, these camp participants are looking for an outlet from or a counterpoint to their more conventional and controlled routines. The CCC, a conference well beyond the pale of typical professional gatherings, provides the perfect vehicle for their needs. As one professional confessed during a late night reverie:

> I don't learn shit here, I spend my time fucked up and away from the wife and kids … I look at this bullcrap enough in company (referring to the business he owns). I don't need more of it for recreation.

4) Deviants. In ethereal hacker culture, "black hats" would be considered a sub-set of the larger deviant subgroup; however, not all "deviants" would be considered "black hats." Deviants differ from black hats in that their outlaw self-perception goes beyond and is not necessarily solely tied to computing attacks. They choose to live on the fringes of normative behavior, adopting a lifestyle that is unconventional in relation to general social norms. Deviants differ from dorks in that they possess no desire to be accepted on anyone's terms but their own. The dork craves acceptance into the normative majority, but in lieu of that ideal, uses acceptance in their outsider sub-group as a surrogate. Deviants differ from professionals in that they have no normative life to which they return. The professional may behave as a deviant by using the CCC as a time anchor for such aberration, but they do not continue as the "outlaw" when the camp breaks and they must return home. The deviant, on the other hand, has adopted a lifestyle. In discussing their affiliation to the CCC, deviants do not speak of community in the sense of belonging but rather as a manifestation of collective tolerance. They may be accepted, but it is not the concern of the deviant to be so. Rather, as one "deviant" confided, they simply want to be "left alone to be themselves and compute." As "Flower," a male deviant so tagged by his CCC traveling group for wearing print sarongs and ornate jewelry, elaborated:

> I don't belong with them … we simply arrived here together … it's not to say I don't like them … I just don't care if they like me … I am who I am … they need to deal with it.

5) Politicals. Politicals anchor themselves to hacker culture for identity, ascribing the label to themselves and to the collective as a badge of honor and, most importantly, as a signifier of purpose. This is not unlike the other categories of campers that were observed at the CCC. To the political, however, it is not enough that the collective serves as an outlet for individual purposes that may be commonly shared if not routinely coordinated. For the political, it is the group's existence that empowers, and it is the coordinated and unified collective effort that provides their individual identities to the larger network. Speaking broadly, politicals want the hacker group to "get things done"; they epitomize the "hacktivism" described in the earlier section on general hacker culture. Politicals want to mobilize the community toward larger goals and they revel in the idea that, even despite their communal fringe status, they can achieve goals beyond what is feasible within established and entrenched economic and political institutions. Judging from the researchers' personal experiences with different hacker communities, politicals seem to be particularly prevalent among European hacker groups.

As an example, one needs to look no further than the keynote address at the CCC 2011 to recognize and appreciate the existence of hacker politicals and their general nature. The address, entitled "Hackers in Space: A Modest Proposal for the Next 23 Years," was given by Jens Ohlig, Lars Weiler, and Nick Farr, three such political players, and focused on the group's desire to organize a space program run and manned by hackers. It called for a utilization of the existing infrastructure of "hackerspaces" for the community-driven, gradual exploration of outer space at a time when nation-states are abandoning their space programs (Chaos Communication Camp 2011b).[5] The address was given in an abandoned East German military aircraft hangar surrounded by the rusted artifacts of a by-gone Cold War era. The location of the address affirmed the "outsider" status of the proposed movement, yet the intent was clear: to organize this loosely affiliated gathering toward a practical political end. Other political objectives routinely discussed at the CCC concerned freedom of information and individual right to privacy. As one hacker, "Viking" stated:

> There is real power in this group ... a real opportunity to do things ... and there are a few of us who are working to make this fact apparent to the morons that come to these things.

6) *Cling-Ons.* Cling-ons participate in the community but mostly as peripheral spectators rather than as camp regulars. Whether camping or not,

---

5. The Hacker Space program proposal was divided into three phases, which "we feel can be accomplished in the next 23 years. Phase one is the launch of an open, free and globally accessible satellite-based network built by hackers as the ultimate defense against terrestrial censorship of the Internet. If that sounds too easy, let's go to phase two: Put a hacker into orbit. This will be the preparation for phase three. By 2034, we plan on landing a hacker on the moon" (Chaos Communication Camp, 2011b).

cling-ons seek out others for interactional meaning and direction. Cling-ons, typically less skilled than other groups, arrive to interact with others in an attempt to garner attention that their status does not warrant, much in the style of the social gadfly. However, these attention-seeking efforts sometimes lead to tensions with other attendees, who see cling-ons as not warranting their attention and who consequently deny them the acceptance they so desperately seek. For example, "Joe," an interviewed day participant, attended the camp with no intention of working on a project, just to talk to others. However, his persistent attempts to interact annoyed all others in the observed hacker groups in a highly consistent manner. Seemingly oblivious to his lack of acceptance, "Joe" nonetheless continued to engage various people sporadically yet relentlessly. As one regular stated, echoing the sentiments of many others:

> What is with that guy ... why come here and isolate yourself by being annoying? I am sure he can do that at home.

As a sub-group of cling-ons, "groupies"(within hacker culture also more negatively referred to as "scene whores," a term denoting conference groupies whose primary interest does not rest on technology-related themes of the conference, but instead centers on garnering attention from male attendees) are predominantly female companions of hackers, oftentimes tied exclusively to a particular male CCC participant. They signify their allegiance to specific male players through demonstrations of intense attention to "their man" while at the same time displaying a pointed aloofness toward other campers. They rarely talk to anyone in the general gathering and, owing to their detached demeanor, receive few initiators (as would be the case for a very low status individual occupying temporary space within the community by virtue of their companion's status). Although groupies attend to the CCC participant with whom they came, their companions rarely reciprocate to avoid being associated with a lower status individual. Indeed, the participants linked to the groupies appear to studiously avoid their companion except when seeking affirmation. Most commonly, the camping hackers will ask for their groupie's agreement or support in a conversational point or for the acquisition of food. When Crash asked a camper accompanied by a groupie about his companion, he blankly stated:

> She is here to be with me ... the camp means nothing to her personally.

The Emergent Grounded Hacker Culture

Mead (1938) noted that individuals and social collectivities create ongoing repertoires that serve as general guidelines for future conduct. Going beyond the more common notion of "norms as prescribed rules," Mead noted that individuals do not experience ongoing repertoires as static objects. Rather, such repertoires include patterns of conduct that become perceived as problematic and so invite adaptations geared toward the avoidance of unwanted consequences (see McPhail 1991, 193–194). In the world of hackers, potentially problematic consequences are not restricted to events that could disrupt the camp. Many probable unwanted consequences also involve outside attitudes, attacks, and damages.

The hacker community and those individuals who govern camp dynamics continually modify cultural repertoires. Participation in ongoing gatherings allows hackers to notice patterns of behavior whereby particular acts become perceived as so uniform and consistent that an expectation for that routine action becomes ingrained and anticipated. When consensus in regard to such recognition emerges, implicit rules are formed and "insider/outsider" ascriptions are applied to individual participants. Those who know the expectations are perceived as a part of the group and accorded due recognition and interactional opportunity. Those who do not are marginalized in subtle but important ways, and are thereby at least partially removed from the camper community. Some codes appeared campsite specific, calling for particular coordinated acts linked to the specific circumstances of a physical place. Clean-up procedures, for example, varied from place to place, depending on literal physical lay-out, camper priorities, and other site idiosyncratic factors.

However, the grounded theory method utilized in this study revealed particular codes of conduct that appeared more universal in that they were repeatedly mentioned in interviews and frequently observed across the entire camp, regardless of physical definition of place, ownership criteria, or in-group variations. Such codes pertain to three general processes of conduct: 1) technology-attitude response patterns — codes concerning individual perceptions of and reactions to computers and computing; 2) interpersonal action dynamics — codes referring to initiation-response patterns constructed among campers; and, 3) looking-glass self-sequences — codes relating to Cooley's [1902] (1922) highly noted depiction of the self as consisting of imagination (appearance) and judgment (labeling appearance).

Technology-attitude response patterns involve two general identifications, "ownership" and "ambivalence." Computer ownership first and foremost applies to the manifest principle that the collective of campers truly appreciates computer-technology and its manifold applications. Conversation about hardware, software, and their various uses, applications, and advantages were rife throughout the camp. Appreciation of others' computing capabilities and software developments were normative. However, campers also viewed certain ap-

plications and activities as fully proprietary and certain access and inquiries
were viewed as forbidden to the extent that the campers themselves sanctioned
violations aggressively. Campers who were solemnly concerned with ownership have, with great commotion, escorted recalcitrant interlopers out of their
camping area. Despite these sometimes intense displays of ownership toward
computing work and equipment, camp regulars also express "ambivalence" in
regard to their participation in the camp and their technology. As one hacker
stated while modifying his CCC identification badge (a programmable, full-
featured microcontroller development board shaped like a rocket ship designed
to be hung on the lapel):

> I am sitting here taking pride in the fact I have modified this self-
> indulgent piece of shit into an even more self-indulgent piece of shit ...
> hacking ... It gives life such meaning.

Another hacker, while trying to get his portable mainframe working, expressed a familiar cry of exasperation that would resonate with anyone who
works in computer-technology:

> God ... I hate computers!

Interpersonal action dynamics deal with hackers' reactions to other hackers
and include at least three processes relevant to overall group functioning, co-
hesion, and the economy of the camp. First, hackers perceive a strong sense of
communalism among themselves, despite their oftentimes competitive relationships. Deep feelings of obligation among campers represent an overall desire to share the responsibilities involved in creating and maintaining the camp
community. To some degree, the apparent communalism stems from shared
histories that were developed prior to and independent from the camp. Even
so, during the CCC, the participants exhibited commitment toward the common good of the group and imposed standards of commitment by which each
attendant was expected to abide and expected others to abide by.

For example, while looking for a place to plug in a phone charger late one
night, Crash was offered an outlet by a stranger and was then invited to sit and
talk at the campsite while the mobile's batteries replenished. During the conversation, the sole adjacent tent opened and a third party came to join the discussion. While the initial offer in and of itself demonstrated a drive toward
the common good, the appearance of the third camper made this point even
more salient. As it turned out, the tent's inhabitant knew neither Crash nor
the person who gave Crash the opportunity to charge his phone. The gathered
group were all strangers to each other: one who had a need, one offering resources that were not specifically his to offer to meet that need, and another

completely comfortable that his resources were offered without his permission in the transaction that occurred. Laissez-faire communalism was manifest in purest form and highest expectation. The cohesiveness of the group was preserved and enhanced as new relationships were formed. The communal functioning of the camp was further confirmed as technological resources were replenished and campers were supported in their private agendas when, in following the manifest economic traditions of the camp, Crash went to buy beer to share with the interloper who invited him to recharge and the owner of the outlet by which his goal was achieved. As indicated by this example, communalism is a key component to hacker conventions and is often one of the social forces that helps keep the cohesiveness of the temporary local community together.

Secondly, campers also demonstrated overt interactional acknowledgements of authority, both formally in relation to camp organizers and informally in regard to emergent communal standards. While camp organizers imposed few rules, expectations about parking, campsite propriety, and event admissions were observably enforced and willingly acknowledged. The informal standard seemed to be an acceptance of these few restrictions in order to enjoy the peaceful unfettering of other types of restrictions. Much like America's "Burning Man" art festival, tolerance from formal authorities was the norm within the confines of the camp as long as legally questionable activities were kept within the gates. As one camper put it:

> It is like Woodstock man … We can do what we want because we are all in it together … no one will bother you because you are not a bother.

Informal authority was of two types, both of which were derived from a consensual acknowledgement and a willingness to accept and adhere to the negotiated will and inter-subjective reality of the gathering. The first of the two types rests in established reputation or accomplishment of the individual camper. The three researchers met several individuals who, because of their efforts toward the camp, the Chaos Computer Club, or their general hacker credentials, were deferred to in conversation and yielded to in choice of course of action. While it is not unusual to give special credence to those "with clout" in any social, professional, or political gathering, it was, nonetheless, surprising to see the fervor with which these individuals, due to their status that was derived primarily from their technical knowledge, were supported. Establishing themselves within the online hacker community prior to the camp appeared to augment their capacity to exert their agendas on the larger group within the confines of a specified geography or defined temporality. The second source of authority came from the will of the group itself. Despite the general informality, unofficial expectations nevertheless abounded and were openly enforced by the collective. As one camper put it:

> The most important thing is the group … it will take care of itself … it will define what the camp will be and what it won't be …

The third code of conduct observed at CCC 2011 is associated with demonstrating a competent looking-glass self-concern about how one contextualizes him/herself within the camp. The researchers observed a consistent display of self-demonstration in the course of camper participation in the collective. Campers developed both self-aggrandizing and self-deprecating styles as they immersed themselves into the emergent culture. Displays minimizing self-worth seemed especially common in the group of regulars. Statements such as, "I play with computers way too much" and "This isn't a life, it is an obsession" were routinely uttered and were evidenced across all visited camp sites. At the same time, emasculating attacks were commonplace. Calling another male attendee a "bitch" or "gay" represented standard jibes and, in relation to specific camp sites, served as an important ascription for the establishment and maintenance of alpha status, even though most campers recognized the dominance as occurring within a very small pond of success. Apparently, the status processes involved in face-to-face communication at hacker conferences helped to mitigate status conflicts that arise online due to the limitations imposed on the ability to communicate verbal and non-verbal cues that signal status among parties engaged in face-to-face communications. Such emasculating assails worked to establish the individual's ascendancy both in relation to his peers and to his own self-identification. As one camper uttered to Crash when "Viking" began calling out for more beer:

> Someone is going to get raped and it won't be me …

Two ascriptions were manifest in this simple statement. The first recognized "Viking's" dominance in his larger group of listeners and the second, "the camper's" own looking-glass self-concern and implied feeling of personal status.

The Vocabulary of Motives

Joining the hacker culture at the CCC is unlike becoming a member of a mainstream organization or interest-based club (e.g., Toastmaster's, Cub Scouts, fantasy football leagues). To self-identify as a hacker is more akin to becoming part of a lifestyle subculture as opposed to a simple affinity group. This being the case, like with street gang members, outlaw motorcyclists, or cultish parishioners, a vocabulary of motives emerges that distinguishes and categorizes the individual within and in relation to the group. Jankowski (1991) describes such a vocabulary for street gangs that has been echoed by various researchers across the years (e.g., Skolnick 1990; Vigil 1988). In relation to hackers, seven distinct motives for camp participation were consistently and repeatedly observed and identified across various times and settings throughout the CCC. These motives would often set into motion the types of personal interaction the individual hackers would have with each other and frequently provided the basis for "tags" assigned to individuals in terms of their hacker handles or camp identities.

1) Material Resources. A quest for material gains and/or networking opportunities was the most consistently sited reason for attending the camp. The CCC provided an excellent occasion for participants to establish contacts that might lead to employment or paid consultantships, and it also gave campers an ideal venue to sell specific items to the collective of camp participants. As one camper put it,

> Some of these dudes would pretend otherwise … — but it is a market here … — we all are pitching something …

2) Validation. From the perspective of the general public, "hacking" is oftentimes naïvely or one-dimensionally defined as illegal or at least counterproductive computer use or data manipulation. The contrasting perception that hacking is the exact opposite — a socially valuable activity that advances both society and technology — was an important and affirming reason for participants to attend the camp. This was most profoundly apparent at the keynote address that centered around the speakers' dream of putting a "hacker in space." The presenters fervently emphasized that the hacker collective could do what the world governments could not or would not do — reinvigorate the manned space programs (Chaos Communication Camp 2011b). With each pronouncement, "We can launch a hacker satellite," "We can put a hacker in space," "We can put a hacker on the moon!," the gathered audience would cheer wildly for the encouraging potentialities of hacking and hacker group activities.

3) Belonging. The feelings of aloneness and of being a social isolate in life outside the camp were palpable in many of the conversations around the camp. While a sense of belonging can certainly be garnered though online means of social networking, and while it is recognized that affinity is becoming more commonly established in cyberspace, there is still a need for face-to-face human contact, even in a predominantly online-based community such as hackers. As one camper suggested, "Man, it gets me away from my screen … out of the dark ..." During the conversation, Crash joked and said in a voice meant to imitate the main character in the classic film *The Elephant Man* (a story of a disfigured man outcast by society who seeks emotional connection and personal contact), "I am human!" The respondent laughed and confirmed, "You got that right."

4) Creating. It was generally acknowledged across the collective that the act of creation was actively encouraged and facilitated throughout the camp. Whether through group brainstorming leading to an evolution of shared ideation or because of individual inspiration sparked by the experience of the collective, creation was a prominent theme describing a motive for camp attendance. The creative process was commonly expressed through the development or reapplication of software and hard technologies. Campers also involved themselves heavily in the creation of art for specific aesthetic expression. Light boards, music manipulations, organic camp artifact displays, and even tent designs all emerged for the camp's enjoyment and as a hacking art outlet. When asked about the aesthetic aspect of hacker culture, one hacker suggested,

> Hacking is art ... math is art ... technology is art ... you just need the right audience to appreciate the expression.

5) Self-identification. While the broader self-identification as a hacker is manifest simply by attending the camp, there are more nuanced identities that are expressed within the collective and serve to give definition to self and to one's outlook on hacking. Whether a partier, an artist, or a political, these motivations become integral to the individual's identity as a camp participant and as part of their reputation after they have left the camp. As one participant suggested,

> This place tears down all that avatar (a term referring to adopted hacker handles) shit and lets or makes you show who you are ... yeah ... whether you want it known or not.

6) Time to resist. The camp provides the individual an opportunity to take a different path from others whose lives or life choices they view as objectionable. Padilla (1992) discusses this in relation to juvenile gang members and suggests that, in this case, the resistance is primarily against their parents and what they perceive as a limited existence of work and struggle. Thompson (1965) alludes to the same motivation in outlaw motorcycle gang members in their attempt to break free from the "square" middle class lifestyle that serves as an anathema to their individual existences. The point of resistance to the hacker and as displayed within the camp can be political or personal or both. The politics of hacking are evident and expressly discussed in terms of libertarian attitudes and progressive views on freedom of information as a fundamental necessity for any truly democratic society. Personal resistance focuses on a myriad of issues concerning middle class expectations, others' judgments of personal looks or status, or occupational doldrums. As one camper stated, "I am not just a programmer … this is my cool." As another pointed out while referring to a "celebrity hacker" who had brought a camera crew with him to record his camp experience,

> That guy wants to prove himself more than he is … filming it makes him think he isn't mediocre in what he can do.

7) Fun and lulz. Finally, attendance at the camp was arranged purely for fun, for the enjoyment of the community, and for the company of likeminded people. Like any conference, old relationships were reaffirmed or rekindled and new ones were established. Conversations, laughter, drinking, and drugs were all abundant in the scene and made for a festive atmosphere, as were pranks played for the generation of "lulz," (i.e., "the joy of disturbing another's emotional equilibrium" (Schwartz 2008)). When asked why he was attending, one camper looked at Crash as if he were asking a question with such a self-evident answer as for it to be absurd:

> Look around man … who wouldn't want to be here … this is fucking fun.

Conclusion

In a broad sense, the CCC is a professional, yet affinity-based gathering that relies on emergent rules, cooperative associations, and recognizable roles to function. As with other such gatherings, the rules and roles within the CCC change and emerge over time. Still, and as in other, more conventional gatherings, there are some consistencies that exist and persist to allow for stability in the group and ultimately for the collective's fundamental existence.

However, beyond broad similarities, the particular differences between the CCC and other organizational conventions stand out as points of interest to sociological investigators. In the context of the CCC, ethereal association, before, after, and even during the gathering, must be considered in the full understanding of the emergent culture. Who, as a participant, one becomes, how one becomes recognized as a specific type of participant, and what factors contribute to the acknowledgement of such identification, contribute significantly to the dynamics of the camp.

The process of attaining recognition as an authentic regular entails the sharing and integration of complex repertoires rather than being principally tied to space and time. Indeed, the regularity ascribed and achieved, derived from prior connections to and understandings of a predominantly cyberspace-based community, is then transposed and translated to the particular space and time of the camp. While sharing many commonalities, from the researchers' personal observations it is also apparent that obvious differences exist between different hacker conventions (e.g., ShmooCon, DefCon, SyScan, Chaos Camp, etc.). Future studies should further compare and contrast these different conventions (see Bachmann 2010; Holt 2007).

As increasing numbers of people utilize Internet-based social platforms and other electronic means to connect to each other, and as their sense of community becomes less linked to time and space anchors, the process of becoming a regular is becoming more detached from the markers that other ethnographers have traditionally observed in established places and at discrete times. The idea of anonymous regularity, while more applicable to Internet-based interactions and the various means of social networking they offer, nevertheless becomes readily apparent in both the face-to-face encounters and the cultural patterns observed at the CCC. Thus, the need to understand collective identity as a fusion and transformation resulting from the collision of the ethereal with the more traditional forms of regularity becomes the task of the modern-day ethnographer and sociologist.

The social Web, oftentimes termed Web 2.0, has noticeably affected social life in innumerable ways. Its most popular platform, "Facebook," for instance, was launched in February 2004 and as of February 2012[update], has more than 845 million active users. With their availability on many mobile devices, Web 2.0 platforms allow users to continuously stay in touch with acquaintances worldwide wherever there is access to the Internet. They also work by uniting people with common interests and/or beliefs. Although some argue that these platforms can be beneficial to one's social life, others maintain that they can cause increased antisocial tendencies because they substitute for direct, face-to-face communications. It is against this backdrop that the subculture of the Chaos Computer Club and all similar associations must be evaluated. It is simply no longer possible to view emergent participant identity and group cultural reality as happening in the vacuum of spatial and temporal confines. The anonymous regularity of social networking is important to the understanding of both and is increasing in its influence on the definition of any group or personal experience. Hence, rather than fitting the stereotypical perception as a loner dork, hackers almost appear as social innovators and many aspects of more ethereal hacker culture will soon become, at least gradually, incorporated into more traditional groups and cultures.

Woodstock Art and Music festival, billed as "An Aquarian Exposition: 3 Days of Peace and Music," was held at Max Yasgur's farm in New York's Catskill Mountains from August 15 to August 18, 1969. During the weekend, 32 musical acts played outdoors to the cheers of 500,000 concertgoers. It is considered one of the most pivotal moments in popular music history and a turning point in youth culture. Given the large attendance and the primitive conditions of the camp, the festival was remarkably safe and peaceful. And, meeting with the idealism of the 1960s, Woodstock fit the motivations, goals, and expectations for attending. It was the sense of social acceptance in the crowd that makes it one of the most important cultural events of its time. Ultimately, Yasgur saw it as a victory of peace and love. It was an amazement that such a large number of people could spend three days with only music, love and peace as sole personal foci. The CCC has often been referred to as the Woodstock of Hacker Conferences and indeed shares a similarity of atmosphere with the historic music festival. However, the ethereal nature of the CCC that is derived from the fact that the camp is a meatspace gathering of a predominantly online-based community eliminates the true communal nature inherent to the "happening" of the 1960s. The ties of regularity drawn from the ongoing past, present, and future online interactions of the conference-goers disallows the organic freedom of collective social evolution that typified the real Woodstock. The Chaos Computer Club community and camp both exist in cyberspace first and foremost and must adapt themselves to a face-to-face reality. As one CCC participant noted while hunched over a laptop and simultaneously monitoring his network card for potential intrusions:

> Look at it man, we came out of our caves, we will go back into them soon and we sit as if we were in them now … Whatever you are looking at in terms of the group, it started existing before we came here and what this group does will be decided long after we leave … hackers are tied continually on the web.

References

Adler, Patricia A., and Peter Adler. *Membership Roles in Field Research.* Newbury Park: Sage Publications, 1987.

Bachmann, Michael. *What Makes Them Click? Applying the Rational Choice Perspective to the Hacking Underground.* Orlando: University of Central Florida Press, 2008.

Bachmann, Michael. "Deciphering the Hacker Underground: First Quantitative Insights." In *Corporate Hacking and Technology-Driven Crime: Social Dynamics and Implications,* edited by Thomas J. Holt and Bernadette H. Schell, 105–126. Hershey: IGI Global.

Bachmann, Michael. "The Risk Propensity and Rationality of Computer Hackers." *International Journal of Cyber Criminology* 4, no. 2 (2011): 643–656.

Bachmann, Michael, and Jay Corzine. "Insights into the Hacking Underground." In *Volume 5: Proceedings of the Futures Working Group: The Future Challenges of Cybercrime*, edited by Toby Finnie, Tom Petee and John Jarvis, 32–43. Quantico: Federal Bureau of Investigation, 2010.

Bechar-Israeli, Haya. "From Bonehead to cLoNehEAd: Nicknames, Play, and Identity on Internet Relay Chat." *Journal of Computer-Mediated Communication* 1, no. 2 (1995).

Blevins, Kristie R., and Thomas J. Holt. "Examining the Virtual Subculture of Johns." *Journal of Contemporary Ethnography* 38, no. 5 (2009): 619–648.

"Blinkenlights." Project Blinkenlights. Accessed January 10, 2012, http://blinkenlights.net/.

Burkhalter, Bryon. "Reading Race Online: Discovering Racial Identity in Usenet Discussions." In *Communities in Cyberspace*, edited by Marc A. Smith and Peter Kollock, 60–75. London: Routledge, 1999.

"Chaos Communication Camp: Main Page." Chaos Communication Camp. Last modified July 19, 2011.http://events.ccc.de/camp/2011/.

"Chaos Communication Camp: Hackers in Space." Chaos Communication Camp. Last modified July 19, 2011. http://events.ccc.de/camp/2011/Fahrplan/events/4551.en.html.

"Chaos Computer Club: Satzung des CCC e.V." Chaos Computer Club. Last modified July 18, 2009. https://www.ccc.de/de/club/statutes.

Charmaz, Kathy. "Grounded Theory." In *Contemporary Field Research: Perspectives and Formulations, 2nd ed.*, edited by Robert M. Emerson. Prospect Heights: Waveland Press, 2001.

Chiesa, Raoul, Stefania Ducci, and Silvio Ciappi. *Profiling Hackers: The Science of Criminal Profiling as Applied to the World of Hacking*. Boca Raton: Auerbach Publications, 2008.

Cooley, Charles H. *Human Nature and the Social Order*. New York: Charles Scribner's Sons, 1902/1922.

Dinello, Daniel. *Technophobia!: Science Fiction Visions of Posthuman Technology*. Austin: University of Texas Press, 2005.

Doane, Randal. "The Habitus of Dancing: Notes on the Swing Dance Revival in New York City." *Journal of Contemporary Ethnography* 35, no. 1 (2006): 84–116.

Emerson, Robert M., Rachel I. Fretz, and Linda L. Shaw. *Writing Ethnographic Fieldnotes*. Chicago: University of Chicago Press, 1995.

Fine, Gary A. *With the Boys: Little League Baseball and Preadolescent Culture*. Chicago: University of Chicago Press, 1987.

Fine, Gary A. "Mobilizing Fun: Provisioning Resources in Leisure Worlds." *Sociology of Sport Journal* 6, no. 4 (1989): 319–334.

Fine, Gary A. *Shared Fantasy: Role Playing Games as Social Worlds.* Chicago: University of Chicago Press, 2002.

Fine, Gary A., and Sherryl Kleinman. "Rethinking Subculture: An Interactionist Analysis." *American Journal of Sociology* 85, no. 1 (1979): 1–20.

Fox, Kathryn J. "Real Punks and Pretenders: The Social Organization of a Counterculture." *Journal of Contemporary Ethnography* 16, no. 3 (1987): 344–370.

Furnell, Steven. *Cybercrime: Vandalizing the Information Society.* London: Addison-Wesley, 2002.

Glaser, Barney G., and Anselm L. Strauss. "Awareness Contexts and Social Interaction." *American Sociological Review* 29, (1964): 669–679.

Glaser, Barney G., and Anselm L. Strauss. *Awareness of Dying.* Chicago: Aldine Transaction, 1965.

Glaser, Barney G., and Anselm L. Strauss. *The Discovery of Grounded Theory: Strategies for Qualitative Research.* Chicago: Aldine Transaction, 1967.

Glaser, Barney G., and Anselm L. Strauss. *Time for Dying.* Chicago: Aldine Transaction, 1968.

Goffman, Erving. *Behavior in Public Places: Notes on the Social Organization of Gatherings.* New York: Free Press of Glencoe, 1963.

Goffman, Erving. *Frame Analysis: An Essay on the Organization of Experience.* Cambridge: Harvard University Press, 1974.

Hessler, Richard M. *Social Research Methods.* St. Paul: West Publishing, 1992.

Holt, Thomas. J. "Subcultural Evolution? Examining the Influence of On- and Off-Line Subcultural Experiences on Deviant Subcultures." *Deviant Behavior* 28, no. 2 (2007): 171–198.

Holt, Thomas J. "The attack dynamics of political and religiously motivated hackers." In *Proceedings of the Cyber Infrastructure Protection Conference, New York, June 4–5, 2009.* Carlisle: Strategic Studies Institute of the U.S. Army War College (2009): 159–180.

Holt, Thomas J. "Crime On-Line: Correlates, Causes, and Context." In *Crime On-Line: Correlates, Causes, and Context,* edited by Thomas J. Holt, 3–28. Raleigh: Carolina Academic Press, 2010.

Holt, Thomas J., and Max Kilger. "Techcrafters and Makecrafters: A Comparison of Two Populations of Hackers." In *Proceedings of the WOMBAT (Worldwide Observatory on Malicious Behavior and Attack Threats) WISTDCS (Workshop on Information Security Threats Data Collection and Sharing), Amsterdam, April 21–22, 2008.* Washington, DC: IEEE Computer Society (2008): 67–78. http://www.computer.org/csdl/proceedings/wistdcs/2008/3347/00/3347a067-abs.html.

Jankowski, Martin S. *Islands in the Street: Gangs and American Urban Society.* Berkeley: University of California Press, 1991.

Jordan, Tim, and Paul Taylor. "A Sociology of Hackers."*Sociological Review*46, no. 4 (1998): 757–780.

Jordan, Tim, and Paul Taylor. *Hacktivism and Cyberwars: Rebels with a Cause?* London: Routledge, 2004.

Karp, David A., Gregory P. Stone, and William C. Yoels. *Being Urban: A Sociology of City Life, 2nd ed.* New York: Praeger Paperbacks, 1991.

Katovich, Michael A., and Monica J. Hardesty. "The Temporary." In *Studies in Symbolic Interaction, Volume 7,* edited by Norman K. Denzin, 333–352. Greenwich: JAI Press, 1987.

Katovich, Michael. A., and William A. Reese. "The Regular: Full-Time Identities and Memberships in an Urban Bar."*Journal of Contemporary Ethnography*16, no. 3(1987): 308–343.

Kilger, Max. "Digital Identity and the Ghost in the Machine." Unpublished paper presented at 22nd Chaos Communication Congress, Berlin, Germany, December 28, 2005. http://events.ccc.de/congress/2005/fahrplan/events/549.en.html.

Kinkade, Patrick. T., and Katovich, Michael. A. "Beyond Space: On Being a Regular in an Ethereal Culture." *Journal of Contemporary Ethnography*, 38, no. 1 (2009): 3–24. doi: 10.1177/0891241607312266.

Kovacich, Gerald L. "Hackers: Freedom Fighters of the 21st Century." *Computers and Security* 18, no. 7 (1999): 573–576.

Levy, Steven. *Hackers: Heroes of the Computer Revolution.* New York: Doubleday, 1984.

Lofland, John, and Lynn H. Lofland. *Analyzing Social Settings: A Guide to Qualitative Observation and Analysis, 3rd ed.* Belmont: Wadsworth, 1995.

McPhail, Clark. *The Myth of the Madding Crowd.* New York: Aldine, 1991.

Mead, George H. *The Philosophy of the Act.* Chicago: University of Chicago Press, 1938.

Meyer, Gordon, and Jim Thomas. "The Baudy World of the Byte Bandit: A Postmodernist Interpretation of the Computer Underground." In *Computers in Criminal Justice,* edited by Frank Schmalleger, 31–67. Bristol: Wyndham Hall, 1990.

Miller, Jody. *One of the Guys: Girls, Gangs, and Gender.* New York: Oxford University Press, 2000.

Mills, Charles W. "Situated Actions and Vocabularies of Motive."*American Sociological Review* 5 (1940): 904–913.

Moreu, Rafael. (1995). *Hackers: Boot Up or Shut Up!* Directed by Iain Softley. Burbank: Metro-Goldwyn-Mayer, 1995 (film).

Naughton, John. *A Brief History of the Future: The Origins of the Internet*. London: Phoenix, 2000.

Nhan, Johnny, and Michael Bachmann. "Developments in Cyber Criminology." In *Critical Issues of Crime and Criminal Justice: Thought, Policy, and Practice*, edited by Mary Maguire and Dan Okada, 164–182. Thousand Oaks: Sage, 2010.

Oldenberg, Ray. *The Great Good Place: Cafes, Coffee Shops, Bookstores, Bars, Hair Salons, and Other Hangouts at the Heart of a Community*. New York: Paragon House, 1989.

Padilla, Felix M. *The Gang as an American Enterprise*. New Brunswick: Rutgers University Press, 1992.

Pease, Ken. "Crime Futures and Foresight: Challenging Criminal Behaviour in the Information Age." In *Crime and the Internet*, edited by David S. Wall, 18–30. London: Routledge, 2001.

Putnam, Robert D. *Bowling Alone: The Collapse and Revival of American Community*. New York: Simon & Schuster, 2000.

Ragin, Charles C. *Constructing Social Research*. Thousand Oaks: Pine Forge, 1994.

Riesman, David, Nathan Glazer, and Raoul Denney. *The Lonely Crowd: A Study of Changing American Character*. New Haven: Yale University Press, 1961.

Rogers, Marcus K. "A Two-Dimensional Circumplex Approach to the Development of a Hacker Taxonomy." *Digital Investigation*3, no. 2 (2006): 97–102.

Schell, Bernadette H., John L. Dodge, and Moutsatsos, Steve S. *The Hacking of America: Who's Doing It, Why, and How*. Westport: Quorum Books, 2002.

Schell, Bernadette H., and Thomas J. Holt. "A Profile of the Demographics, Psychological Predispositions, and Social/Behavioral Patterns of Computer Hacker Insiders and Outsiders." In *Online Consumer Protection: Theories of Human Relativism*, 192–213. Hershey: IGI Global, 2009.

Schell, Bernadette. H., and Clemens Martin. *Cybercrime: A Reference Handbook*. Santa Barbara: ABC-CLIO, 2004.

Schell, Bernadette H., and June Melnychuk. "Female and Male Hacker Conferences Attendees: Their Autism-Spectrum Quotient (AQ) Scores and Self-Reported Adulthood Experiences." In *Corporate Hacking and Technology-Driven Crime: Social Dynamics and Implications*, edited by Thomas Holt and Bernadette Schell, 144–169. Hershey: IGI Global, 2010.

Schrutzki, Reinhard. "Die Hacker Ethik." In *Das Chaos Computer Buch*, 166–180. Hamburg: Rowohlt, 1989.

Schutz, Alfred. "The Stranger."*American Journal of Sociology* 49 (1944): 499–507.

Schwartz, Mattathias. (2008, August 3). "The Trolls Among Us." *The New York Times Magazine*, August 3, 2008. http://www.nytimes.com/2008/08/03/magazine/03trolls-t.html?_r=1&pagewanted=all.

Sennett, Richard. *The Fall of Public Man.* New York: Knopf, 1977.

Simmel, Georg. "The Metropolis and Mental Life." In *On Individuality and Social Forms: Selected Writings*, edited by Donald Levine. Chicago: University of Chicago Press, 1903/1951.

Simmel, Georg. In *The Sociology of Georg Simmel.* Translated and Edited by Kurt H. Wolff. Glencoe: Free Press, 1950.

Skolnick, Jerome H. *Gang Organization and Migration.* Sacramento: Office of the Attorney General of the State of California, 1990.

Snow David A., and Leon Anderson. *Down on Their Luck: A Study of Homeless Street People.* Berkeley: University of California Press, 1993.

Stone, Gregory P. "Appearance and the Self." In *Human Behavior and Social Processes*, edited by Arnold M. Rose. Boston: Houghton Mifflin, 1962.

Strauss, Anselm L., and Juliet M. Corbin. *Basics of Qualitative Research: Grounded Theory Procedures and Techniques.* Newbury Park: Sage, 1990.

Strauss, Anselm L., and Barney G. Glaser. *Anguish.* Mill Valley: Sociology Press, 1970.

Sykes, Gresham. *The Society of Captives: A Study of a Maximum Security Prison.* Princeton: Princeton University Press, 1958.

Taylor, Paul A. *Hackers: Crime and the Digital Sublime.* New York: Routledge, 1999.

Taylor, Paul A. "Hackers—Cyberpunks or Microserfs?" In *Cybercrime: Law Enforcement, Security and Surveillance in the Information Age*, edited by Douglas Thomas and Brian D. Loader, 36–55. London: Routledge, 2000.

Taylor, Paul A. "Hacktivism—Resistance is Fertile?" In *The Blackwell Companion to Criminology*, edited by Colin Sumner, Chapter 26. Oxford: Blackwell, 2004.

Thomas, Douglas. Hacker Culture. Minneapolis: University of Minnesota Press, 2003.

Thomas, Douglas. "Notes from the Underground: Hackers as Watchdogs of Industry." *USC Annenberg: Online Journalism Review*, February 17, 1998. www.ojr.org/ojr/business/1017969515.php.

Thompson, Hunter S. "The Motorcycle Gangs." *The Nation* 200, no. 20, May 17, 1965: 22–526.

Thornton, Sarah. *Club Cultures: Music, Media, and Subcultural Capital.* Boston: Blackwell-Polity Press, 1995.

Turgeman-Goldschmidt, Orly. (2008). "Meanings that Hackers Assign to Their Being a Hacker." *International Journal of Cyber Criminology* 2, no. 2 (2008): 382–396.

Twist, Jo. "Cracking the Hacker Underground." *BBC News*, November 14, 2003. http://news.bbc.co.uk/1/low/technology/3246375.stm.

Vigil, James D. *Barrio Gangs*. Austin: University of Texas Press, 1988.

Voiskounsky, Alexander E., and Olga V. Smyslova, "Flow-Based Model of Computer Hackers' Motivation." *CyberPsychology & Behavior* 6, no. 2 (2003): 171–180.

Wilson, Brian, and Michael Atkinson. "Rave and Straightedge, the Virtual and the Real: Exploring Online and Offline Experiences in Canadian Youth Subcultures." *Youth & Society* 36, no. 3 (2005): 276–311.

Williams, J. Patrick. "Authentic Identities: Straightedge Subculture, Music, and the Internet." *Journal of Contemporary Ethnography* 35, no. 2 (2006): 173–200.

Wolcott, Harry F. *The Art of Fieldwork*. Walnut Creek: Alta Mira, 1995.

Yar, Majid. Cybercrime and Society. London: Sage, 2006.

3

The Evolution of Online Piracy: Challenge and Response

Johnny Nhan

Significant technological and legal developments have shaped the history of Internet piracy, or the unauthorized download or distribution of digital copyrighted works online. The seemingly endless enforcement and counter-enforcement of piracy reflects the dynamic structural, cultural, and legal evolution associated with applying forms of social control online. Specifically, digital distribution technologies often dictate legal actions, which in turn affect technology. Hollywood, interested in protecting its intellectual property, is often at odds with media consumers who want unrestricted and often free access to content and technology companies who need these consumers to purchase their products. This paper examines the historical developments of Internet piracy through complex structural, technological, legal, and cultural interplay amongst different groups that hold different ideals for the Internet. Technological, legal, and enforcement perspectives will give a more nuanced and holistic view of the developments in online piracy.

The evolution of Internet media piracy is marked by several significant cycles that begin with technologies that facilitate piracy and end with industry responses. Significant technological periods include the following: (1) The change from physical media (hard goods) to digital media (soft goods), (2) media files hosted directly on websites, (3) the Napster era of early peer-to-peer (P2P) networks, and (4) the *BitTorrent* P2P file sharing era. Corresponding to the technological advancements, industry strategies have evolved in several stages: (1) Doing nothing, (2) filing litigation against index sites, (3) bringing aggressive suits against individual end users, and (4) proposing legislative changes to the law. Concurrently, production industries have utilized both public policing and private security firms. The struggle to contain online piracy highlights not only the difficulties in policing the online space, but also the cultural and structural frictions that accompany attempts to apply social control online.

Review of the Literature

Research on Internet media piracy has come from a variety of sources, ranging from computer scientists and engineers to economists and criminologists. Social science scholars have focused mainly on individual motivations, legal implications and harm, and the enforcement of Internet piracy. This interdisciplinary research reveals a variety of behavioral motivations.

Individual Motivations and Factors Influencing Participation in Piracy Activities

Many studies have surveyed college students and young adults, groups known for high levels of illegal file sharing (Einav 2008). For example, a survey of 500 college students found respondents valued purchased music significantly more than downloaded music, suggesting they were unlikely to have purchased it in the first place (Rob and Waldfogel 2004). Studies also show that students believe in a separate moral code when it comes to file sharing and pirating. A study of students at two religiously affiliated campuses found no differences in that students' moral acceptance of downloading copyrighted software and music compared with the acceptance of students at secular institutions (Siegfried 2005).

Criminologists have attempted to apply criminological theories towards explaining motivations for piracy. Hinduja (2006) applied *social learning theory*, *self-control theory*, and *general strain theory* to explain the prevalence of intellectual property theft. He found general strain theory, which explains crime as a result of decisions by rational individuals with blocked legitimate means to pursue *innovative* and deviant means in order to obtain their goals (Merton 1936; Agnew 1992), does not adequately explain music pirating activities. Instead, he found piracy rates highest amongst individuals with low self-control coupled with higher online technical skills (Hinduja 2006). Malin and Fowers (2009) tested the predictability of college piracy using high school students' level of self-control by applying Gottfredson and Hirschi's (1990) general theory of crime. They found biological sex, Internet experience, and affiliation with deviant peers to be the most significant factors that influence piracy (Malin and Fowers 2009).

Higgins (2007a) found a link between low self-control and rational choice that influences a person's propensity for piracy. A sample of college students were surveyed using different scenarios that measured self-control and factors that influence rational choice (shame, perceived value, morals, external sanctions, and prior piracy activities) with digital piracy. He found the link between low self-control and digital piracy to be mediated by perceived value and other factors related to rational choice (Higgins 2007a). Higgins (2007b) also predicted low self-control and biological sex contributed significantly to initial levels and rates of change in pirating activities. He found male students to be more likely to initially apply neutralizations in order to pirate music and remove any considerations or perceptions of criminality.

International studies on the motivations for media piracy are equally diverse. A study in Taiwan found that singer/band idolization positively impacted purchase decisions (Chiou, Huang, and Lee 2005). A software piracy study in Germany cited an increase in knowledge of external consequences, fear of personal legal consequences, and a downward trend in software prices as explanations for a significant reduction piracy from 2003 to 2006 (Nill, Schibrowsky, and Peltier 2010). The same study found that file sharers often justified piracy with Robin Hood-like wealth redistribution attitudes and peer-oriented social norms which perceive downloading software as illegal, but generally acceptable. A study in Hong Kong found that software pirates perceived the lack of punishment, high availability of pirated material, and the cost of legitimate software as being too high as significant factors for piracy (Moores and Dhillon 2000). The harm caused by file sharing reflects the lack of consensus among motivations for piracy.

Researchers have found individual motivations for digital piracy are often influenced or facilitated by a variety of environmental and other external factors. Some consider unauthorized file sharing a normalized activity. Cos, Johnson, and Richards (2008) apply Cohen and Felson's (1979) *routine activities theory* to explain the normalization of file sharing, attributing it to the many conditional opportunities online, such as the availability of a suitable targets, lack of guardianship, and motivated offenders.

Researchers found attitudes that affect the likelihood of piracy were influenced by peer groups. For instance, a study of over 2,000 university undergraduate students who illegally downloaded music found that normative peer beliefs and behaviors in the university environment trumped law breaking attitudes (Ingram and Hinduja 2008). The study linked peer-influenced behavior with individual *techniques of neutralization* (Sykes and Matza 1957), such as denials of harm, victimization, and responsibility, to explain the students' dismissal of any real harm associated with piracy (Ingram and Hinduja 2008; Moore 2011). Similarly, Higgins, Wolfe, and Marcum (2011) examined the longer term effects of *techniques of neutralization* in a longitudinal study of digital music piracy amongst college students using Latent Trajectory Models (LTM) and found variability in piracy rates and a general decrease over time as students reflected on the criminality of their behavior.

Perceptions of digital music itself can influence individual decisions to engage in piracy. Yu (2010) compared perceptions of stealing with digital music piracy. Using a sample of students from six universities, he found that despite negative correlations with general morality and stealing, moral justifications for piracy replaced general morality. Yu's findings suggests a perception of substantive difference between online and offline crime. These findings are consistent with perceptions of the Internet as a space disconnected from "reality," where earthly rules and legal notions of property do not apply, as discussed later.

Technology itself can facilitate piracy activities. Holt and Morris (2009) compared piracy rates between college students who owned a digital music device (MP3 player) with those who did not. They observed that MP3 player ownership compounds deviant peer associations in significantly increasing the likelihood of individual involvement in digital music piracy activities. Holt and Morris' (2009) findings suggest that an individual is more likely to pirate music after acquiring devices such as an iPod.

Other disciplines offer different perspectives on digital piracy that further enrich criminological understandings and theoretical research. Smith and Telang (2009) take a more economic approach to understanding digital piracy by charting DVD sales with concurrent alternative, free outlets, such as over-the-air television broadcast and unauthorized peer-to-peer versions of the movie. They noted a spike in DVD sales after the airing of a movie, suggesting that the presence of free alternatives does not significantly impact individual decisions to pursue piracy. Smith and Telang's findings complement those of Ramayah, Ahmad, Chin, and Lo (2009), who tested a causal model of Internet piracy behavior amongst college students using a structural equation model investigating the effects of habit, affect, and intention on actual piracy behavior. They found habit to have a strong effect on piracy. Moreover, respondents remained undeterred despite acknowledgement that it is illegal, citing that "downloading information from the Internet should be free and it is full of fun and joy" (Ramayah et al. 2009, 212).

As the above examples of the research have shown, individual motivations for piracy are varied and often difficult to categorize and understand, which reflects the complexity of activities, social interactions, and normative values online. Moreover, the complexity of digital piracy is reflected by the lack of consensus in terms of the actual harm created, which ranges from little or no harm to potentially threatening the existence of the industry.

The Impact and Harm of Piracy

The estimated costs and impact of digital piracy and its distribution have been significantly different between the industry and scholars. Studies commissioned by the Motion Picture Association of America (MPAA) have drawn criticism and doubt about the true financial impact of piracy on ticket sales, with some pointing to record profits of *The Avengers* movie despite bootlegged versions made via camcorders available during its opening weekend (Tassi 2012; Galloway 2012). According to the study, the major U.S. motion picture studios lost an estimated $2.3 billion in 2005 from Internet piracy worldwide, costing over 141,000 in lost jobs (Siwek 2006). A similar study on sound recording piracy found losses of $12.5 billion in 2006, constituting over 71,000 jobs directly from both the industry and retail outlets (Siwek 2007). Both studies correlate each download to the full price of a movie or music album or song. However, critics have pointed out that individuals who downloaded those movies may not have ever intended on its purchase, implying that those figures supported by the motion picture and recording industry are wildly overstated (Rob and Waldfogel 2004). Schechter, Greenstadt, and Smith (2004) estimate the cost of piracy by using an economic multiplier effect, calculated by adding the initial extraction cost to the per-copy distribution cost multiplied by the size of the distribution network.

Some scholars point out the ideological impact of piracy on competition. Gu and Mahajan (2004) propose that common price discrimination models, which target poorer consumers with competitive prices, may actually reduce company profits in the long run. They reason that by allowing file-sharers to pirate material the industry eliminates smaller companies. This finding is consistent with the MPAA's view that piracy can actually reduce competition by making products produced by smaller companies "compete" against pirated versions of expensive products (Smith and Telang 2009; Nhan 2010). These findings are contrary to the common notion that piracy forces producers to make better products. Different enforcement strategies often reflect divergent understandings of the root causes and costs of piracy.

Enforcement of Piracy Laws

The Recording Industry Association of America (RIAA) and MPAA's legal enforcement of piracy laws has drawn attention from different scholars. In the late 1990s and early 2000s, the RIAA's aggressive stance on individual file sharers in particular has drawn sharp criticism from the public and some artists.

Bhattacharjee, Gopal, Lertwachara, and Marsden (2006) found that threat of prosecution does result in lower levels of file sharing but does not impact the availability of music files on P2P networks. Harbaugh and Khemka (2001) argue that aggressive enforcement of expensive products only affects existing customers and actually gives greater incentive for low-level and marginal buyers to pirate material. Bachmann (2011, 155) metaphorically described the lack of deterrence as attempting to sue the "genie back in the bottle."

A replacement effect has largely undermined the effectiveness of Hollywood's litigation strategies. Legal attacks against early P2P indexing services, such as Napster in the early 2000s, have resulted in more sophisticated file sharing technologies taking its place, such as The Pirate Bay and *Cyberlockers* ("Policing Internet Piracy" 2011). Aggressive piracy law enforcement has led to a cycle of endless conflicts between P2P operators and file-sharers with Hollywood production companies. In addition to litigation strategies, Hollywood has employed different enforcement strategies that use public and private security.

The U.S. considers piracy a major economic problem. In 2009, the Obama Administration recognized piracy as a threat to economic recovery and appointed Victoria Espinel as the U.S. Intellectual Property Enforcement Coordinator, who stated, "Protection of our innovation and protection of our creativity is an essential part of our plan for economic recovery" (Corbin 2010). Particularly, she underscored the threat of piracy by foreign countries and cited China in particular as a major source of copyright infringement activities. Espinel has sought to pass international laws as well as increase collaborative enforcement efforts.

Several large-scale international operations have been executed to fight piracy. For example, in 2001, the U.S. spearheaded *Operation Buccaneer*, a collaborative effort between the U.S. Customs Service, FBI, and agencies from six countries to fight international software, game, and movie piracy. Agents raided dozens of locations in the U.S. and other countries, resulting in the takedown of a warez site *DrinkOrDie* and arrests of members of the highly organized "elite Internet pirate organization" that ran the site (Associated Press 2001; U.S. Department of Justice 2001). In 2004, The FBI, U.S. Department of Justice, and Interpol conducted a similar collaborative campaign named *Operation Fastlink*, which has yielded similar arrests and convictions on several warez release groups, which pirated computer software, games, movies, and music (U.S. Department of Justice 2004). In 2009, Operation Fastlink yielded 60 felony convictions (FBI 2009). Despite such large-scale collaborative efforts, digital piracy remains a significant problem.

In California, the RIAA and MPAA have formed partnerships with public law enforcement agencies throughout the state. Both organizations are part of a high-tech crimes consortium of specialized federal, state, county, and local policing agencies. Scholars have studied this collaborative model of security using a *nodal governance* theoretical framework, which identifies the roles, assets, and relationships of each security stakeholder (Nhan and Huey 2008; Nhan 2010).

Hollywood has discretely employed the services of private high-tech security firms. The security company MediaDefender, for example, employed disruptive technologies, such as seeding decoy or corrupt files in P2P networks to slow down traffic, which interfered with file-sharing activities. These "torrent poisoning" strategies, however, have largely been ineffective and P2P networks have developed anti-corruption detection methods. Moreover, retaliatory efforts by Internet hackers resulted in the source code for MediaDefender's antipiracy system being released on to P2P networks, including a file which contains a leaked phone conversation between MediaDefender employees and the New York State Attorney General's Office (Schonfeld 2008). The cycle of skirmishes between Hollywood and file-sharers is the framework for the evolution of piracy.

Timeline

This paper attempts to create a brief history using a framework based on significant cycles in technologies and legal strategies. Through these evolutionary shifts, one can tease out the dialectical relationship between Hollywood and Internet users in order to show major cultural differences that dictate transitions in technologies and enforcement/legal strategies.

The Digital Transition: From Hard Goods to Soft Goods

The transition from physical media ("hard goods") to digital media ("soft goods") represents the first salvo in many piracy conflicts. In 1996, the Motion Picture Experts Group (MPEG), with the support of the Industry Standards Organization (ISO), developed a codec for audio compression, Audio Layer 3, or "MP3." The MP3 format allowed users to compress large audio files to a much smaller size for easier transportation during a time when most users connected through dial-up modems. In the years following the codec's release, free MP3 playing software, such as Winamp, became popular. By 1999, the first MP3 portable playing device was created, which ushered in a new era in music consumption.

The growth of the Internet facilitated the development and eventual ubiquity of MP3 files. According to Internet World Stats, an organization which tracks

Internet usage and population statistics, Internet usage grew from 16 million users in 1995, constituting 0.4% of the world's population to 2.11 billion in 2011, or roughly 30.4% of the world's population (www.internetworldstats.com/emar-keting.htm). Internet connection speeds also grew significantly. The Pew Internet and American Life Project found high-speed broadband connections grew from roughly 2% in 2000 to nearly 55% in 2008 (Horrigan 2008). By comparison, dial-up usage declined from approximately 35% in 2000 to approximately 10% in 2008. The adoption of high-speed Internet, coupled with MP3 compression technology, facilitated the rapid growth of online music piracy. This digital transition also has social and cultural significance.

Technology has often been a driving force behind social change (Heidegger 1977). Technological development often reflects power and affects material relations. Technology can serve as an impetus for discourse in these areas. According to Sterne (2006), MP3s contextualize legal, political, economic, and broader cultural dimensions of file-sharing by breaking the traditional use/exchange-value system presented by Karl Marx, where the value of a product is derived from the utility of its use as well as its exchange. According to Sterne (2006) MP3s are akin to "recorded music without commodity form," a problem compounded by an erosion of exchange value for the music labels since "they are not paid for and therefore do not require much labor," further exacerbated by "free, easy, and large-scale exchange" (p. 831). In essence, digital music fundamentally differs from other forms of copyright protection. When MP3s were coupled with the global online distribution network of the Internet, its distribution grew exponentially. However, it would be years before it drew the attention of Hollywood.

As users increasingly digitized and distributed music online, media and software companies were busy fighting piracy offline. A wide range of anti-piracy measures were in place, ranging from crackdowns on illegally copied magnetic and optical discs being shipped and sold on the streets, to research on copyright protections built into the media. Nevertheless, digital music was initially distributed unrestricted on the web. Simply put, the success of the MP3 format caught Hollywood, which was focused on large profits from optical disks, by surprise.

Website Hosting Music

Websites directly distributed digital music files freely throughout the latter half of the 1990s, where users downloaded them with impunity. Hollywood was slow in recognizing and reacting to digital distribution as a threat to their business. Consequently, the music labels were slow to lobby for changes in laws and solicit the help of law enforcement. Instead, recording labels focused on protecting against threats from pirates of optical media. In the early 2000s, the RIAA was aggressive in seizing and arresting illegal CD distributors in major cities. The RIAA conducted over 250 large busts and seizures in 2002 and over 230 in 2003 (www.grayzone.com).

Several popular websites emerged during the late 1990s and early 2000s. Mp3.com became the top MP3 distributor in 1998 when it allowed users to download full albums directly from its website. To bypass any potential legal troubles, the site required users to prove ownership of music by either purchasing the CD from the website or putting a CD in the computer's drive. By 2000, the music hosting website had over 10 million registered users downloading from a database of over 45,000 albums. When the company went public in 1999, it raised over $370 million. Mp3.com's success drew the attention of the RIAA, which sued and won for copyright infringement at the tune of $750 to $30,000 per violation, essentially destroying the business (King 2000). Consequently, increasingly sophisticated and larger distribution networks quickly filled the vacuum that was created by the legal attacks by the RIAA and other production entities.

Peer-to-Peer: The Napster Era

The P2P network architecture became popular in late 1990s to resolve two main issues associated with web hosting. First, as MP3 music files gained popularity, demands for network bandwidth and storage increased substantially. In P2P networks, files are stored on individual computers (peers) and exchanged directly through the HTTP Internet protocol. Indexing services, such as Napster, merely facilitated connections and monitored network traffic amongst different users, which saved company bandwidth. Secondly, P2P networks served a legal function by moving data files away from a central server and to individual computers. P2P networks, such as Napster, argued that they only served a passive indexing role for users to share indiscriminate files. Policing a system with the millions of files being exchanged daily by transient users, they argued, was too much of a burden (*Metallica et al. v. Napster* 2000; *A&M Records v. Napster* 2000). At its peak in 2001, 2.79 billion music files were traded through Napster in the month of February (Lowe 2003). Moreover, users of Napster typically log in to the service for less than one hour (Saroiu, Gummadi, and Gribble 2003).

Prior to the widespread use of Napster, which provided an easy P2P interface for users to share digital music, digital files were distributed through Internet Relay Chat (IRC) channels. In 1998, Jarkko Oikarinen wrote the IRC protocol to allow for simultaneous communications amongst users in thousands of chat rooms. Music file transfers initially required users to communicate with each other online in order to initiate peer-to-peer file transfers (Cooper and Harrison 2001). Users interested in obtaining a specific song or album typically entered a chat room, found another user with the desired files, communicated with that person and struck a deal. IRC piracy was initially used to illicitly distribute and share computer software ("warez"), creating a subculture or "scene" that was largely based on vouching for another user (Cooper and Harrison 2001). File transfers were later facilitated by File Transfer Protocol (FTP) servers automated by IRC robots, or "bots," to users in each channel. Despite the automation and organization of FTP servers, the piracy scene consisted of more advanced Internet users who navigated an assortment of piracy sources, such as IRC or USENET channels (Cooper and Harrison 2001). Moreover, these more covert channels required users to sort through a variety of file types and execute scripts, which may be difficult to the casual computer user. However, Napster created an exclusively MP3 centralized location using a user-friendly graphical interface which led to the exponential proliferation of unauthorized music piracy in the general population.

Hollywood perceived Napster's massive file sharing as a substantial threat to their CD sales and pursued legal action. The first lawsuit came from the rock band Metallica, who discovered one of its singles was available for download via Napster before its official release. Napster defended its passive position and pointed to the fact that it did not generate revenue from the exchange of files. Nevertheless, a district court in Northern California underscored the music industry's position that by brokering a real time index of available music files, Napster was essentially acting as a music piracy service (McCourt and Burkart 2003). Another similar lawsuit reinforced the outcome of Metallica's case. In this lawsuit, filed the same year by A&M Records against Napster (239 F. 3d 1004), the Ninth Circuit Court of Appeals upheld the District Court's ruling in finding that mass distribution of music adversely affected CD sales and undermined prospective future digital ventures by Hollywood. Consequently, a federal judge placed an injunction which ordered Napster to police and enforce all instances of copyright infringement. In 2001, under intense legal pressure, Napster agreed to settle out of court and transform itself into an officially licensed digital outlet. However, with a pay model in place, Napster's traffic quickly faded, leading to an evolution of other P2P services.

Peer-to-Peer: BitTorrent Era

In the early 2000s, BitTorrent, a new file sharing protocol, became popular. Unlike Napster, BitTorrent ("torrent") allows for multiple sources to download and upload simultaneously instead of going through a single server, which yielded higher traffic throughput. While Napster kept an index of music files on its server, BitTorrent services relied on a variety of sources for finding files. Torrents serve as true peer-to-peer indexing services that merely direct traffic from individual users who host the files. A user initially contributes to the database with a file, or "seeds," while others download, or "leech." Once a download is completed, the once leecher becomes a seeder of the file, growing the number of sources of the file exponentially. Parts of the file can be obtained from multiple sources simultaneously in packets, creating redundancy and optimizing for slower traffic. As a result, BitTorrent was faster, more robust, and truly decentralized. By 2004, BitTorrent services accounted for over 50% of all P2P traffic, due to its wide availability to the public, ability to filter out bad or "fake" files, and ability to handle large surges of traffic (Pouwelse, Garbacki, Epema, and Sips 2005).

Dozens of BitTorrent sites emerged during this era, each with hundreds of thousands to millions of users. Perhaps the most famous site is *The Pirate Bay* (TPB), which gained notoriety with its open disputes with Hollywood production studios. In 2003, TPB quickly became one of the most popular torrents on the Internet, offering users not just music, but full movies, software, games, and other content in an easy-to-use interface. Like other BitTorrents, Hollywood targeted TPB despite it being thousands of miles away in Sweden, a country known for its lax copyright laws.

The Pirate Bay is best known for its open defiance of Hollywood's legal actions. Under pressure from the MPAA, Swedish police raided and confiscated TPB's servers in 2006, causing a service disruption. However, Pirate Bay administrators reopened the site in a matter of days with remote servers, with double the traffic. Moreover, the site returned with a logo of a pirate ship sinking the Hollywood sign. In 2007, TPB failed to permanently insulate itself from prosecution when it proposed to establish itself as a sovereign state by attempting to buy an unincorporated sea fort off the coast of England. Nevertheless, the site continued to operate despite active attempts by Hollywood to abolish its existence. In 2009, three Pirate Bay site operators were convicted of violating Swedish copyright law, sentenced to one year in jail each, and ordered to pay fines of millions. Despite the legal trouble, the site still operates—even touting itself as "The world's most resilient bittorrent site" while boldly listing legal threats and their responses on their website (http://thepiratebay.org/legal). For example, when council from DreamWorks informed TPB of violations of the Digital Millennium Copyright Act in 2004, which prohibits circumvention of copyright technologies, Pirate Bay administrators responded with:

As you may or may not be aware, Sweden is not a state in the United States of America. Sweden is a country in northern Europe. Unless you figured it out by now, US law does not apply here. For your information, no Swedish law is being violated.

TPB's actions are part of a larger legal challenge-response cycle. Legal strategies have evolved in response to more clever ways by file sharers to circumvent legal moves. Hollywood has applied a three-pronged legal strategy: (1) litigation targeting individual users, (2) influencing Internet service providers (ISPs), and (3) changing legislation.

Litigation

Unable to stem the tide of illegal file sharing, the RIAA drew public disdain when it began suing individual file sharers for copyright infringement in 2003. This tactic began when the RIAA sued four college students for copyright infringement for running a file-sharing network from their dormitories. Facing the possibility of being fined $150,000 each, they quickly settled out of court, with fines ranging from $12,000 to $17,500. This success began several years of suing hundreds of users each year. The strategy initially appeared to be mildly successful, as P2P traffic on popular sites dropped significantly in 2003. However, closer examination shows that P2P traffic has never declined but merely migrated to different networks (Karagiannis et al. 2004).

In the wake of legal setbacks on cases where the RIAA attempted to force ISPs to turn over lists of user identities, Hollywood filed a series of "John Doe" lawsuits against computer users known only by their IP addresses. ISPs, such as Verizon, argued that the subpoenas which did not require court review threatened customer privacy. In 2004, John Doe cases found early success as 233 out of 382 defendants settled out of court for an average of $3,000 each (Roberts 2004). However, the public and media began questioning the legitimacy and effectiveness of the RIAA's strategy when reports surfaced showing that a grandmother and 12-year-olds were being sued, suggesting that even suing high-volume file sharers only gave a false sense of security (Sag 2006). In 2008, the RIAA abandoned its strategy, which critics described as a public relations disaster that did little to stop online piracy (McBride and Smith 2008).

In order to enhance enforcement, major Hollywood entertainment companies have pressured ISPs to monitor illegal P2P activities. In 2011, the RIAA implemented a "six strikes" plan that places increased penalties for individuals who are caught illegally sharing content, which starts with warnings that can escalate to suspension of Internet services. In the past, the RIAA has sued ISPs, who have an incentive for keeping their customers, for turning a blind eye to copyright infringement activities. For instance, in 2003, the RIAA filed a lawsuit against Verizon for its refusal to respond to subpoenas to identify its clients who they suspected of trafficking copyrighted material (351 F. 3d 1229).

A third controversial strategy used by Hollywood that has drawn public attention is their proactive stance on enacting legislation. Copyright law in the United States has existed for decades. The original intent of contemporary copyright law in the U.S. is to protect intellectual property, ranging from literature and artwork to products. In 1976, Congress amended existing copyright law to take into account technological advances in intellectual property, namely sound recordings, film, television, and radio. These protections, scholars argue, serve an instrumental purpose by allowing authors to create content that contributes to social value and where authors are compensated for their efforts (Sterk 1996). Despite existing copyright laws, Hollywood sought to enhance existing legislation and enact new legislation to deal with file sharing and digital distribution.

Congress added three key pieces of legislation to existing copyright law that have made acts of file sharing highly punitive. First, the No Electronic Theft Act (17 U.S.C. and 18 U.S.C.), known as the NETAct, enacted in 1997, increased the maximum penalties for unauthorized replication of copyrighted material ("criminal infringement") to up to 3 years and $250,000. Trafficking in counterfeit goods can bring a maximum penalty of 10 years and $2 million. Second, the "Sonny Bono Act," enacted in 1998, amended Title 17 Copyright Right Act to extend the copyright protection period for an additional 20 years. Third, the Digital Millennium Copyright Act (DMCA) (Pub. L. No. 105-304, 112 stat. 2860), also enacted in 1998, gave Hollywood the tools to tackle some of the unique aspects of digital music, such as making circumventing copyright protection technologies a criminal act. Despite these three significant pieces of legislation, Hollywood has continued to pursue legislative changes.

At the time of this writing, two pieces of proposed legislation have drawn an Internet firestorm. Senate Bill 968, known as The Preventing Real Online Threats to Economic Creativity and Theft of Intellectual Property Act of 2011 (PROTECT IP Act or PIPA) and the Stop Online Piracy Act (SOPA) are mainly designed to stop foreign distribution and sales of copyrighted material by restricting access to websites that host unauthorized content. PIPA, which broadly defines infringement to include illegal distribution of digital content or circumventing anti-piracy technologies, when used in conjunction with SOPA, which addresses the aforementioned TPB non-U.S. jurisdiction defense by mandating U.S. service companies, such as Google, MasterCard, and PayPal payment services, is designed to withhold services and payment to these organizations.

The rationale behind the bill is, "If you can't force overseas sites to take down copyrighted work, you can at least stop U.S. companies from providing their services to those sites" (Pepitone 2012, 1). However, the bill has sparked concerns by tech companies over liability and privacy issues since it essentially makes companies responsible for content uploaded by users.

Due to provisions in PIPA/SOPA, many concerned individuals see the bills as slippery slopes that can potentially escalate to increasing Internet policing and, ultimately, censorship. The bill can potentially monitor and limit U.S. traffic to certain sites by blocking or redirecting certain domain names that contain pirated material, without any form of due process. In addition, Internet security experts have raised concerns with interfering with the Internet's directory service, leading to the provisions being removed (Lee 2012). The White House has also voiced its opinion on SOPA after a massive Internet opposition to the bill. According to the official White House Blog, "Any effort to combat online piracy must guard against the risk of online censorship of lawful activity and must not inhibit innovation by our dynamic businesses large and small" (Espinel, Chopra, and Schmidt 2012). An Internet "blackout" date was enacted on January 18, 2012, by several prominent websites in order to show opposition to the bills, including Wikipedia. However, several senators who once supported PIPA, as a measure to protect U.S. jobs, have reversed their position under strong pressure from technology and web services companies and netizens. This conflict has once again pitted technology companies, such as Google and Wikipedia, who publicly oppose the bill, against Hollywood.

Internet Culture

Deeply rooted and inherent contradictions in the Internet subculture can explain Hollywood's friction with technology companies and Internet users. The Internet was conceived as an open space for the free and unfettered exchange of ideas. According to Leonard Kleinrock (2004, 195), one of the forefathers of the Internet, the early vision of the Internet includes the following principles: (1) its technology was to be ubiquitous, (2) always accessible, (3) always on, (4) accessible from any location and device, and (5) be invisible. Moreover, he lists the positive characteristics that include principles such as, no one controls it, no one can turn it off, it provides a means to share works and ideas, it is empowering, and it is owned by no one (Kleinrock 2004). Internet rights advocate John Barlow cemented these principles with his *Declaration of Independence of Cyberspace* that underscores the principles of freedom and rejects formal social controls online in 1996 (https://projects.eff.org/~barlow/

Declaration-Final.html). Internet users as whole, therefore, perceive the actions of Hollywood studios as attempting to privatize, commoditize, and censor this open space, which are clear violations of Barlow's declaration. Moreover, strict content-owner control hampers the product development of technology companies (Lasica 2005).

Laws enacted in favor of Hollywood are seen as a direct affront to the core principles of Internet freedom, which is often used to further justify piracy and other activities. For instance, the DMCA is often viewed in an anticompetitive instrument used by the wealthiest and most powerful entities, which also undermines technological advances (Lasica 2005). Silicon Valley, which requires constant changes and advancements in technology, therefore, is reluctant to adopt the Hollywood model of proprietary content protection. However, according to Lasica (2005), this antagonistic relationship has eroded, as technology companies have waned in their role as consumer advocates for several reasons. First, technology companies have consolidated with media companies, such as Sony's electronics and movie roles. Second, technology companies refusing to cooperate with Hollywood could mean more governmental mandates. Finally, computer companies seeking larger roles in entertainment digital technologies, such as digital televisions, have become more reliant on Hollywood for content.

Conclusion and Limitations

This paper has shown that the history of Internet piracy reflects deep-rooted divergent views on the purpose of copyright and the Internet space. In a larger sense, the application of laws to social control of this space has drawn sharp divisions from the Internet community and Hollywood. Government has been caught in the middle, with pressure from both Hollywood and the growing masses of the public. As the title of the paper suggests, we are in an endless cycle where every new file-sharing technology (challenge) brings another round of copyright protection technology and lawsuits (response). The solution to the problem is still unclear as we move forward in the digital world.

This paper focuses on significant events related to music and movie piracy. However, it is not a comprehensive history of Internet piracy and excludes several significant parts, such as software piracy and more detailed court cases. Software piracy is a significant and costly problem that warrants more specific attention. Similar to the challenge and response cycles between the music and movie industry with pirates, software companies face a seemingly endless cycle of software updates (patches) followed by circumvention software (cracks) and so on. This level of sophistication requires attention that is beyond the scope of this paper and should be explored in future works.

In addition, less mainstream channels for file sharing are not discussed, such as secured private high-speed networks, or "darknets." Like software piracy, these sophisticated distribution channels require the level of attention that is beyond the scope of this paper. An examination of darknets can explain the motivations, structure, and technologies of top-level pirates and the distribution chain from the movie theater to the end consumer (Biddle, England, Peinado, and Willman 2002). Nevertheless, the material presented in this paper serves to contextualize conflicts between Hollywood and the general public in a general timeline. Clearly, more scholars from all disciplines need to conduct research in this area in order to understand and craft long-term solutions to the growing problem.

References

Agnew, Robert. "Foundation for a General Strain Theory of Crime and Delinquency," *Criminology* 30, no. 1 (1992): 47–87.

Associated Press. "Feds Zero in on Piracy Ring." *Wired*, December 11, 2001. http://www.wired.com/politics/law/news/2001/12/49026.

Bachmann, Michael. "Suing the Genie back in the Bottle: The Failed RIAA Strategy to Deter P2P Network Users." In *Cyber Criminology: Exploring Internet Crimes and Criminal Behavior*, edited by Karuppannan Jaishankar, 155–172. Boca Raton, FL: CRC Press, 2011.

Bhattacharjee, Sudip, Ram D. Gopal, Kaveepan Lertwachara, and James R. Marsden. "Impact of Legal Threats on Online Music Sharing Activity: An Analysis of Music Industry Legal Actions," *Journal of Law & Economics* 49, no. 1 (2006): 91–114.

Biddle, Peter, Paul England, Marcus Peinado, and Bryan Willman. "The Darknet and the Future of Content Distribution," *Microsoft Corporation*. Paper presented at the ACM Workshop on Digital Rights Management, Washington, D.C., November 18, 2009. http://msl1.mit.edu/ESD10/docs/darknet5.pdf.

Chiou, Jyh-Shen, Chien-yi Huang, and Hsin-hui Lee. "The Antecedents of Music Piracy Attitudes and Intentions," *Journal of Business Ethics* 57 (2005): 161–174.

Cohen, Lawrence E., and Marcus Felson. "Social Change and Crime Rate Trends: A Routine Activity Approach," *American Sociological Review* 44 (1979): 588–608.

Cooper, Jon, and Daniel M. Harrison. "The Social Organization of Audio Piracy on the Internet," *Media, Culture, & Society*, 23 (2001): 71–89.

Corbin, Kenneth. "White House IP Boss: Digital Piracy Costs U.S. Jobs," *Datamation*, October 5, 2010. http://www.datamation.com/secu/article.php/3906846/White-House-IP-Boss-Digital-Piracy-Costs-US-Jobs.htm.

Cox, Raymond W., Terrance Johnson, and George E. Richards. "Routine Activity Theory and Internet Crime." In *Crimes of the Internet*, edited by Frank Schmalleger and Michael Pittaro, 302–316. Upper Saddle River, NJ: Prentice Hall, 2008.

Einav, Gali. "College Students: The Rationale for Peer-To-Peer Video File Sharing." In *Peer-to-Peer Video: The Economics, Policy, and Culture of Today's New Mass Medium*, edited by Eli M. Noam and Lorenzo M. Pupillo, 149–162. New York: Springer, 2008.

Espinel, Victoria, Aneesh Chopra, and Howard Schmidt. "Obama Administration Responds to We the People Petitions on SOPA and Online Piracy." *The White House Blog*, January 14, 2012. http://www.whitehouse.gov/blog/2012/01/14/obama-administration-responds-we-people-petitions-sopa-and-online-piracy.

Federal Bureau of Investigation. "60th Felony Conviction Obtained in Software Piracy Crackdown Operation Fastlink," March 6, 2009. http://www.fbi.gov/newhaven/press-releases/2009/nh030609b.htm.

Galloway, Stephen. "Who Says Piracy Costs the U.S. $58 Billion a Year?" *The Hollywood Reporter*, May 11, 2012. http://www.hollywoodreporter.com/news/piracy-costs-megaupload-kim-dotcom-318374.

Gu, Bin, and Vijay Mahajan. "The Benefits of Piracy: A Competitive Perspective." Paper presented at the Workshop on Information Systems and Economics, Washington, D.C., December 11–12, 2004. http://opim-sun.wharton.upenn.edu/wise2004/sat612.pdf.

Harbaugh, Rick, and Rahul Khemka. "Does Copyright Enforcement Encourage Piracy?" *Claremont Colleges Working Paper* 14 (2001). http://papers.ssrn.com/sol3/papers.cfm?abstract_id=244949.

Heidegger, Martin. *The Question Concerning Technology and Other Essays*. New York: Harper & Row, 1977.

Higgins, George E. "Digital Piracy, Self-Control Theory, and Rational Choice: An Examination of the Role of Value," *International Journal of Cyber Criminology* 1, no. 1 (2007a): 33–55.

Higgins, George E. "Digital piracy: An Examination of Low Self-Control and Motivation Using Short-Term Longitudinal Data," *CyberPsychology & Behavior* 10, no. 4 (2007b): 523–529.

Higgins, George E., Scott E. Wolfe, and Catherine D. Marcum. "Music Piracy and Neutralization: A Preliminary Trajectory Analysis from Short-Term Longitudinal Data." *International Journal of Cyber Criminology* 2, no. 2 (2008): 324–336.

Hinduja, Sameer. *Music Piracy and Crime Theory*. El Paso, TX: LFB Scholarly Publishing, 2006.

Holt, Thomas J., and Robert G. Morris. "An Exploration of the Relationship between MP3 Player Ownership and Digital Piracy," *Criminal Justice Studies* 22, no. 4 (2009): 381–392.

Horrigan, John. "Home broadband adoption 2008." *Pew Internet & American Life Project*, July 2, 2008. http://pewresearch.org/pubs/888/home-broadband-adoption-2008.

Ingram, Jason R., and Sameer Hinduja. "Neutralizing Music Piracy: An Empirical Examination." *Deviant Behavior* 29, no. 4 (2008): 334–366.

Karagiannis, Thomas, Andre Briodo, Nevil Brownlee, KC Claffy, and Michalis Faloutsos. "Is P2P Dying or Just Hiding?" Paper presented at the IEEE Global Internet and Next Generation Networks (Globecom'04), Dallas, Texas, November 29–December 4, 2004.

King, Brad. "RIAA Wins Suit against MP3.com." *Wired*, April 4, 2000. http://www.wired.com/techbiz/media/news/2000/04/35933.

Kleinrock, Leonard. "The Internet Rules of Engagement: Then and Now." *Technology & Society* 26, no. 2 (2004): 193–207.

Lasica, Joseph D. *Darknet: Hollywood's War against the Digital Generation*. Hoboken, NJ: John Wiley & Sons, 2005.

Lee, Timothy B. "Even without DNS Provisions, SOPA and PIPA Remain Fatally Flawed." *Ars Technica*, January 18, 2012. http://arstechnica.com/tech-policy/news/2012/01/even-without-dns-provisions-sopa-and-pipa-remain-fatally-flawed.ars?utm_source=rss&utm_medium=rss&utm_campaign=rss.

Lowe, Sue. "New Tune for Napster." *Fairfax Digital*, October 7, 2003. http://www.theage.com.au/articles/2003/10/06/1065292529108.html.

Malin, Jenessa, and Blaine J. Fowers. "Adolescent Self-Control and Music and Movie Piracy." *Computers in Human Behavior* 25 no. 3 (2009): 718–722.

McBride, Sarah, and Ethan Smith. "Music Industry to Abandon Mass Suits." *The Wall Street Journal*, December 19, 2008. http://online.wsj.com/article/SB122966038836021137.html.

McCourt, Tom, and Patrick Burkart. "When Creators, Corporations and Consumers Collide: Napster and the Development of On-Line Music Distribution." *Media, Culture & Society* 25 (2003): 333–350.

Merton, Robert K. "The Unanticipated Consequences of Purposive Social Action." *American Sociological Review* 1 no. 6 (1936): 894–904.

Moore, Robert. Digital File Sharing: An Examination of Neutralization and Rationalization Techniques Employed by Digital File Sharers. In *Cyber Criminology: Exploring Internet Crimes and Criminal Behavior*, edited by Karuppannan Jaishankar, 209–228. Boca Raton, FL: CRC Press, 2011.

Moore, Trevor T. and Gurpreet Dhillon. "Software Piracy: A view from Hong Kong." *Communications of the ACH* 43 no. 12 (2000): 88–93.

Nhan, Johnny. *Policing Cyberspace: A Structural and Cultural Analysis.* El Paso, TX: LFB Scholarly Publishing, 2010.

Nhan, Johnny, and Laura Huey. "Policing Through Modes, Clusters and Bandwidth." In *Techno-Crime: Technology, Crime, and Social Control,* edited by Stephane Leman-Langlois, 66–87. Portland, OR: Willan Press, 2008.

Nill, Alexander, John A. Schibrowsky, and James W. Peltier. "Factors that Influence Software Piracy: A View from Germany." *Communications of the ACM* 53 no. 6 (2010): 131–134.

Pepitone, Julianne. "SOPA Explained: What It Is and Why It Matters." *CNN Money,* January 17, 2012. http://money.cnn.com/2012/01/17/technology/sopa_explained/index.htm.

"Policing Internet Piracy: Accessories After the Fact." *The Economist,* November 26, 2011. http://www.economist.com/node/21540281.

Pouwelse, Johan, Pawel Garbacki, Dick H. J. Epema, and Henk Sips. "The Bittorrent P2P File-Sharing System: Measurements and Analysis." Paper presented at the 4th International Workshop on Peer-to-Peer Systems (IPTPS'05), Ithaca, New York, February 24–25, 2005.

Ramayah, T., Noor H. Ahmad, Lau G. Chin, and May-Chiun Lo. "Testing the Causal Model of Internet Piracy Behavior among University Students." *European Journal of Scientific Research* 29 no. 2 (2009): 205–216.

Rob, Rafael, and Joel Waldfogel. "Piracy on the High C's: Music Downloading, Sales Displacement, and Social Welfare in a Sample of College Students." *National Bureau of Economic Research* (2004). http://www.nber.org/papers/w10874.

Roberts, Paul. "RIAA Sues 532 'John Doe' File Swappers." *InfoWorld,* January 21, 2004. http://www.infoworld.com/t/business/riaa-sues-532-john-doe-file-swappers-970.

Sag, Matthew. "Twelve Year-Olds, Grandmothers, and Other Good Targets for the Recording Industry's File Sharing Litigation." *Northwestern Journal of Technology and Intellectual Property* 4 no. 2 (2006): 133–155.

Saroiu, Stefan, P. Krishna Gummadi, and Steven D. Gribble. "Measuring and Analyzing the Characteristics of Napster and Gnutella Hosts." *Multimedia Systems* 9 (2003): 170–184.

Schechter, Stuart E., Rachel A. Greenstadt, and Michael D. Smith. "Trusted Computing, Peer-to-Peer Distribution, and the Economics of Pirated Entertainment." *Economics of Information Security* 12 (2004): 59–69.

Schonfeld, Erick. "The Futility of Fighting Media "Pirates"—How MediaDefender got Hacked." *TechCrunch,* February 10, 2008. http://techcrunch.com/

2008/02/10/the-futility-of-fighting-media-pirates%E2%80%94how-mediadefender-got-hacked/.

Siegfried, Robert M. "Student Attitudes on Software Piracy and Related Issues of Computer Ethics." *Ethics and Information Technology* 6 no. 4 (2005): 215–222.

Siwek, Stephen E. "The True Cost of Motion Picture Piracy to the U.S. Economy." *Institute for Policy Innovation Policy Report 186* (2006). http://www.ipi.org/IPI/IPIPublications.nsf/PublicationLookupFullTextPDF/293C69E7D5055FA4862571F800168459/$File/CostOfPiracy.pdf?OpenElement.

Siwek, Stephen E. "The True Cost of Sound Recording Piracy to the U.S. Economy." *Institute for Policy Innovation Policy Report 188* (2007). http://ipi.org/IPI/IPIPublications.nsf/PublicationLookupFullTextPDF/51CC65A1D4779E408625733E00529174/$File/SoundRecordingPiracy.pdf?OpenElement.

Smith, Michael D., and Rahul Telang. "Competing with Free: The Impact of Movie Broadcasts on DVD Sales and Internet Piracy." *MIS Quarterly* 33 no. 2 (2009): 321–338.

Sterk, Stewart E. "Rhetoric and Reality in Copyright Law." *Michigan Law Review* 94 no. 5 (1996): 1197–1249.

Sterne, Jonathan. "The MP3 as Cultural Artifact." *New Media & Society* 8 no. 5 (2006): 825–842.

Sykes, Gresham M., and David Matza. "Techniques of Neutralization: A Theory of Delinquency." *American Sociological Review* 22 no. 6 (1957): 664–670.

Tassi, Paul. "The Avengers Demonstrates Piracy's Overstated Effect on Ticket Sales." *Forbes*, May 8, 2012. http://www.forbes.com/sites/insertcoin/2012/05/08/the-avengers-demonstrates-piracys-overstated-effect-on-ticket-sales/.

United States Department of Justice (2001). "Federal Law Enforcement Targets International Internet Piracy Syndicates: Multiple Enforcement Actions Worldwide Snare Top "Warez" Leadership." http://www.justice.gov/opa/pr/2001/December/01_crm_643.htm.

United States Department of Justice (2004). "Justice Department announces international Internet piracy sweep: 'Operation Fastlink' is the Largest Global Enforcement Action Ever Undertaken against Online Piracy." http://www.justice.gov/opa/pr/2004/April/04_crm_263.htm.

Yu, Szde. "Digital Piracy and Staling: A Comparison on Criminal Propensity." *International Journal of Cyber Criminology* 5 no. 2 (2010): 239–250.

4

Understanding Online Work-at-Home Scams through an Analysis of Electronic Mail and Websites

Sarah Turner, Heith Copes, Kent R. Kerley, and Gary Warner

Fraud has been a concern since the advent of modern economic systems. Historically, fraud involved direct interaction between victims and offenders, such as telephone-based communications or face-to-face interactions (Kitchens 1993; Knutson 1996; Stevenson 1998). The increase in the use of electronics for business and personal reasons has provided new opportunities for fraud (Grabosky, Smith, and Dempsey 2001; Wall 2001; Wire Fraud 2010). Offenders are now able to access a much larger number of victims faster and with fewer resources by using the Internet than by using previous mediums (Savona and Migone 2004). This growth in opportunities is likely responsible for the rise in fraud over the past decade (Shover and Hochstetler 2006; Symantec 2010).

The reliance on email for communication in recent decades has made it an ideal place to search for targets. Fraudsters have increasingly turned to spam email messages to facilitate their illegal behaviors. By using this approach, offenders are able to send massive amounts of unwanted emails with little or no direct costs. For example, large-scale distribution of spam messages, referred to as "spam campaigns," may include millions of emails sent around the world in only a few hours. Some estimate that spammers send 130.5 billion email messages each year, which accounts for 89.1% of all email sent (Symantec 2010).

Many spam campaigns have a clear intent to defraud individuals of their money, property, or personal information (Yu 2011). There are multiple types and uses of spam, most of which are responsible for financial damages (i.e., pharmaceutical spam or phishing emails). However, many of these types of spam emails have not been studied widely, especially from a social science perspective. Here we focus on "work-at-home" spam as an emerging form of online fraud. This fraud solicits participation in a variety of scams that promise "big money" for just a few hours of work per day, all of which can be done at home. In one recent example of this type of fraud, Google sued Pacific WebWorks for trademark infringement, dilution, unfair competition, and federal cyber piracy (ABC News 2009). The 2009 suit alleged that Pacific Web-Works victimized consumers by prominently displaying the Google logo, by suggesting sponsorship by Google, and by urging consumers to obtain a kit designed to help them work at home with Google products. According to Google officials, thousands of individuals had been tricked into sending payment information and then were charged for hidden fees and renewable subscriptions. The average loss per consumer was just under $100 (ABC News 2009).

Despite being responsible for significant financial losses, relatively little is known about online work-at-home fraud. Given the relative anonymity of the offenders and the significant monetary damages associated with this fraud, our goal in this exploratory study is to identify the common characteristics of a representative sample of work-at-home spam derived from a proprietary database. In doing so we shed light on trends in this type of fraud, techniques fraudsters use to enhance the legitimacy of the proposition, and elements of the solicitations that may be attractive to potential victims.

Work-at-Home Scams

A work-at-home scam is a fraudulent opportunity where the goal is to extort money from victims by luring them with offers to be employed at home. Typically the offer involves performing simple tasks for a short amount of time each day while earning an amount that far exceeds market value. These scams encompass many work-at-home opportunities, such as secret shoppers, stuffing envelopes, multi-level marketing (i.e., pyramid schemes), product sales, processing medical or insurance claims, or repackaging and shipping.

One example is a "secret shopper" scam in which potential employees are required to pay upfront fees that will cover training materials and/or membership to a database of secret shoppers from which corporations can hire. The secret shopper scheme usually is advertised as not requiring any previous experience, special training, or advanced education. In these scams fraudsters prey on victims by advertising the ability to earn money simply by shopping.

The "employees" are provided a check or money order to purchase merchandise at specific retailers and, on average, are offered 10% of each check or money order as compensation. After purchasing the requested items with the provided funds and writing a report on their shopping experience, the shoppers then ship the purchased items to a designated location and send the remaining money by wire transfer (ABC News 2008). This type of secret shopping arrangement incorporates elements of a "re-shipping scam" and a "cashier's check scam." Both scams are used to launder money or goods, as well as to extort money by having victims cash potentially fraudulent checks. In addition to financial losses, victims may suffer identity theft and face criminal charges based upon the type of work being performed (Internet Crime Complaint Center 2010).

As with any emerging fraud, reliable data on the incidence, prevalence, and economic impact of work-at-home scams is not readily available. This lack of data contributes to a lack of knowledge (for both the legislature and public) about the crime, which makes developing effective policy difficult. While there is a substantial "dark figure" associated with any type of fraud (Titus and Heinzelmann 1995), preliminary data on work-at-home fraud can be gleaned from the intelligence reports of many major companies. According to Symantec (2010), work-at-home spam is now ranked as the fifth most prevalent type of spam and is estimated as being responsible for 4,306,500,000 (3.3%) spam messages during the year 2010. Results from the 2010 Symantec Intelligence Report can be used to estimate the impact of work-at-home spam using the number of messages and typical startup fee of $19.95 or greater. Thus, if only 1/1000 of 1% (430,640) of individuals who received a work-at-home spam email paid a one-time startup fee of $19.95, it would create over $8.5 million in monetary losses.

Online Fraud in Context

While there is a lack of information about the nature and content of work-at-home spam, there are several recent studies of fraudulent online schemes, many of which involve spam email. Yu (2011) studied the broad topic of Internet spam messages to determine their content, format, techniques, and compliance with the Federal Trade Commission's 2004 CAN-SPAM Act. The researcher gathered 3,983 spam messages from five separate Gmail accounts for a four-month period during 2010. Nearly half of all the messages were written in HTML, over one-third used images, and nearly 60% were written in English. Interestingly, of the nearly 4,000 messages, only 108 did not have a clear violation of the CAN-SPAM Act. Nhan, Kinkade, and Burns (2009) studied spam email via an analysis of two email accounts over a three-month time period. During the months in which the accounts were active, 476 unsolicited emails were received and identified as potentially fraudulent. The researchers then categorized the messages along a broad range of variables such as businesses or industries mentioned, profession of sender, personal information provided by sender, nature of the message, amount of money involved, amount of return expected on investment, and the target information requested. Overall, they found that fraudsters tended to prefer a "social engineering" method of obtaining victims' personal and financial information, as opposed to more direct inquiry about sensitive information.

Edelson (2003) studied the 419 Nigerian advance fee fraud scam to identify key characteristics of those emails. The 419 scam is a unique form of fraud that is perpetrated through letters, fax, email, and websites. These scams are a concern not only for the estimated five billion dollars lost worldwide during the 1990s, but also for the enormous volume of spam fraudsters send and the associated security risks. Analyzing the headers of 1,000 emails, Edelson found that the 419 emails operated primarily, but not exclusively, from West Africa and Europe. Emails typically contained multiple methods of communication (i.e., telephone numbers, fax numbers, pagers, and emails) and the content often ended in the middle of a paragraph. To combat the concerns associated with this spam, Edelson recommends that email providers employ better filtering methods to prevent the emails from being sent.

Holt and Graves (2007) focused on other types of advance fee fraud. They conducted a qualitative analysis of 412 advance fee fraud emails received in two separate inboxes over two years. The purpose of Holt and Graves' study was to analyze the message syntax and to identify any traits or patterns that increased the likelihood of victimization. The authors compared multiple aspects of the email structure and content to identify both common and unique characteristics so they could better identify advance fee fraud emails. The findings suggest that 419 scammers attempt to include data that can increase impressions of legitimacy by employing unique phrasing throughout each email, enticing subject lines, or appeal to victims by mentioning potential monetary earnings. Their findings were used to improve knowledge of Internet fraud and identity theft by the general public as well as by law enforcement agencies. In addition to encouraging Internet service providers to employ better filtering methods, the authors advocate public awareness programs and more empirical research to identify any similarities between victims as a possible means of understanding the enticements.

Hu, McInish, and Zeng (2010) investigated how spam emails that promoted stock tips might influence the decision-making processes of active stock traders. The researchers gathered over 40,000 spam messages touting 785 firms in 580 spam campaigns over a nearly three-year period. The five key aspects of the spam messages analyzed were target price of the stock, message length, email source, incentives for purchase, and whether the businesses touted were international. Of these five aspects, Hu et al. (2010) found that target price and international businesses were the two most important aspects. Specifically, stock trading was most likely to be impacted by the spam campaigns when a short-term price of the stock was mentioned and when the businesses touted were U.S.-based. Rege (2009) added to the literature by examining fraudulent online dating sites from 2000 to 2009. Specifically, the researcher identified 170 online documents from dating sites, news and media sites, anti-scam commissions, law enforcement agencies, and government agencies for analysis. The purpose was to develop a typology of cyber offenders involved in online dating scams, which includes their techniques, motivation, and organization.

In this paper we build on these previous studies to explore work-at-home fraud. That is, we explore trends in this type of fraud, techniques of the fraudsters, and elements of the solicitations that may be attractive to potential victims. We analyze a representative sample of work-at-home spam messages and corresponding websites derived from a proprietary database. In addition to expanding the limited amount of research on work-at-home spam, the present study will identify key characteristics of work-at-home emails and websites.

Data and Methodology

This pilot study examines work-at-home emails and their embedded website links derived from the University of Alabama at Birmingham's Spam Data Mine. The Spam Data Mine receives over 1.5 million messages daily and its resources have been used for research in spam, phishing, and malware (Wardman and Warner 2008; Wei, Sprague, and Warner 2009; Wei, Sprague, Warner, and Skjellum 2010). We began our study in January, 2011, by focusing on the two most recent months of data from the Spam Data Mine. Because the data mine has such a large collection of emails, Structured Query Language (SQL) was used to narrow the results based on the subject lines of the emails and the month in which they were sent. Subject lines such as "work from home," "job available," "stay at home," and "extra cash" were used in the queries to return a relevant list of work-at-home emails. This database query yielded 8,014 emails for November, 2010, and 7,200 emails for December, 2010. The results from the subject query returned a subject line and unique identifier[1] for each email. We drew a representative sample of emails from each month with a 95% confidence interval and a 10% sampling error. Given that each month had a population between 5,000 and 10,000, we needed to select at least 95 emails from each month to achieve a representative sample (Salant and Dillman 1994). We then oversampled slightly to reach 100 emails per month, for a total sample of 200.

Each selected identifier number was used to find the body of the email in the Data Mine. Once the corresponding emails were located, the content was checked to ensure it advertised for a work-at-home opportunity. Emails were considered fitting sampling criteria if they contained content relating to any form of a work-at-home opportunity. If so, the emails were exported, the subject recorded for analysis, the website links included in the message content were documented, and the corresponding email was tagged as having contained an active link.

Any website address appearing in the body of the email was then selected as a second source of data. Documented website addresses were pasted into an Internet browser to capture screenshots and Whois information for the work-at-home sites.[2] The website links were followed as quickly as possible because these sites have a high rate of change. This is due, in part, to "black lists" (i.e., lists of websites deemed scams or potential threats that are not only available to the public but also are sent to email and Internet service providers), email recipients alerting their email providers of potential scam emails, and Internet Service Providers blocking or shutting down suspected scam sites. Using this method we identified a total of 59 websites embedded in the 200 emails.

We determined that the best methodological approach for this data was content analysis, and thus developed separate coding sheets for the emails and the websites. While similar in coding content, the nature of the formats dictated that we code them differently. Whereas the emails were better suited for textual analysis, the websites also contained numerous images that could be analyzed. For the emails, we sought information about the financial details mentioned, claims of legitimacy, use of personalization or flattery, and locations from which the emails were sent. When coding for legitimacy we looked

---

1. The unique identifier is a tag assigned to every email received in the data mine. This is to expedite queries and allow better organization within the database. Each tag include the date received as well as the time, an example is iid.10Nov01.1111.

2. Whois.domaintools.com is a free website that offers information about an IP address or website such as website registrar, name server, contact information for the domain owner, create/expiration/update dates for websites, and much more.

for characteristics such as whether the sender provided a physical address or other contact information, whether they mentioned well-known legitimate companies, and whether they mentioned other solicitations that could be scams. When coding for personalization we focused on mentions of the sender's or recipient's gender, mentions of the recipients' names, or the use of flattery (e.g., describing the recipients as "smart" or as "good business people").

When coding the websites we sought to determine the overall format of the websites. The websites came in one of six variations: news website, piggyback on legitimate cites, a "regular" website advertising work at home offers, offering a service/item to assist in your work at home success, a website requiring the visitor to either input personal data or request information on the product/service being described, or other/unknown. There were more testimonials in websites than in email so we coded for the number of testimonials and the gender of those giving them. When coding for the financial details from websites we included dollar amounts that appeared in the text and those that appeared in images (e.g., photos of checks). Finally, we coded websites for claims of legitimacy. These included whether well-known legitimate companies were mentioned and if so, how many, if other scams were mentioned, and the location on the website where these mentions were found.

Once coding for email and message content was completed, information about the legitimacy of the email and websites was collected. Information about each website address was collected using Whois.domaintools.com, FlagFox, and the UAB Geolocator. This information included screen shots, the IP address of the domain, the domain name, Whois data, the Compete rank[3], and the actual geographic region to which the IP address belongs. The Whois data included the location of the IP address owner, when the website was created, when it expires, and the ICANN registrar (i.e., the person to whom the domain was registered and the person responsible for the website). To collect information on the legitimacy of the email we reviewed the header of the email to establish if the email had been "spoofed" (faked or forged IP address or domain), where the IP originated from, and any discrepancies between the "from" email address and the "reply to" address.

Identifying the originating IP and header information was accomplished with the same steps. Some email clients provide the sender's IP address as "Originating IP" inside the email header, but other email providers do not. It is in those instances that the IP can be found by working backwards to the ap-

---

3. Compete is a monthly ranking system that counts unique visitors of websites. The websites with the most visitors have higher ranks.

parent originating IP by comparing the "received from" lines and then verifying that the supplied IP addresses resolve to the reported domains. If the lines did not match then the header had most likely been spoofed. In some instances, the email service providers for the recipients of the scam emails recognized that the header had been spoofed and/or was part of a spam campaign. If there was any uncertainty while manually classifying a header, the tools Ping, Whois, or the online application IP Address Location were used for verification.[4]

Once the originating IP and domain were identified (if possible), that information was then compared to the "from" tag to again check for any attempts at spoofing. The "from" tag was then compared to the "reply to" tag to check for consistency. This comparison was necessary because if the "from" address was spoofed to look like it came from a well-known company or group, the scammer would need to have a different "reply to" email address to access any replies received from that email.

Analysis of Emails

Table 1 provides a summary of the content of the email messages. The first element recorded for the emails was whether the message was comprised of text and no link, a link and no text, or both a text and a link. The majority of the emails (77%) contained both text and a link in the message body, 20% consisting of text only, and 3% consisted of links only. The emails with text offered more details of the scam being promoted than emails with links. Although a large percentage of the website links were not active, we note that 74% of the emails requested a response via a website. Approximately 28% of the emails used HTML graphics and nearly 90% used a "testimonial" about the work opportunity. The median length of email message was 151 words.

In Table 2 we describe the extent to which the emails were personalized and targeted to potential victims. As shown in Table 2, we found that 49% of the messages did not include any reference to the gender of the email sender (i.e., they were not signed or used the advertised company or group name in closing). Those that included the gender of the sender were almost twice as likely to be male than female. In situations where the gender was identified, it was typically through the introduction of the email, and in most instances (77.5%) there was no mention of any professional credentials of the sender (i.e., no formal closing or mention of a job title or position). The majority (90.5%) of

---

4. Because of how the emails are stored in the data mine, it was not possible to retrieve the full header of every email.

Table 1. Message Content of Work-at-Home Email

	Frequency	Percent
Message consists of		
Text only	40	20.0
Link only	6	3.0
Text and Link	154	77.0
Response method		
Website	148	74.0
Email	52	26.0
HTML graphics		
Yes	55	27.5
No	145	72.5
Testimonial		
Yes	177	88.5
No	23	11.5
Message Length (words)		
Range	0–1113	
Median	151	
Average	98.65	
Mode	105	

emails did not contain a gender-specific greeting, whether it was a name or other, such as "Hey Daniel," or "good morning ma'am." When gender was mentioned it was equally split.

In some circumstances, scammers personalized the email, either by including the recipient's email address in the message, the recipient's name,[5] or

---

5. In most instances it was not possible to know if the included name was that of the recipient or a randomly generated one; however, if a name was present, it was coded as having been personalized.

Table 2. Personalization and Targeting of Work-at-Home Email Content

	Frequency	Percent
Sender Gender		
Male	65	32.5
Female	37	18.5
Unknown	98	49.0
Recipient Gender		
Male	10	5.0
Female	9	4.5
Unknown	181	90.5
Greeting Personalization		
Yes	35	17.5
No	165	82.5
Flattery		
Yes	49	24.5
No	151	75.5

by using a less formal, friendlier writing style such as "Hey, I know money's been tight and you've been busy working which sucks since you never have time to hang out anymore."[6] While theoretically a more personal greeting may increase the probability of a response, 82.5% of senders did not personalize the message.

We also sought to determine the extent to which senders used flattery to entice recipients. Flattery such as "only intelligent individuals were given this opportunity," can make the recipient feel emotionally linked to the sender and could increase the likelihood of response. For example, the scammer may give the impression that this work-at-home opportunity is only available to the "upper echelons of society" or to "intelligent members of society." Approximately 25% of the emails contained this writing style. This component of

---

6. This example, as well as others we present throughout, is drawn from emails in our sample.

work-at-home scam emails is an example of other tools offenders may use to convince people to try a program.

We also examined several elements of the legitimacy of the message. Harley and Lee (2009, 5) have noted the importance of "brand association" in online scams because "it is considered an effective technique that allows scammers to directly steal information or be able to use social engineering to persuade users to disclose financial information." As shown in Table 3, 32% of the emails included the mention of a major company. Also, the same amount (32%) of emails mentioned the program's legitimacy. Two examples of legitimacy claims were:

"I want to tell you about a REAL job you can do from anywhere you are-for well-known, legitimate companies who pay well, pay fast, and really need people who are willing to be reliable for them."

Table 3. Message Legitimacy Claims in Work-at-Home Email

	Frequency	Percent
Scammer mentions a legitimate company		
Yes	64	32.0
No	136	68.0
Scammer mentions other scam/legitimacy of this program		
Yes	64	32.0
No	136	68.0
Mailing Address included		
Yes	108	54.0
No	92	46.0
Personal sender information listed		
Yes	45	22.5
No	155	77.5
Grammar and spelling errors		
Yes	77	38.5
No	123	61.5

"What's more, I'd like you to know that this is not one of those scams or schemes. No way. In fact, more than 630,239 U.S. citizens now make a fulltime ... or part-time ... income this way. Plus, it's been raved about in the media. For example ... CNN News says it's, 'A great way to make extra cash.'"

Such claims demonstrate methods the scammers may use to entice potential victims and to put wary victims at ease.

Another aspect of legitimacy coded was the presence of a physical address or sender information. The presence of a physical address would imply that there is a true physical location, thus giving potential victims a sense of ease because not only is this potential work opportunity online, but also there is a physical location for the user's security. If anything goes wrong, that address could be reported to law enforcement officials. Slightly over half (54%) of the emails contained a physical address. Only 22.5% gave personal information on the sender.

Misspellings are also a potential identifier of work-at-home scams and should be "red flags" for potential victims. We found that 38.5% of emails contained obvious grammatical and spelling errors. These errors were in the form of Internet shorthand (i.e., leet speak) or a simple misspelling such as "Amerycans."

In Table 4 we summarize key financial aspects of the emails. The "fees required" emails added not only a sense of legitimacy, but also provide an indication of how much financial impact these types of scams may cause. The maximum amount of potential earnings mentioned in the email messages was $136,808.00 and the minimum was $160.00. By having such a large amount ad-

Table 4. Financial Aspects of Work-at-Home Email

	Frequency	Percent
Potential Monthly Earnings		
Range	$160.00–$136,808.00	
Median	$3,200.00	
Associated Fees		
Mentioned	12	6.0
Free	15	7.5
Not Mentioned	173	86.5

vertised, interest in the product may increase, but some people will then believe that the offer is "too good to be true." With median potential monthly earnings of $3,200 per month, it appears that the scammers were somewhat realistic in their promises and generally kept the monthly earnings range between $1,500 and $5,000 per month. Some fees were also mentioned in efforts to boost legitimacy and also to convince victims that paying a small start-up fee is nothing in comparison to the large salaries they will soon be earning. However, the large majority of emails (86.5%) did not mention a fee and 7.5% of the emails stated that the program was free.

Several of the emails contained multiple email addresses, one in the "from," "reply to," and one included in the email body. As displayed in Table 5, these email addresses were analyzed for legitimacy or having being sent from a well-known email server such as Google. Domains that are well-known for legitimacy are

Table 5. Branding and Legitimacy Work-at-Home Email

	Frequency	Percent
Established Domains		
Aim.com	1	1.41
AOL.com	5	7.04
Att.net	4	5.63
Bellsouth.net	1	1.41
Gmail.com	25	35.21
Habitat.org	3	4.23
Hotmail.com	14	19.72
Live.com	3	4.23
MSN.com	1	1.41
Yahoo.com	14	19.72
Spoofed		
Yes		
Verified	28	13.9
Suspected	31	15.4
No	142	70.6

known as established domains. Some of the documented established domains included: Gmail.com, AOL.com, Bellsouth.net, Habitat.org and Hotmail.com.

Many of the obtained addresses were sent from established domains; however, this does not indicate that the program is legitimate as most email accounts are available to the public for free and the message header can be forged to look like the email is from a well-known source (Wei, Sprague, and Warner 2009). Approximately 14% of analyzed emails were verified as being spoofed or forged to hide the sender's identity and another 15% were suspected to be spoofed but were unable to be verified. We note that 70% had not been forged, although there are many tools available to scammers to more thoroughly forge a header.

Analysis of Websites

We separated the website layouts into six categories based on the structure of the webpage (see Table 6). The least common type of website recorded was a legitimate website hosted by a legitimate organization that had nothing to do with the spam email. This is referred to as piggybacking (3.39%). Piggybacking websites (see Figure 1) allows scammers another way of appearing legitimate to potential clients. For example, one email included a link to a prestigious research institute's website and offered a work-at-home position through this website. Victims would then see the website and believe the email to be legitimate even though the "reply to" email address in the original email would not match the address associated with the website. If potential victims visit the re-

Table 6. Layout of Work-at-Home Websites

	Frequency	Percent
Layout		
Piggyback	2	3.39
News Report	6	10.17
Requires information/log in	30	50.85
Regular website advertising a good	5	8.47
Make purchase to work at home	14	23.73
Other/Unknown	2	3.39

search institute's website to confirm the company and details mentioned in the email, the illegitimacy of the promoted organization would be obvious.

Figure 1. Example of Piggybacking Website

Another approach to the website designs was the news report variation (see Figure 2). These websites were created to resemble local news stations' websites. This layout typically included testimonials, multiple images with "clients," checks, comments, headings such as "Local Mom Makes $710/Week," and links to legitimate news sites such as Central News Network (CNN). Local news layouts were structured as real news reports and in doing so, may have added a sense of legitimacy to the promoted opportunity. Most even had a number of

Figure 2. Example of News Report Website

comments from "readers" at the bottom of the pages (see Figure 3). The local news layout comprised about 10% of all websites in the sample.

Just over 50% of the websites required users to provide some form of information (i.e., email address, name, phone number) to obtain access to the site and to receive information about the work-at-home opportunity. Many asked users to sign up for a "risk free kit" that involved providing personal information and a small payment (see examples of these websites in Figures 4 and 5).

Another variation of websites that were recorded is the "regular" format. These websites were coded by appearing to be a website simply advertising work at home opportunities and accounted for about 8% of the analyzed sites. These sites contained no mention of purchasing any products or being required to sign up for anything. Figure 6 is an example of what was considered a "regular" website.

The fifth criteria for categorizing a website was whether or not that site was advertising goods or services for purchase in order to gain access to work at home materials. This category accounted for 23.73% of the recorded websites. Websites were classified as requiring payment based on the presence of having to pay a fee whether it was for a membership fee, CD, guide book, or other in order to have access to the advertised work at home materials. Figure 7 is an example of a website classified under this category.

The final category of website format was "other." This category accounted for about 3% of the retrieved websites. Websites in this group are those that had errors where no links were available to get any additional information (in-

Figure 3. Reader Comments from News Report Website

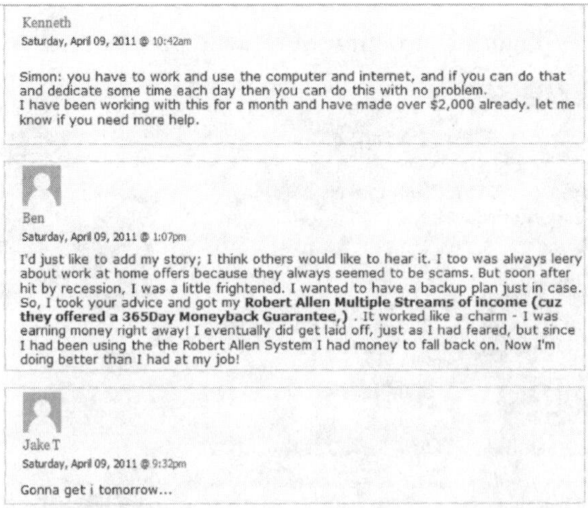

Figure 4. Work-at-Home Website Asking for Personal Information

Figure 5. Work-at-Home Website Asking for Registration

Figure 6. Example of Work-at-Home "Regular" Website

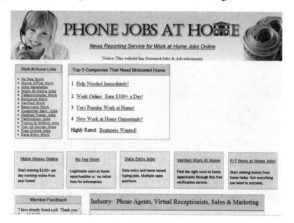

Figure 7. Example of Website Asking to Make a Purchase

dicating the site may have been used for malware) or the site talks about working from home but did not actually provide an avenue in which to engage in a work at home scam (i.e., dead links or poorly written website code). Figure 8 is an example of such a site that had no working links, did not request any additional information, and did prompt visitors to make a purchase or sign up for a membership.

In addition to the layout of the work-at-home websites, we sought to identify the type of work being offered (see Table 7). Many websites advertised work-at-home opportunities and the ability to make large amounts of "easy money," but never elaborated the exact process whereby money could be made. We were. however, able to group the websites into six categories. The first dis-

Figure 8. Example of "Other" Type of Work-at-Home Website

tinct avenue of work was advertising and it accounted for 13.56% of the employment. The work was classified as advertising if the site mentioned anything about gaining popularity for a website, posting links, or distributing advertisements. The second group is called "work" and consists of any website that seemed to offer actual tasks (i.e., typing, telemarketing, survey taking). This group constituted 10.17% of the websites. The third group comprised 23.73% of the websites and work under this category could not necessarily be established because individuals needed to pay a fee to learn the secret or gain access to the work at home materials. The fourth group is largest at 38.98% and is similar in nature in that these work opportunities could not be defined because users had to sign up or create an account to ascertain what the actual

Table 7. Advertised Work Opportunities in Work-at-Home Websites

	Frequency	Percent
Layout		
Advertising	8	13.56
Work (i.e., typing or telemarketing)	6	10.17
Not specified—purchased required	14	23.73
Not specified—sign up/log in required	23	38.98
Not specified at all	3	5.08
Other	5	8.47

job requirements were. The fifth group (5.08%) pertained to websites that did not specify the type of work at all; there were no indications of what participants would be doing. The sixth group (8.47%) is classified as "other." These websites indicated that the work-at-home businesses would soon be in touch with users or other.

In Table 8 we describe the use of testimonials and gender in the sampled websites. The criteria for testimonials on the websites included: number of testimonials, gender, and locations (if they were located in the text, sidebars, or in a comment section). There are more criteria for website testimonials because much of the data was gained through images and emails cannot support such large files.

Table 8. Testimonials and Gender in Work-at-Home Websites

	Frequency	Percent
Testimonial Genders		
Male	13	44.8
Female	16	55.2
Number of Testimonials (Median)		
In the Text	2	
In the Sidebars	5	
In the Comments	8	

Testimonials were included for coding because of the implication of how popular or legitimate a program seemed. By having seemingly ordinary people state how easy or effective a program is potential victims may be lulled into a false sense of security by seeing other people use this program. Some websites also contained comment sections where potential users or skeptics voiced their comments, concerns, and praise. Testimonials were located in several locations on work-at-home sites, such as the text of the website, in sidebars, and in comment sections. The gender of the person to whom the testimonials were attributed was not significantly different as men were responsible for about 45% and women comprised the remaining 55%.

Next we addressed the financial aspects of the websites (see Table 9). Websites were coded for the amount of money mentioned in the title or heading of the page, amounts mentioned in the text, any start up fees, and if there was

Table 9. Financial Matters in Work-at-Home Websites

	Frequency
Amount Mentioned In Website Title	
Maximum	$136,808.00
Minimum	1,000.00
Amount Mentioned in Text	
Maximum	$136,808.00
Minimum	800.00
Median	5000.00
Check Photo	
Maximum	$8782.57
Minimum	400.00
Start-up Costs	
Not Mentioned	42
Mentioned	17
Maximum	$100.00
Minimum	7.00

a photo of a check on the website. The work-at-home websites in our sample contained more references to financial matters than emails because the websites were able to host more content in different forms, such as pictures of money, large fonts at the top of the website indicating how much money a person could make, the amount of startup costs, and pictures of earned checks. In many cases, these websites had a title at the top of the page that stated the name of the program and how much a person can make using the advertised product. The maximum amount mentioned in the website headings was $136,808.00 and the minimum recorded was $1,000.00. The text consisting of the body of the website also contained potential earning amounts with a maximum of $136,808.00, minimum of $800.00, and median of $5,000.00. Scammers also included images of checks (see Figure 9) with the highest amount recorded as $8,782.57 and the lowest as $400.00. However, to make the promised money and to receive a check with your name on it, some scams required

Figure 9. Image of Check Found on Work-at-Home Website

You could be making checks like this

start-up or membership fees. Most of the websites did not mention any fees[7] (71.2%), but there was a smaller percentage (28.8) that did and those start-up fees ranged from $7.00 to $100.00.

As summarized in Table 10, claims of legitimacy were also made in the website content, although it was more common (57.6%) for a scammer to avoid mentioning a legitimate company on the site than it was for them to make their websites look supported by reputable companies (42.4%). The same pattern follows in whether a scammer mentioned a different scam or stated the legitimacy of the program being promoted. More offenders did not mention other scams or defend the legitimacy of their own (62.7%) than those who did (37.3%). Websites that included a company name typically mentioned two groups in the text and five groups in the header. The most commonly advertised groups were Apple, ABC, Adidas, and MSNBC.

In Table 11 we include other important information about the source and history of the websites. Of the 59 sampled websites, 55 of the website domains were unique and 4 were repeated. There were 49 unique IP addresses and 10 duplicated IPs that originated from over 30 countries. The oldest website was created September 28, 1996, the newest website was created December 07, 2010, and the most common year of creation for these websites was 2000. This is significant because work-at-home websites typically have an extremely high rate of turnover. The age of the domains may indicate several things, such as

---

7. It is important to note that some of the work-at-home websites required potential users to create a log-in account before any details of the program were released. It would be ideal to register at each site that required a log in so to uncover any start up fees, but for each site the authors would have to enter an email address, wait for the confirmation email, sign in, and such. So as this is a pilot study, it has been left to future research to undertake that task.

Table 10. Legitimacy of Work-at-Home Websites

	Frequency	Percent
Legitimate company mentioned		
Yes	25	42.4
No	34	57.6
Mentions other scams or the program's legitimacy		
Yes	22	37.3
No	37	62.7
Number of companies mentioned		
In Text	1–7	
Median	2	
In Header	1–7	
Median	5	

Table 11. Information About Work-at-Home Websites

	Frequency	Percent
Website Link		
Unique Sites	55	92.7
Repeated Sites	4	7.3
IP Address		
Unique	49	83.1
Repeated	10	16.9
Length of Existence		
Oldest	September 28, 1996	
Newest	December 07, 2010	
Most common year of creation	2000	

1) the original website had been hacked to suit the scammer's needs and the website owner was unaware, 2) the scammer was exceptionally lucky and no one complained about the site to an Internet Service Provider, or 3) the scammer constantly updated and changed the appearance of the website thus making it more difficult to identify as illicit. The IP addresses were also entered into the UAB Geolocator to identify where the websites were being hosted. The results of this query indicated that the websites were registered to a total of 5 countries (United States, Germany, China, United Kingdom, and British Columbia) with 49 of the 59 websites hosted through companies in the United States.

Finally, in addition to using Whois.domaintools.com for domain information, Compete Rank was used to identify the standing of each possible domain (see Table 12). Compete Rank is an online ranking system that ranks each website based on the number of unique visitors it receives each month. The highest ranking for the analyzed sites was 1,597, with a total of 1,217,570 unique visitors each month. The lowest recorded rank was 4,617,375, with a total of only 43 unique visitors to the website each month. The median ranking was 83,043 with 23,366 unique visitors per month.

Table 12. Compete Rankings of Work-at-Home Websites

	Rank	Visitor Count
Compete Rank		
Maximum	1,597	1,217,570
Minimum	4,617,375	43
Average	400,862	134,541
Median	83,043	23,366

Discussion and Conclusions

The goal of this paper was to provide an exploratory analysis of work-at-home emails and websites. Through this analysis, we sought to identify the common characteristics for this type of fraud, as well as common techniques used by the offenders to make the solicitations attractive to potential victims. Our study indicates that a typical work-at-home email is from an unspecified sender to an unspecified recipient. Email subjects are worded persuasively to increase the likelihood that individuals will open the email and visit the website (if supplied and active) and then fall prey to the fraud. The work-at-home emails consist of text and, in some cases, hyperlinks to a website with additional information about the scam. The length of the message will usually be short and without any misspellings. The email will contain some claim of legitimacy, such as a testimonial, mention of another scam, or mention/impersonation of a reputable company. Additionally, the "From" information is likely to have been spoofed. There may be some mention of the work-at-home position as being "easy money" and even include a potential earning amount; however, the email typically will not list the start-up fees.

Work-at-home websites are typically found in three layouts: news reports, advertisements, or piggybacking. The content for the websites will, for the most part, not elaborate on how to achieve work-at-home success without first requiring a startup fee or the creation of a log-in account. Website content will contain monetary amounts that can be found at the top of the websites as well as within the text or sidebars. Additionally, most websites will not include pictures. Similar to the email content, legitimacy claims are common on websites through the form of testimonials and either mentioning or displaying logos of reputable companies.

Before offering the research and policy implications of our study, we note that readers may question whether we are generalizing all work-at-home business arrangements as fraudulent. We are aware that not every work-at-home opportunity is a scam. Legitimate opportunities exist, but they can be difficult to identify because of the vast number of illegitimate ones. Christine Durst, Chief Executive Officer of StaffCentrix, a company that specializes in home-based careers, recently noted that among "the 5,000 home job leads StaffCentrix screens weekly, there is a 54 to 1 scam ratio" (Blake 2009). This means that individuals looking for work-at-home opportunities must exercise extreme caution when searching for employment. This could include looking at the job requirements, because if there are none or the company is requiring participants to pay upfront fees then it is most likely fraudulent. Individuals can also call the advertised company's main office to verify its existence and location. This should always be performed no matter how well-known the company is and if there is still doubt, individuals can contact the Better Business Bureau or the Federal Trade Commission. Another indication of a scam is the trite, yet accurate, guideline that "if it sounds too good to be true, it probably is." As a general rule, businesses are not going to pay someone with no experience an inordinate amount of money to perform a menial task for only a few hours of work per day.

The area of work-at-home spam is relatively new and offers many avenues for additional research. With larger sample sizes over longer periods, a more accurate portrait of work-at-home spam could be formed. Trends within spam campaigns could be identified though larger sample sizes obtained over a greater time period by identifying when a spam campaign is the most popular, such as news reports being more prevalent during the spring, or piggybacking scams being noticed more in the fall. The domain names for work-at-home websites could be monitored for repeat usage or similarity. Also, patterns between email senders' IP addresses could be established by identifying which IP is responsible for which specific work-at-home campaign. This data could also assist in establishing spam campaign trends. By working with agencies, such as the Federal Bureau of Investigation's Internet Crime Complaint Center (IC3), researchers may also be able to gather information from the victims of these scams. If victim contact is made, then it would be possible to obtain first-order accounts of why victims fell prey to these scams. There are myriad research opportunities in the field of work-at-home fraud and this exploratory study was intended to catalyze this line of research.

Our findings point to several policy implications. First, results from our study could be used to create or supplement educational programs about online fraud more generally, and work-at-home fraud specifically. These programs could contain information we found regarding the structure, format, goals, and impact of the fraudulent emails and websites we analyzed. Such educational programs could be offered by the law enforcement community, consumer protection agencies, and university researchers, and could increase awareness of fraud as well as offer steps to avoid falling prey. In addition to creating awareness and resistance strategies for online fraud, our study results could be used to promote appropriate consumer responses to victimization. Online fraud victims often are reticent to report, and even when motivated struggle to identify the proper authorities or organizations to whom they should report. National victimization reporting databases such as the Internet Crime Complaint Center (www.ic3.gov) could be better publicized, as could state and regional efforts such as Operation Swordphish in Alabama (https://swordphish.cis.uab.edu/new).

Second, our results could be used to facilitate a cooperative effort between law enforcement officials (in particular at the federal level) and major Internet search providers (e.g., Google) to prevent and control online work-at-home fraud. For example, our study found a consistent pattern in the images, email text, and website testimonials in many work-at-home frauds. If these common patterns were shared with law enforcement officials and Google, it is possible that the fraudulent websites could be flagged and/or deleted from an online search index much sooner than in the past. Our findings may also help these groups identify the source of online kits that contain files needed to create work-at-home scams.

References

ABC News. "Cops Warn of 'Secret Shopper' Scam." March 7, 2008. http://abcnews.go.com/TheLaw/wireStory?id=4407858.

ABC News. "Google work-at-home scammers hauled to court." December 9. 2009. http://www.abs-cbnnews.com/technology/12/09/09/google-work-home-scammers-hauled-court.

Baker, Wayne E., and Robert R. Faulkner. "Diffusion of Fraud: Intermediate Economic Crime and Investor Dynamics." *Criminology* 41 (2003): 1173–1206.

Blake, John. CNN, "How I got taken by a work-at-home scam." Last modified January 07, 2009. http://articles.cnn.com/2009-01-07/living/home.scams_1_work-at-home-scammers-data-entry-job?_s=PM:LIVING.

Edelson, Eve. "The 419 Scam: Information Warfare on the Spam Front and a Proposal for Local Filtering." *Computers & Security* 22 (2003): 392–401.

Grabosky, Peter N., Russell G. Smith, and Gillian Dempsey. *Electronic Theft: Unlawful Acquisition in Cyberspace.* Cambridge, UK: Cambridge University Press, 2001.

Harley, David and Andrew Lee. "A Pretty Kettle of Phish: Something Phishy in your Email? What you Need to Know about Phishing Fraud." ESET Antivirus and Security White Papers. Accessed March 25, 2012. http://go.eset.com/us/resources/white-papers/Pretty_Kettle_of_Phish.pdf.

Holt, Thomas J., and Danielle C. Graves. "A Qualitative Analysis of Advance Fee Fraud E-Mail Schemes." *International Journal of Cyber Criminology* 1 (2007): 137–154.

Hu, Bill, Thomas McInish, and Li Zeng. "Gambling in Penny Stocks: The Case of Stock Spam Emails." *International Journal of Cyber Criminology* 4 (2010): 610–629.

Internet Crime Complaint Center. 2010 Internet Crime Report. Accessed November 15, 2011. www.ic3.gov/media/annualreport/2010_ic3report.pdf.

Kitchens, T. L. The Cash Flow Analysis Method: Following the Paper Trail in Ponzi Schemes. *FBI Law Enforcement Bulletin* 62 (1993): 10–13.

Knutson, M. C. The remarkable criminal financial career of Charles K. Ponzi. Accessed November 15, 2011. (1996) http://www.usInternet.com/users/mcknutson.

Nhan, Johnny, Patrick Kinkade, and Ronald Burns. "Finding a Pot of Gold at the End of an Internet Rainbow: Further Examination of Fraudulent Email Solicitation." *International Journal of Cyber Criminology* 3 (2009): 452–475.

Operation Swordphish. Accessed April 1, 2012. https://swordphish.cis.uab.edu/new.

Rege, Aunshul. "What's Love Got to Do with It? Exploring Online Dating Scams and Identity Fraud." *International Journal of Cyber Criminology* 3 (2009): 494–512.

Salant, Priscilla and Don A. Dillman. *How to Conduct Your Own Survey.* New York: John Wiley and Sons, 1994.

Savona, Ernesto U., and Mara Mignone. "The Fox and the Hunters: How IC Technologies Change the Crime Race." *European Journal on Criminal Policy and Research* 10 (2004): 3–26.

Shover, Neal and Andy Hochstetler. *Choosing White-Collar Crime.* Cambridge, UK: Cambridge University Press, 2006.

Symantec MessageLabs. 2010 Annual Security Report. Accessed November 1, 2011. http://www.symanteccloud.com/mlireport/MessageLabsIntelligence_2010_Annual_Report_FINAL.pdf.

Titus, Richard and Fred Heinzelmann. Fraud Victimization—The Extent, the Targets, the Effects. Technical Report. United States Department of Justice, National Institute of Justice. (1995). Washington, DC: Government Printing Office. Accessed November 8, 2011. http://www.ncjrs.gov/pdffiles/frau.pdf.

Wire fraud. Accessed November 10, 2011. http://fraud.laws.com/wire-fraud.

Wall, David S. "The Internet as a Conduit for Criminals." In *Information Technology and the Criminal Justice System*, edited by April Pattavina, 77–98. Thousand Oaks, CA: Sage, 2004.

Wardman, Brad and Gary Warner. "Automating Phishing Website Identification through Deep MD5 MatchinG." Paper presented at the eCrime Researchers Summit, Atlanta, GA, 2008.

Wei, Chun, Alan Sprague, and Gary Warner. "Clustering malware-generated spam emails with a novel fuzzy string matching algorithm." Proceedings of the Association of Computing Machinery Symposium on Applied Computing, Honolulu, HI, 2009.

Wei, Chun, Alan Sprague, Gary Warner, and Anthony Skjellum. Identifying new spam domains by hosting IPs: Improving domain blacklisting. Paper presented at the 7th Annual Collaboration, Electronic Messaging, Anti-Abuse, and Spam Conference, Mountain View, CA, 2010.

Yu, Szde. "Email Spam and the CAN-SPAM Act: A Qualitative Analysis." *International Journal of Cyber Criminology* 5 (2011): 715–735.

5

Internet Child Pornography: Legal Issues and Investigative Tactics

Marcus K. Rogers and Kathryn C. Seigfried-Spellar[1]

The protection of children has historically been an important part of any so-ciety; the same holds true today (Finkelhor, Mitchell, and Wolak 2000). With the incredible growth in science and technology over the last two decades, there has been an increased emphasis on the protection of children (Finkelhor, Mitchell, and Wolak 2000; Seigfried-Spellar, Lovely, and Rogers 2010). The Internet and its accompanying technologies (e.g., the World Wide Web, Twit-ter, FaceBook) have introduced some complexity and possible new avenues for the potential abuse of children and other historically victimized segments of our population. The notion that the Internet has become both a tool for advancing our society and culture as well as a tool for criminal or nefarious pur-poses is well documented (Ferraro and Casey 2005; Rogers and Seigfried-Spellar 2009; Taylor 1999, September; Wolak, Finkelhor, and Mitchell 2009). Crimi-nals and other deviant segments of society have traditionally been early adopters of technology as a means to extend and improve their criminal tradecraft (Fer-raro and Casey 2005). Information and Internet technologies are no excep-tion to this. One only has to look at the various media reports on identity theft, credit card fraud, or some other electronic banking attack for confirmation.

As it relates to the notion of protecting children, the Internet and its tech-nologies have been in the media forefront. Federal, state, and local law en-forcement agencies have created specialized units and task forces (e.g., Internet Crimes Against Children (ICAC) Task Force) to investigate crimes against chil-

---

1. The authors contributed equally to this work.

dren where the attacker has used technology to target their victims (Breeden and Mulholland 2006). The Federal Government has passed new legislation (e.g., the Adam Walsh Act) and provided funding to centers that focus on combating child exploitation (National Center for Missing and Exploited Children) (Finkelhor, Mitchell, and Wolak 2000; Wolak et al. 2008).

Despite these seemingly proactive approaches to child protection, very little if any research has been conducted on the nature of these types of crimes and on the characteristics of these offenders (Lanning and Burgess 1984; Quayle and Taylor 2005). While there has been some empirically based research (such as Durkin and Bryant 1999; Jenkins 2001), most of the evidence cited to justify the focus on the Internet and its technologies is anecdotal or single case in nature. This has resulted in a gap in our understanding of the offenders, uncertainty regarding how to protect the victims, and ignorance as to how best to investigate, prosecute, and deter these types of offences (Ferraro and Casey 2005; Taylor and Quayle 2003).

There has been some limited debate as to whether there is truly an increase in pedophilia and sexual deviancy that can be attributed to the corresponding increase in society's dependency on technology and the Internet. Current research indicates that regardless of the correlation versus causation debate, consumers of online child pornography are using Internet technologies to further their deviant sexual behavior (Taylor and Quayle 2003; Wolak, Finkelhor, and Mitchell 2009).

As an attempt to shed some much-needed light on this societal issue, this chapter examines the role that the Internet and internet-related technologies play in child pornography, pedophilia and sexually deviant Internet based paraphilia. We examine the emerging typology of online consumers of child pornography and how this is being manifested in the technology and online behaviors exhibited by these individuals. The chapter provides a brief overview of the context and possible scope of online child paraphilia, summarizes the current research related to investigative profiles of online predators and consumers of child pornography, advances in understanding and categorizing offenders and their offences, provides suggestions for modifying current sentencing guidelines and provides guidance on using digital evidence in support of these types of investigation. Two cases studies are also included to illustrate the concepts discussed.

Scope and Context

As was stated in the introduction, the threat of online predators and the correlation between the Internet and pedophilic behavior has caused much alarm in the law enforcement and general public domains. One would assume that given the fact that so much media and political attention has been focused on this, that we would have statistics and meaningful metrics regarding the frequency and prevalence of these activities or that we would have a body of empirical research regarding offender characteristics, victimology, and the effectiveness of investigative techniques. Sadly, this is not the case (Seigfried-Spellar, Lovely, and Rogers 2010; Wolak, Finkelhor, and Mitchell 2009; Wolak et al. 2008). As was previously stated, there does not seem to be a large body of research or evidence based public or law enforcement policy regarding this type of criminal behavior (Wolak, Finkelhor, and Mitchell 2009). To be fair, federal agencies such as the FBI have published various law enforcement related reports (Lanning 2001; Lanning and Burgess 1984) dealing with predatory offenders and consumers of child pornography, but these reports are restricted to those cases that have been officially reported to authorities; like other sex crimes, pedophilic related or predatory offender crimes tend to be under reported (Wolak, Finkelhor, and Mitchell 2009; Wolak et al. 2008).

This lack of statistics has resulted in some dubious and obviously inflated claims by organizations that have taken on the task of trying to protect children and/or educate parents as to the risks of the Internet to children and adolescents. As an example of some these claims, several websites provide the following statistics (Enough 2009; Media 2009):

- Average age of first Internet exposure to pornography—11 years old;
- Largest consumers of Internet pornography—35–49 age group;
- 15–17-year-olds having multiple hard-core exposures—80%;
- 8–16-year-olds having viewed porn online—90% (most while doing homework);
- 7–17-year-olds who would freely give out home address—29%;
- 7–17-year-olds who would freely give out email address—14%; and
- Children's character names linked to thousands of porn links—26 (Including Pokemon and Action Man).

It is unknown where these statistics came from or how the sample was selected (assuming some type of actual empirical/survey based research was conducted), as no information was available on the methodology or sampling procedures. At first glance these statistics seem very frightening, with 80% of adolescents having hardcore experiences, and 11-year-olds viewing pornography. Even if these statistics are valid and reliable, they do not tell us anything about the risk of these children and adolescents becoming victims of online predators or about the consumption of child pornography. Other websites offer even more disturbing supposed statistics (Healthymind 2009):

- 100,000 websites offer illegal child pornography;
- Child pornography generates $3 billion annually;
- Largest consumer of Internet pornography is the 12–17 age group.

These statistics are equally frightening, but again, where did they come from? How can we possibly know or estimate the annual revenue from child porn; do these individuals and businesses file tax returns with their respective countries? How did they confirm the age range for the consumers of child porn? Unfortunately, as is the case with emotionally and politically charged topics, personal, corporate, and political agendas can get in the way of meaningful metrics and statistics that are essential for garnering a true understanding of the risks to children and adolescents and the actual role that the Internet and its technologies play (e.g., Quayle and Taylor 2005; Skenazy 2009). As Lanning so eloquently stated:

> Some professionals [dealing with child sexual abuse], however, in their zeal to make American society more aware of this victimization, tend to exaggerate the problem. Presentations and literature with poorly documented or misleading claims about one in three children being sexually molested, the $5 billion child pornography industry, child slavery rings, and 50,000 stranger-abducted children are not uncommon. The problem is bad enough; it is not necessary to exaggerate it. Professionals should cite reputable and scientific studies and note the sources of information. If they do not, when the exaggerations and distortions are discovered, their credibility and the credibility of the issue are lost (Lanning 1992, 15).

From a global perceptive, the problem of child pornography only escalates due to the differences in national and international legislatures. The possession, distribution, and production of Internet child pornography is criminally sanctioned in several countries, such as the United States and United Kingdom; however, it is not illegal but is, in fact, readily available in others. For example, Japanese law only criminalizes the production or distribution of child pornography, thereby allowing personal possession without intent to distribute. In addition, similar laws accepting the personal use of child pornography are prevalent in Russia, Thailand, and Korea (Akdeniz 2008). On the other hand, several international entities have criminalized the possession, distribution, and production of Internet child pornography all together, such as the European Union, Council of Europe, and United Nations (Akdeniz 2008). The Canadian Criminal Code has included "viewing" or "accessing" as a criminal offense, even if the individual did not permanently possess (e.g., download) the child pornography image. Overall, child pornography has become a global problem due to advancements in technology and the differences in regulatory policies and sanctions.

The lack of reproducible empirical research in this area often leads to difficulties in determining the real severity of the offence, the danger posed by the offender, and what sentences are appropriate or in the United States, constitutional (Akdeniz 2008). Therefore, it is important to turn our discussion to possible solutions to this gap in knowledge.

The COPINE Project

In 1997, funding from the European Commission ignited the Combating Paedophile Information Networks in Europe (COPINE) project to research and explore the relationship between technology, more specifically the Internet, and the victimization of children (Taylor, Holland, and Quayle 2001). As part of the COPINE project, researchers began to quantitatively analyze and review child pornography images collected by offenders in order to explore the level of child victimization and severity of possession for the offenders. In 2001, Taylor et al. developed a continuum or categorization system, which placed seemingly innocent, non-sexualized images at one end of the spectrum while the sexually explicit and aggressive images appeared at the polar end. COPINE's continuum includes 10 levels based on the increase in severity of the child's sexual victimization: indicative, nudist, erotica, posing, erotic posing, explicit erotic posing, explicit sexual activity, assault, gross assault, and sadistic/bestiality (Taylor et al. 2001).

Level 1, or the indicative category, refers to any non-pornographic or innocent image, such as the advertisements for Disneyland. The nudist category (Level 2) includes images of naked or semi-naked children in appropriate nudist settings from a legitimate source (Taylor et al. 2001), such as an Art gallery or family photo album. Level 3, or the Erotica category, refers to images secretly taken of children in safe environments with varying degrees of nakedness, such as pictures covertly taken of children playing at the park or on the beach. However, the images contained in Levels 1, 2, and 3 are usually not considered "chargeable" offenses due to the lack of obscenity or difficulty in identifying the context or intent of the image (e.g., child pornography vs. real family photographs; Taylor et al. 2001).

Levels 4, 5 and 6 specifically refer to images where the children are deliberately posed. In Level 4 (posing), the images involve children that are intentionally posed in either complete, partial, or no clothing. According to Taylor et al. (2001), the amount, context, and organization of the Level 4 images may suggest whether or not the collector has a sexual interest in children. In addition, Level 5 (erotic posing) refers specifically to the deliberate sexual nature of the child's pose, which may include varying degrees of nakedness (e.g., child's legs are spread open). The explicit sexual posing category (Level 6) includes images, which stress the child's genital areas, once again, regardless of the degree of nakedness. As the categories increase in the level of child victimization, the legality of the images becomes more cohesive with current legal definitions of child pornography. Again, Levels 4 and 5 may or may not be considered illegal; however, there still exists a psychological abuse due to the broken boundaries between the adult and child. With Level 6, images are more likely to be considered chargeable depending on the age of the minor. Currently, the majority of international and national legislature defines a minor as under the age of 18 years (Akdeniz 2008).

Finally, for most international and national legislatures, it is illegal to possess, distribute, or produce images of minors in Levels 7, 8, 9, and 10 of the COPINE continuum. These categories include images in which the level of victimization is considered to be more severe because of the direct interaction between the victim and the producer, which involves both physical and psychological abuse. Level 7, or explicit sexual activity, involve images of "touching, mutual and self-masturbation, oral sex, and intercourse by a child" (Taylor et al., 2001, 101), which do not involve the participation of any adult. In the assault category (Level 8), the child is sexually assaulted by an adult through digital touching. Level 9 (gross assault) includes grossly indecent images in which an adult is sexually assaulting the child by penetrative sex, masturbation, or oral sex. Finally, Level 10 (sadistic/bestiality) refers to images in which (1) the child is being "tied, bound, beaten, whipped, or otherwise subject something that involves pain" or (2) images of a child involved in some form of sexual activity with an animal (Taylor et al. 2001).

Overall, the continuum suggested by Taylor et al. (2001) is the best descriptive analysis to date regarding the types of child pornography images available via the Internet. As the spectrum suggests, not all child pornography images are the same, especially in regards to their level of victimization. In addition, the classification system includes images that may or may not be criminally sanctioned. By not solely focusing on the pictures that are illegal, science can begin to emphasize the psychological perspectives of the offender (Taylor et al. 2001). In the end, the preferred type of image and the collection itself may provide researchers with a better understanding of the offenders' personality traits and psychological characteristics.

In addition, Taylor et al. (2001) suggest each level should be assessed regarding size, novelty, and the age of the victim. The size and quality of the offender's collection may indicate their level of involvement in child pornography. For instance, the collection may reveal the offender's sexual interest with children or level of addiction or obsession with the Internet. In addition, the presence of novel images may indicate the offender's ability to network on the Internet. In essence, the more novel the images, the more involved the offender may be in the Internet child pornography rings. Finally, younger children are more likely to be the victims of child pornography because they are easier to control and manipulate, and research indicates the age of children involved in pornography is decreasing (Taylor 1999). Overall, the level of severity within each category of the COPINE continuum may differ depending on these three additional factors.

The Courts and COPINE

The COPINE classification system has influenced research on this topic as well as legislative decisions regarding the sentencing of child pornography offenders. For instance, Frei, Erenay, Dittmann, and Graf (2005) gathered data on 33 male child pornography offenders in Switzerland who were identified and arrested by law enforcement for using the Internet child pornography company, "Landslide Production Inc," which required the clients to provide identifiable information. The authors conducted a qualitative analysis of the pornographic material collected by the offenders using the COPINE classification system. Almost half of the offenders (45%) collected Level 9 images, or gross assault, and 27% of the offenders collected Level 10 images or "sadistic/bestiality" pictures. 9% of the offenders collected erotica (Level 3) images, 3% collected erotic posing (Level 5) images, and 3% collected explicit sexual assault (Level 7) images. Finally, 12% of the offenders either did not collect any child pornography, or the level of the child pornography images was unknown due to lack of data. Thus, the majority (72%) of the offenders collected images, which depicted greater levels of child victimization as indicated by the COPINE classification scale (Frei et al. 2005).

In 2002, the COPINE scale was adopted and modified into England and Wales' sentencing guidelines for child pornography related offenses. *In R v. Oliver and others*, the Court of Appeal determined the seriousness of a child pornography offense should be based on the "nature of the material involved and the extent of the offender's involvement with it" (*R v. Oliver and others* 2003). Based on the COPINE classification system, the "nature of the material" was defined in the Oliver image description scale as five categories: (1) erotic posing with no sexual activity, (2) sexual activities involving a child or children, (3) adult and child non-penetrative sexual activity, (4) adult and child penetrative sexual activity, and (5) sadism or bestiality (Akdeniz 2008). Levels 1, 2, and 3 of the COPINE scale, which involve less sexual victimization, were not included in the Oliver image description scale.

In addition, England and Wales adopted sentencing guidelines, which assess the content (i.e., level) and amount (i.e., quantity) of the images seized in child pornography related offenses based on the Oliver image description scale (Akdeniz 2008). In addition, the sentencing guidelines take into account the various child pornography offenses (i.e., possession, distribution, or production) as well as whether the child in the image is a real or computer-generated victim. In general, images involving real children, in contrast to computer-generated images, are considered by the courts as a more serious offense (Akdeniz 2008). Taking these four factors into consideration, the Oliver guidelines may suggest a punishment anywhere from a fine to a ten-year maximum sentence. However, as indicated by their name, the Oliver guidelines are merely "rules of thumb" for the courts to consider; the judges have discretionary power to contemplate other aggravating factors, such as the defendant posting the images in a public domain of the Internet. In 2004, the *R v. Thompson* guidelines further clarified the Oliver guidelines by requiring indictments to include either an exact or representative count of the number of images at each level of the Oliver image description scale (*R v. Thompson* 2004). This guideline resulted from questions regarding the definition of "small or large quantities" in the Oliver guidelines (Akdeniz 2008).

In 2005, the Provincial Court of British Columbia, Canada, adopted a similar system as the U.K.'s Oliver image description scale for categorizing the images seized in child pornography cases (see Table 1). According to the adopting court, the guidelines for categorizing images were meant to act as a deterrent for offenders by focusing on the harm experienced by the child in the images (Akdeniz 2008). Despite using a similar nomenclature in which the levels increase in their degree of child sexual victimization, the court documents do not make any reference to the COPINE scale or U.K.'s Oliver images description scale (Akdeniz 2008).

Currently, the United States does not utilize the COPINE scale, or any similar system, in the federal courts. However, the United States Sentencing Commission (U.S.S.C.) developed sentencing guidelines for offenses related to the sexual exploitation of a minor. Specifically, harsher sentences are implemented if the offense involves "material that portrays sadistic or masochistic conduct or other depictions of violence" (U.S.S.C. 2009). In addition, the guidelines recommend harsher sentences for offenses involving collections with a large quantity of images with 10–149 images at the lower end of the spectrum and more than 600 images at the polar end (2009). Overall, the current federal sentencing guidelines in the United States focus on violent images of child sexual victimization and the total number of images in the offender's collection.

Table 1. The Suggested Canadian System for Classifying Images Seized in Child Pornography Related Cases

Level	Description
1	Non-erotic, non-sexualized material including nudity
2	Material where the dominant characteristic demonstrates a sexual purpose
3	Explicit sexual activity and assaults between adult-child, child-child
4	Gross assaults, penetrative assaults involving adults
5	Sadistic images

A Hypothetical Case Study

In order to better understand the classification system developed by Taylor et al. (2001), we created a hypothetical collection of images to clarify the various levels of the continuum. The doll images used for this case study were obtained from an actual law enforcement case in which the defendant was accused of child molestation, and during the investigation, hundreds of hard-copy images were discovered of dolls in various degrees of nakedness. The original case file was provided to the author by the investigating detective with direct orders to use the materials for educational and teaching purposes. The possession of child pornography by academics for the purpose of research is illegal in the United States by federal law. Thus, the hypothetical collection includes both non-child pornography images obtained via the Internet as well as the doll images obtained from a law enforcement case.

To set up the scenario, the reader is to assume the collection of images was obtained during a search of a suspect's computer, who was accused of possessing and distributing child pornography. As show in the Box 1 (from left to right), the collection contains the following images:

- the Coppertone girl, a famous ad for an American sunscreen;
- a doll with her arms raised above her head, which reveals her underpants;
- Olympia Nelson, then at the age of six, photographed nude by her mother, which appeared on the cover of an Australian art magazine (Marks, 2008);
- a young girl with her dress pulled down, which reveals her undergarments

- a doll's genitals; and
- two young girls on the beach in bikinis.

The images in Figure 1 will be discussed in the hypothetical order they might appear based on the COPINE's continuum of increased sexual victimization.

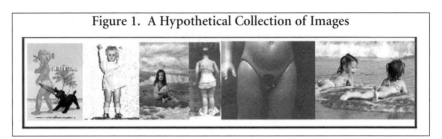

Figure 1. A Hypothetical Collection of Images

Using COPINE's scale, the Coppertone ad is an excellent example of the Level 1 or indicative category. Despite the girl's partial nudity, the image of the Coppertone girl ad is clearly innocent and non-pornographic in nature. Therefore, this image would not be considered illegal by most jurisdictions in view of the fact that it was obtained from a legitimate commercial source. For instance, this type of image would not fall into a category according to the U.K.'s Oliver Image Description Scale. In addition, it would most likely be labeled as a Level 1 image in the Canadian courts, which encompasses images not subject to criminal sanctions (Akdeniz 2008). However, as suggested by Taylor et al. (2001), these types of images should not be ignored by investigators, for the "context or organization of pictures by the collector [may] indicate inappropriateness" (p. 101).

The image of Olympia Nelson, whose nude photograph appeared on the cover of an art magazine, is more controversial than the Coppertone girl. Recently, this photograph sparked controversy as to the distinction between "art" and child pornography (Marks 2008). Although society continues to debate this fine line between legal and illegal, this image is an excellent illustration of the Level 2 or nudist category according to COPINE. In this hypothetical collection, such an image would be labeled a Level 2 because it is from a legitimate, verified source, an art magazine. In most instances, this image would not apply to the U.K.'s Oliver scale, and it would be labeled a Level 1 by Canadian courts.

Next, the image of the two girls on the beach becomes more difficult to classify according to the COPINE continuum. Assuming the image is from a legitimate source, such as the collector's family album, the image would be considered a Level 1 since the girls are semi-naked (wearing bikinis) at an appropriate setting (the beach). However, if this picture was not from the collector's family album, but was instead secretly taken of the two girls while they were playing at the beach, the image would be categorized as a Level 3 (erotica). Thus, the investigators would have to determine the source of the image (i.e., family album or covertly taken) in order to accurately classify the image using COPINE's scale. In addition, investigators should once again consider the amount or context of other images, which are of a similar nature, in order to understand the collector's intent of possessing the innocent images.

Investigators would probably label the image of the doll raising her hands above her head as a Level 4 (posing). She appears to be posed in a non-provocative manner although her underwear is slightly revealed. In addition, this category is not concerned with the degree of nakedness of the child in the image. Although, this image would not be considered illegal in most jurisdictions, Taylor et al. (2001) suggest investigators should be aware of the "amount, context, and organization" of the images, which may suggest the collector has a sexual interest in children (p. 101).

As shown in Figure 1, the image of the partially nude girl with her dress pulled down would best be labeled as a Level 5 (erotic posing) using COPINE's scale. The girl is deliberately posed in a sexualized manner since her dress has been pulled down around her ankles, which reveals her undergarments. Again, this image may or may not be considered a chargeable offense in most jurisdictions. In the U.K., this image may be identified as a Level 1 (erotic posing with no sexual activity) according to the Oliver guidelines. However, this image may be labeled as a Level 2 (material demonstrates sexual purpose) according to the Canadian sentencing guidelines.

Lastly, the image focusing on the doll's genitals would be an example of a Level 6 (explicit erotic posing), since the genital area is clearly emphasized in this image, and no sexual activity is apparent (e.g., touching, masturbation). Images identified at this level are more likely to be considered illegal depending on the age of the minor. Based on the Oliver scale, this image would most likely be labeled as a Level 1, whereas it would fall under the Level 2 category according to the Canadian guidelines.

Criticisms of Court Image Classifications

Overall, the sentencing guidelines in the United States, England and Wales, and Canada, base sentencing decisions on the *quantity* of images as well as the *content* of the images in the collection. More specifically, the guidelines recommend harsher sentences for collections that include more violent images (e.g., sadism). The COPINE continuum was originally developed as a way of discriminating images within a collection by identifying the level of sexual victimization. In addition, it offered a "means of judging severity within the broad offense of possession" while providing a "basis on which systemic picture qualities may be related to offender behavior" (Taylor et al. 2001). For example, utilizing a classification system allows researchers to better understand the trends in child pornography collections; Taylor (1999) suggests the children in child pornography images are becoming younger. In other words, newer images of child pornography feature younger children, which may be related to the imbalance of power between adults and young children (Taylor and Quayle 2003).

The authors' original intention of "judging severity" has clearly been adopted by the courts to mean that collectors with more violent images, or images at the higher levels of COPINE, should receive harsher sentences within their child pornography related offenses. The courts rationalization for the increased punishment is the belief that the *types* of images and *size* of the collection must be reflective of the offender's behavior or personality. First, collections including more violent images may be related to more violent offenders or at least offenders who are at the greatest risk of recidivism. In addition, the sentencing guidelines appear to place some of the blame on the possessors of child pornography because they are fueling a commercial industry; if there were no demand for the sadistic images, there would be no need to produce them. Overall, the sentencing guidelines suggest possessors of child pornography should receive harsher sentences for being a part of this child pornography supply-demand chain.

However, research suggests there is no evidence to support the enhancement of sentences because more violent collections reflect more violent offenders (Beech, Elliott, Birgden, and Findlater 2008; Friendman and Supler 2008; Quayle 2008). According to Friedman and Supler (2008), there is a lack of research or empirical validation for the sentencing guidelines implemented in the United States. That is to say, there is no evidence that collections including more violent images should act as an aggravating factor when determining offender risk for recidivism (Beech et al. 2008).

Secondly, harsher sentences are also recommended for offenses involving larger collections of images. Specifically, the current U.S. sentencing guidelines suggest increasing the base level for offenses involving large collections of images with 10–149 images at the lower end of the spectrum and more than 600 images at the polar end (c.f., U.S.S.C. 2009). However, Basbaum (2010) argues these sentence enhancements should be amended in order to "incorporate a realistic understanding of how file-sharing works and [how] evolving technology permits defendants to download massive numbers of images with little effort or even intent" (3–4). The number of images and use of electronic means for distribution may not reflect the offender's risk for recidivism or level of dangerousness toward children. Technological advances have clearly impacted the prevalence of child pornography by making it easier and more readily available compared to the pre-Internet era. Consequently, the post-Internet child pornography consumer may be different from the pre-Internet child pornography user who had a more difficult and risky time obtaining the materials (c.f., Hessick 2010). Overall, "a defendant [may] download large numbers of child pornography images not so much out of a specific desire ... but simply because it is easy to do so" (Basbaum 2010, 21).

Currently, the sentencing guidelines reflect political agendas and societal panic in response to the increased availability of Internet child pornography (Akdeniz 2008; Basbaum 2010; Friendman and Supler 2008). More research needs to be conducted in order to better understand the relationship between the offenders and their collections. However, if the purpose of the sentencing guidelines is to punish offenders because they are fueling a commercial industry, then it may be appropriate to consider the level of child victimization in the image. After all, as the images become more violent, the child is not only being exposed to emotional or psychological abuse but physiological abuse as well. In addition, the harsher sentences require that the possessor and distributor of the images take some responsibility for the increased demand in images with higher degrees of sexual victimization. Overall, the various guidelines implemented by the United States, United Kingdom, and Canada may be appropriate if they are solely focusing on the level of harm experienced by the child (Beech et al. 2008; Taylor and Quayle 2003).

Classification System for the United States

The United States judicial system is in dire need of an image classification scale based on the COPINE scale. By classifying the images seized in child pornography related offenses, research and empirical data may be generated regarding trends in the content as well as comparisons between cases and countries. In addition, a detailed classification system may assist the various stages of the legislative process from the initial investigation to the sentencing procedures. Based on the previous scales adopted by the U.K. and Canada, we developed a similar classification system, which includes a description and example as well as the individuals involved at each level (see Table 2). We hope this modified scale will ignite academic research and interest for qualitatively analyzing the content of images collected by offenders in the United States. First, new trends in the child pornography market may be identified. In addition,

informed policy decisions regarding the level of severity in the offender's actions and behaviors along with the psychological perspectives of the offender's
sexual interest in the child may be better understood.

Technical Investigations

Prior to an offender coming before the court system, investigators must
identify evidence and determine that, in fact, an offence has been committed.
Investigating online criminal behavior in general is somewhat problematic
(Furnell 2002; Rogers 2005; Rogers, Seigfried, and Tidke 2006; Stambaugh et
al. 2001). Crimes involving technology and technical advances such as the Internet and the World Wide Web require that investigators, be they law enforcement, military or private sector, have a strong understanding of the
underlying structure of networks and networking protocols, operating systems, file systems, storage devices (e.g., hard drives, thumb drives, DVD's)
and software/application development (Rogers and Seigfried, 2004). Each of
these areas is a specialization in and of itself, and to assume that investigators
can be experts in all of these is unrealistic.

Apart from the challenge of having properly trained investigators, the fact that
technology evolves and changes at an incredible rate causes investigators and forensic tool developers to make constant changes to their methods, techniques and
applications. Each time an update is made to an operating system (e.g., Microsoft Windows 7, Apple Snow Leopard), the location of potential evidence,
encryption capabilities and new privacy enhancements (e.g., over writing of
web browser history files, shredding of deleted files) can result in the tool or investigator missing crucial evidence or misinterpreting the context of any evidence
found (Rogers and Leshney 2009; Rogers and Seigfried 2004; Slade 2004).

Size limitations of this chapter preclude us from conducting an in depth
discussion about all possible investigative strategies such as online sting operations, across all platforms.[2] Instead we focus on investigations involving Microsoft Windows and its NTFS file system. The NTFS files system is the most
widely used file system in the world and is the default file system found on
Windows XP, VISTA and Windows 7. In order to assist investigators, several
offender investigative profiles have been developed. These include the Lanning
FBI model, the Krone model and the Rogers and Seigfried-Spellar Hybrid
model (Rogers and Seigfried-Spellar 2009).

---

2. Please see the following for more information (Ferraro and Casey 2005; Hagy 2007;
Hart 2004).

Lanning Model

The model developed by Lanning (2001), is based on the FBI's dichotomous offenders framework. This model uses the primary categories of situational and preferential sexual offender as the two extremes. The motivation of the offender is placed on a continuum of needs consisting of Biological/Physiological Sexual needs, Power/Anger Nonsexual needs, Psychosexual/Deviant Sexual needs (Lanning 2001). Lanning clearly indicates that his model should be thought of in terms of investigative typologies used to assist investigators and not for use in clinical diagnosis or developing psychological profiles.

Lanning's model states that preferential offenders include those with specific preferences or paraphilia that can include a preference for children and pornographic pictures of children, more commonly known as pedophilia (Lanning 2001). He further sub-divides the category of situational offender into: Regressed, Morally Indiscriminate, and Inadequate. Regressed offenders are characterized by low self-esteem, poor coping skills, and seek children as sexual partners to offset their inability to have a mature/age appropriate relationship (Lanning 2001).

Morally indiscriminate offenders are habitual "users and abusers of people" (Lanning 2001, 26). The sexual victimizations fit their pattern of general abuse directed at spouses, offspring, co-workers, etc. The sexual abuse is often opportunistic but the preference is for children. Common examples of this type of offender include incestuous fathers or mothers. Inadequate offenders can be suffering from mental disorders such as psychosis, mental retardation, senility, or other personality disorders (Lanning 2001). The sexual relations with children can be the product of curiosity, insecurity or built up impulses.

Lanning evolved his model to include computer-based offenders (Lanning 2001) (see Table 2). For those situational offenders using computers and computer technology, two additional types were added from his earlier model: "Normal"—adolescent/adult who was curious about sex and pornography and used computers to search for pornography online; and "Profiteer" who makes easy money from commercial opportunities for selling child pornography online (Lanning 2001).

Under the category of Preferential computer offenders, the model again lists two additional types: "Diverse"—offender with a wide variety of paraphilic or deviant sexual interests, but no strong preference for children (referred to as the sexually indiscriminate in his previous model); and "Latent"—individuals with potentially illegal but previously latent sexual preferences (these latent preferences become manifested through online activities such as chats, which weakens their inhibitions; Lanning 2001).

Table 2. Classification System of Images Seized from Child Pornography Cases Suggested for the United States of America by Rogers and Seigfried-Spellar			
*Level	Adult Involved	Description	Example
1	No	No sexual activity; May involve sexual posing	Naked child laying on bed
2	No	Child-child sexual activity or solo masturbation	Child touching his/her genitals
3	Yes	Non-penetrative sexual activity between adult-child	Adult touching a child's genitals
4	Yes	Penetrative sexual assault between adult-child	Sexual intercourse between adult-child
5	Maybe	Sadistic activity or child-animal sexual activity	Child tied and beaten OR bestiality

All levels include varying degrees of nakedness

Krone Model

Similar to Lanning's computer offender typology, Krone's model is used specifically with offenders who are familiar with technology and use technology to view, collect, distribute, and produce child pornography in an online environment (i.e., Internet). The model is based on work that was conducted in Australia, but nothing in the model precludes it from being used internationally. Krone focuses on the type of involvement of the offender, amount of networking, the level of technical expertise, whether the offender took technical precautious to avoid being traced or caught and the nature of the abuse. The model consists of nine types of offenders: Browser, Private fantasy, Trawler, Non-secure collector, Secure collector, Groomer, Physical abuser, and Distributor (Krone 2004).

According to Krone, a browser would fall under the umbrella of Lanning's situational offender. This is one of the only categories in this model that would be considered non-preferential offenders. Browsers stumble upon illicit pictures of children during their web browsing or via spam/rootkits but then fail to get rid of the pictures or intentionally seek more out (Krone 2004). Browsers, generally, do not take steps to secure or hide their activities while online and do not have well-established networks in order to trade pictures. This type of offender does not usually participate in actual contact offenses with children.

Private fantasy offenders are preferential offenders under the Lanning model. They harbor thoughts and fantasies regarding sex with children (i.e., pedophilia) and collect pictures, movies and stories depicting naked children and children engaged in sexual activities (Krone 2004). Again, this group does not actively hide their online behaviors or secure their computer systems against the possibility of being investigated. Private fantasy offenders do not have networks established for trading purposes. These offenders try and keep off the radar of law enforcement and do not usually move onto contact offenses with children.

Trawlers actively seek out child pornography and are considered preferential offenders. The major difference, according to Krone, between trawlers and private fantasy offenders is that trawlers take a more active approach to seeking out child porn. The private fantasy offender sits at a level of intentionality between Browsers and Trawlers. The Trawler also tends not to have a deep network of other offenders established, but may have connections in the "community." Trawlers are a low risk for contact offenses. The level of security and privacy knowledge and techniques are also very minimal (Krone 2004).

Non-secure collectors make use of peer-to-peer networks, chat rooms and other more open sites. These offenders have set up relationships with other offenders for the purpose of trading and collecting. This category does not typically employ any sophisticated security or privacy controls to hide their online activities and is not considered a high risk for contact offenses (Krone 2004).

Secure collectors are more cautious than the non-secure group. They are well connected in the "community" and prefer trusted sources and more secure networks in order to collect and trade their pictures (Krone 2004). They are usually concerned with security and privacy, have moderate to high levels of technical knowledge and abilities and may attempt to cover their tracks. However, this group is still unlikely to commit contact offenses.

The Groomer category is the first level in this model that has a high risk of contact offending. Groomers use technology and the Internet to make initial contacts in order to have sex with children. According to Krone they may have a level involvement across the entire range in the model. Groomers may have complex networks that include children or other offenders looking to actually engage in sexual activity with children. At this level the Krone model is vague as to whether security refers to technology or physical security in the context of the child involved (Krone 2004).

Physical abusers use pornography to facilitate the abuse, have connected networks to establish contact with children and, again, the security component is more focused on the physical contact of the child (Krone 2004). Technology is often involved for use in documenting the abuse in more of a private diary format than for distribution.

Producers are effectively at the top level of the model. They use technology to seek out victims and produce media that can be shared with other pedophiles. The level of networking depends upon whether the media produced is used more for private use or to feed the demands of the "community." They are involved in the actual abuse of the children and security is more related to technology used in the production of the media and the physical security in context of the child involved (Krone 2004). Although not directly listed in the model, it is logical to assume that the technical knowledge of this group would be significant.

Distributors in Krone's model are a bit of an odd category and could also be considered to fall under the category of situational offenders under Lanning's model. Distributors in Krone's model may or may not be pedophiles, but could be thought of as opportunistic business people (similar to Lanning's Profiteers). Money seems to be the primary motive and as such, they have regular clients and producers that they deal with. They do not ordinarily engage in any contact offenses, and as a business, they take steps to protect their computer systems and websites (Krone 2004).

Other researchers have further generalized the typologies of Lanning and Krone into four higher order categories (Beech et al. 2008, 225):

1) individuals who access abusive images sporadically, impulsively and/or out of curiosity;
2) those who access/trade abusive images of children to fuel their sexual interest in children;
3) individuals who use the Internet as part of a pattern offline contact offending; and
4) individuals who access abusive images for seemingly non-sexual reasons (e.g., commercial profit).

Rogers and Seigfried-Spellar Hybrid Model

The hybrid model was first introduced in July 2009 at a workshop conducted by Rogers and Seigfried-Spellar at John Jay College of Criminal Justice in New

York City (Rogers and Seigfried-Spellar 2009). The model was also presented at the US-Indo Conference and Workshop on Cyber Security, Cyber Crime, and Cyber Forensics in Kochi, India, in August 2009. The model extends the work of both Lanning and Krone and focuses on how and where different offenders will store evidence related to their online offenses on their computer systems. The model uses Krone's concept of security employed by the various offender types, but the hybrid model restricts the focus to technology and not physical security. The model is considered a hybrid in that it extends the work of Krone, who expanded the work of Lanning.

The hybrid model is primarily designed as an investigative tool for investigators and not as a diagnostic classification or treatment typology. While the focus is on technology, the model does not deal with networking technologies (e.g., routers, switches, firewalls or other servers that log user activity). It is acknowledged that these areas can provide crucial information, however, the starting point for most investigations is the suspect's computer system.

The model considers the offender's computer system, and specifically the file system, to be analogous to geographical or physical space (Rogers and Seigfried-Spellar 2009). Offenders (and all computer users) interact with metaphors of the real world/physical space. When we log in we are taken to a desktop, we have files, folders, recycle bins. Our data and files are abstracted and presented to us in hierarchies, with various levels of nesting. The basics behind the graphical user interface (GUI) have purposely mimicked the real world that most users (at least older generations) were already comfortable with.

The computer operating systems (e.g., Windows XP, Windows 7, Leopard, Unix) and their file systems (e.g., NTFS, HFS+, EXT3) have other constraints and defaults around where data structures and files are stored. Due to the interaction of the GUI and the file system, there is actually a fairly well mapped out geography of a typical computer's hard drive. This mapping allows the hybrid model to predict the most likely location of evidence given the technical abilities of the offender in question and the operating and file system being used.

The assumption that system defaults for files systems locations of certain data is based on research findings that most online child pornography offenders do not employ any type of encryption, data wiping, or other kinds of security and/or privacy software to cover their activities (Carr 2004; Wolak, Finkelhor, and Mitchell 2005). Studies have also found that the majority of those arrested for child pornography did not have sophisticated computer systems and were not considered to have a high degree of technical knowledge or capabilities (Wolak et al. 2005).

As stated earlier, due to its large market share, our discussion of the hybrid model will be limited to Microsoft Windows operating system (e.g., Windows XP) and the NTFS file system. Table 3B illustrates the model. The first two columns are identical to Krone's, and the third column provides investigators with artifacts that have the highest probability of being of an evidentiary nature. Investigators now have some type of a basic workflow model to help guide their investigations. This workflow is not considered a checklist and is designed to only act as suggested minimum types of data that should be located, examined and analyzed. As was mentioned previously, the artifacts and their locations within the file system are the result of defaults set by the system. However, it should be noted that data, such as pictures and documents, could be relocated by the end user to non-default locations. This is why it is important to understand the technical knowledge of the suspect. If the suspect has a high level of technical knowledge and sophistication, then investigators need to look in non-default locations (other than "C:\Documents and Settings\User Account\ <USERS>").

Table 3A. Lanning Computer Offender Typology

Type	Sub-Category
Situational	Normal adolescent/adult
	Morally indiscriminate
	Profiteers
Preferential	Pedophile
	Diverse
	Latent

Table 3B. Rogers Seigfried-Spellar Hybrid Model

Category	Features	System Artifacts
Browser	Response to spam, accidental hit on suspect site—material knowingly saved.	Internet History logs, Temporary files, Web Cache, Cookies, Default User account folders (e.g., pictures, movies), Thumbnails, Deleted files, Recycle Bin
Private fantasy	Conscious creation of online text or digital images for private use.	Internet History logs, Temporary files, Web Cache, Cookies, Default User account folders (e.g., pictures, movies), Thumbnails, P-2-P folders, Email, Registry/Typed URLS, Deleted files, Recycle Bin, External storage devices, Mobile Phone

Table 3B. Rogers Seigfried-Spellar Hybrid Model, *continued*

Category	Features	System Artifacts
Browser	Response to spam, accidental hit on suspect site—material knowingly saved.	Internet History logs, Temporary files, Web Cache, Cookies, Default User account folders (e.g., pictures, movies), Thumbnails, Deleted files, Recycle Bin
Private fantasy	Conscious creation of online text or digital images for private use.	Internet History logs, Temporary files, Web Cache, Cookies, Default User account folders (e.g., pictures, movies), Thumbnails, P-2-P folders, Email, Registry/Typed URLS, Deleted files, Recycle Bin, External storage devices, Mobile Phone
Trawler	Actively seeking child pornography using openly available browsers.	Internet History logs, Temporary files, Web Cache, Cookies, Default User account folders (e.g., pictures, movies), Non-default folders, Thumbnails, P-2-P folders, Email, Registry/Typed URLS, Deleted files, Recycle Bin, IRC folders, External storage devices, Mobile Phone
Non-secure collector	Actively seeking material often through peer-to-peer networks.	Internet History logs, Temporary files, Web Cache, Cookies, Default User account folders (e.g., pictures, movies), Non-default folders, Thumbnails, P-2-P folders, Email, Registry/Typed URLS, Deleted files, Recycle Bin, IRC folders, External storage devices, Mobile Phone
Secure collector	Actively seeking material but only through secure. Collector syndrome and exchange as an entry barrier.	Internet History logs, Temporary files, Web Cache, Cookies, Default User account folders (e.g., pictures, movies), Non-default folders, Thumbnails, P-2-P folders, Email, Registry/Typed URLS, Deleted files, Recycle Bin, External storage devices, Encrypted folders, IRC folders, Mobile Phone
Groomer	Cultivating an online relationship with one or more children. The offender may or may not seek material in any of the above ways. Pornography may be used to facilitate abuse.	Internet History logs, Temporary files, Web Cache, Cookies, Default User account folders (e.g., pictures, movies), Non-default folders, Thumbnails, P-2-P folders, Email, Registry/Typed URLS, Deleted files, Recycle Bin, External storage devices, Mobile Phone
Physical abuser	Abusing a child who may have been introduced to the offender online. The offender may or may not seek material in any of the above ways. Pornography may be used to facilitate abuse.	Internet History logs, Temporary files, Web Cache, Cookies, Default User account folders (e.g., pictures, movies), Non-default folders, Thumbnails, P-2-P folders, Email, Registry/Typed URLS, Deleted files, Recycle Bin, External storage devices, Digital cameras, Mobile Phone

Table 3B. Rogers Seigfried-Spellar Hybrid Model, *continued*

Category	Features	System Artifacts
Producer	Records own abuse or that of others (or induces children to submit images of themselves).	Internet History logs, Temporary files, Web Cache, Cookies, Default User account folders (e.g., pictures, movies), Non-default folders, Thumbnails, P-2-P folders, Email, Registry/Typed URLS, Deleted files, Recycle Bin, External storage devices, IRC folders, Digital cameras, Mobile Phone
Distributor	May distribute at any one of the above levels.	Internet History logs, Temporary files, Web Cache, Cookies, Default User account folders (e.g., pictures, movies), Non-default folders, Thumbnails, P-2-P folders, Email, Registry/Typed URLS, Deleted files, Recycle Bin, External storage devices, IRC folders, Digital cameras, Mobile Phone

Note: Table A provides reduced version of the model and only provides an overview of the offender type (based on Krone's model) and what system artifacts the investigator should look for. The full model provides the investigator with the location of where these files are kept—assuming the system in question is using the standard defaults (Rogers and Seigfried-Spellar 2009).

Case Study

The utility of the hybrid is best understood in the context of a small case study. The case study looks at an investigation in which the suspect falls into the offender type of "Browser." According to Lanning's typology, a Browser could be classified as a situational "Normal adolescent/adult." According to Krone, Browsers do not usually employ any kind of physical or technical security and are not technically sophisticated (Krone 2004).

Figure 2 shows the directory listing of the Browser's system. The investigation would initially focus on the "Documents and Settings" directory to locate the user accounts on this system. The "Recycler" directory, which contains files that have been placed in the "recycle bin" would also be of interest, as these files are grouped by a unique security ID and can be easily recovered (see Figure 3).

According to Figure 4, in this case the system has three user accounts that are not default system accounts (e.g., all users, guest, administrator).

Figure 5 shows the location of the cookies folder belonging to the user Badguy 1. This folder contains cookie information related to activity of someone logged into the Badguy 1 account. Figure 6 shows the content of the cookies folder. These cookie files are produced when a user visits a particular

Figure 2. Directory Listing

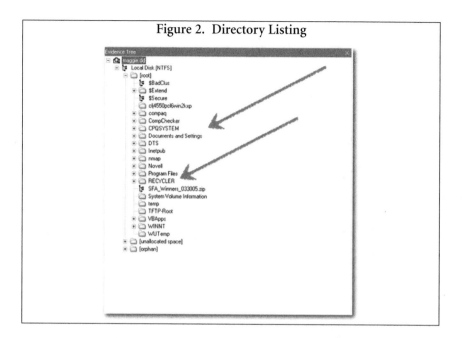

Figure 3. Recycle Bin

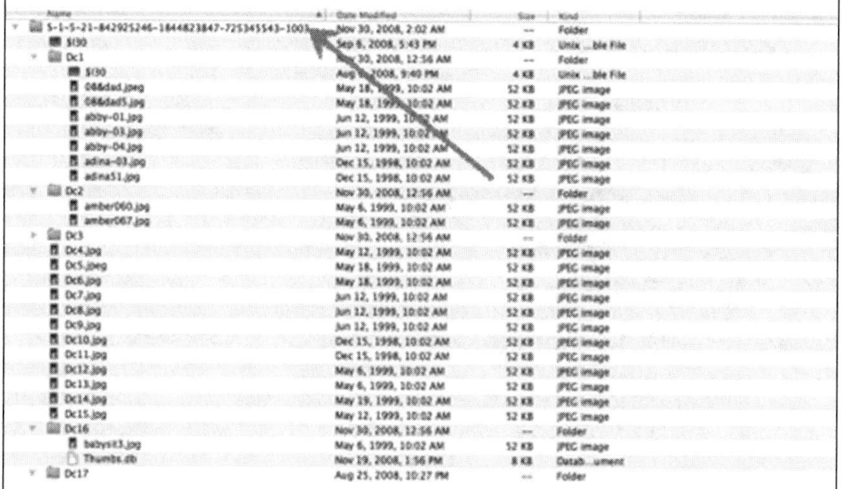

webpage. They are generated by the external webpage but stored locally on the users system. The cookies give an indication of the webpages that have been visited by the suspect and provide information used for marketing purposes.

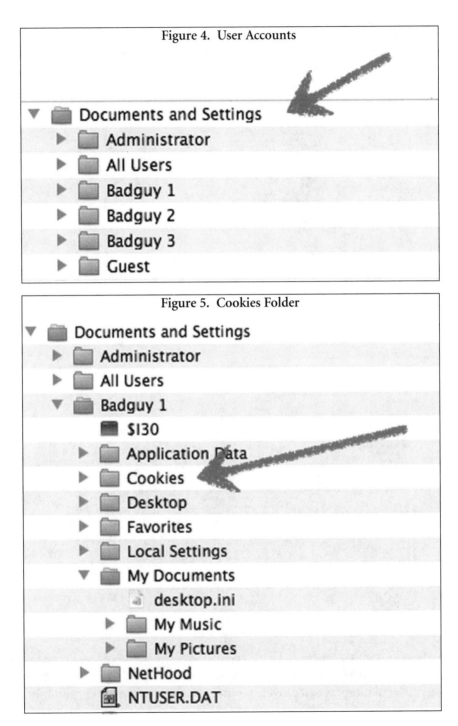

Figure 4. User Accounts

Figure 5. Cookies Folder

Figure 5. Cookies Folder, *continued*

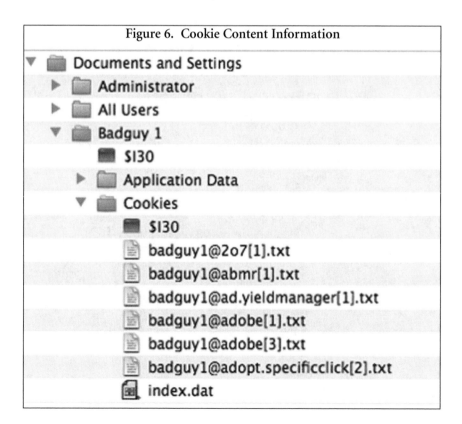

NTUSER.DAT.LOG

ntuser.ini

▶ PrintHood

▶ Recent

▶ SendTo

▶ Start Menu

▶ Templates

▶ Badguy 2

▶ Badguy 3

▶ Guest

Figure 6. Cookie Content Information

▼ Documents and Settings

▶ Administrator

▶ All Users

▼ Badguy 1

$130

▶ Application Data

▼ Cookies

$130

badguy1@2o7[1].txt

badguy1@abmr[1].txt

badguy1@ad.yieldmanager[1].txt

badguy1@adobe[1].txt

badguy1@adobe[3].txt

badguy1@adopt.specificclick[2].txt

index.dat

The Internet history folder shown in Figure 7 contains information related to websites visited, the dates and times of the visit and, depending on the browser, the number of times visited by the user (see Figure 8).

Figure 7. Browser History

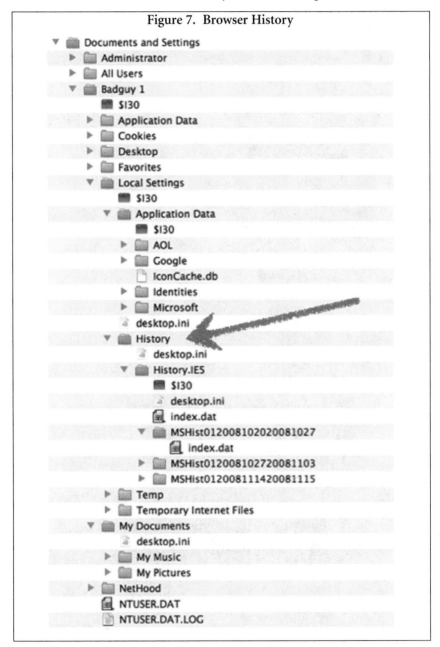

Figure 8. Browser History

We end our case study as this point as it should be clear how the model is used. In an actual case, the investigator would continue to locate the remaining system artifacts as listed in the model.

Conclusions

To say that the Internet poses the largest threat to our children is a gross exaggeration (Skenazy 2009; Wolak, Finkelhor, and Mitchell 2009; Wolak et al. 2008). However, we cannot be blind to the fact that sexual deviants, pedophiles, and other predatory offenders are using technology to find victims, trade pictures, and evolve their criminal tradecraft. In order to effectively deal with online child pornography, we must better understand the technology and those using it (Beech et al. 2008; Rogers and Seigfried-Spellar 2009; Schell et al. 2007; Taylor and Quayle 2003; Wolak et al. 2005; Wolak et al. 2009).

We need to continue our efforts to harmonize international law related to child pornography and eliminate any so-called safe havens for these offenders. But as Taylor et al. (2003) indicated, simply locking these offenders up partially treats a symptom; it does not go after the root cause of the problem. Identifying the root cause of pedophilia or other deviant sexual behaviors is extremely difficult and requires funding and focused research.

In this chapter, we have attempted to provide an overview of the current models related to the offenders and the types of offences they commit. We introduced the work in Europe on COPINE and how a modification of this could be integrated into the United States legal justice system as a better approach for sentencing guidelines. We also looked at the investigative typologies of Lanning and Krone and how these typologies could be used to assist investigators in the form of the Rogers Seigfried-Spellar Model.

It is important to consider child pornography as a wide range of images involving different levels of victimization, rather than pictures that are defined as either legal or illegal. After all, images of children may be collected for sexual purposes despite the purity or lack of sexuality in the materials (Howitt 1995). In the end, the preferred type of images selected by the users may provide clues in understanding their personality traits and psychological characteristics. For instance, by understanding the types of images in the collection, we may be able to improve the criminal courts ability to assess an offender's risk of recidivism. In addition, a modified version of COPINE in the U.S. criminal courts may assist judges who must determine the appropriate level of punishment through sentencing guidelines. Despite legislative attempts at regulating and criminalizing the pornographic materials, technological advances (e.g., computer-generated images) will continue to occur, making research an important part of society's attempt to better understand not only the consumer but the collection of images as well.

The proposed investigative model can greatly assist investigators working on online child pornography cases, by providing some direction and consistency to the investigative process. Obviously, the model needs to be further developed and refined in order to further validate the offender categories, identify overlapping offender characteristics, and ensure the file system artifacts and paths are correct. As the criminal category of online child pornography offenders becomes better understood and studied, it is anticipated that more precise offender categories will become apparent. These typology changes will be reflected in the revised model. The bigger challenge consists of keeping the model current as the technology being used by the offender changes rapidly. Newer software and operating systems (e.g., Windows 7) can have subtle and not so subtle changes to their files system, resulting in different artifacts being created (e.g., Web history, cookies) and different storage locations for this type of evidence (Carrier 2005).

As we struggle to deal with emotional and politically charged topics, such as child pornography, we need to keep in mind that the problem by all accounts is not going away, and technology is becoming ever more integrated into the lives of our children. Therefore, any assistance that can be provided to the courts (in dealing with offenders), to the behavioral sciences community (in treating these individuals), and to the investigators (in collecting better evidence) is sorely needed. As a corollary, this assistance should also provide parents and care givers with a better understanding of the risk to children and how to identify potentially dangerous situations.

References

Akdeniz, Yaman. *Internet child pornography and the law: National and international responses.* Burlington: Ashgate Publishing Co, 2008.

Basbaum, Jesse P. "Sentencing for possession of child pornography: A failure to distinguist voyeurs from pederasts," *Hastings Law Journal* 61 (2010):1–24.

Beech, Anthony, Ian Elliott, Astrid Birgden, and Donald Findlater. "The Internet and child sexual offending: A criminological review," *Aggression and Violent Behavior* 13 (2008):217–228.

Breeden, Bob, and Judie Mulholland. "Investigating internet crimes against children (ICAC) cases in the state of Florida," In *SAC'06.* Dijon, France: ACM, 2008.

Carr, Angela. *Internet traders of child pornography and other censorship offenders in New Zealand.* (2004) Accessed June 27, 2010. http://www.dia.govt.nz/diawebsite.nsf/wpg_URL/Resource-material-Our-Research-and-Reports-Internet-Traders-of-Child-Pornography-and-other-Censorship-Offenders-in-New-Zealand?OpenDocument.

Carrier, Brian. *File system forensic analysis.* New York: Addison-Wesley, 2005.

Enough. *Enough is enough: Protecting our children online* 2009. Accessed November 1 2009. http://enough.org/inside.php?id=2UXKJWRY8.

Finkelhor, David, Kimberly Mitchell, and Janis Wolak. *Online victimization: A report on the nation's youth.* Crimes Against Children Research Center, 2000.

Ferraro, Monique, and Eoghan Casey. *Investigating child exploitation and pornography: The internet, the law and forensic science.* New York: Elsevier Academic Press, 2005.

Frei, Andreas, Erenay, Nuray, Dittmann, Volher, and Graf, Marc. "Paedophilia on the internet—A study of 33 convicted offenders in the canton of lucerne," *Swiss Medical Review* 135 (2005):488–494.

Friendman, Ian, and Supler, Kristina. "Child pornography sentencing: The road here and the road ahead," *Federal Sentencing Reporter* 21 (2008):83–89.

Furnell, Steven. *Cybercrime: Vandalizing the information society.* Boston: Addison-Wesley, 2002.

Hagy, David. *Investigations involving the internet and computer networks.* Washington: Department of Justice, 2007.

Hart, Sarah. *Forensic examination of digital evidence: A guide for law enforcement.* Washington: National Institute of Justice, 2004.

Healthymind. *Internet pornography statistics* 2009, Accessed November 1, 2009. http://www.healthymind.com/s-porn-stats.html.

Hessick, Carissa Byrne. "Disentangling child pornography from child sex abuse," *Washington University Law Review* 88 (2010):853–902.

Howitt, Dennis. "Pornography and the paedophile: Is it criminogenic?" *British Journal of Medical Psychiatric* 68 (1995):15–27.

Jenkins, Philip. *Beyond tolerance: Child pornography online.* New York: New York University Press, 2001.

Keith, Durkin, and Clifton Bryant. "Propagandizing pederasty: A thematic analysis of the on-line exculpatory accounts of unrepentant pedophiles," *Deviant Behavior* 20 (1999):103–127.

Krone, Tony. *A typology of online child pornography offending.* Canberra: Australian Institute of Criminology, 2004.

Lanning, Kenneth. *Child sex rings: A behavioral analysis for criminal justice professionals handling cases of child sexual exploitation, 2nd Edition.* Washington D. C.: National Center for Missing and Exploited Children, 1992. Accessed October 1, 2009. http://www.skeptictank.org/nc72.pdf.

Lanning, Kenneth. *Child molesters: A behavioral analysis 4th Edition.* Washington D. C.: National Center for Missing and Exploited Children, 2001.

Lanning, Kenneth, and Ann Burgess. "Child Pornography and sex rings," *FBI Law Enforcement Bulletin* January, 1984.

Marks, Kathy. "Art or abuse? Fury over image of naked girl." *The Independent* 2008, July 8. Accessed August 1, 2009. http://www.independent.co.uk/news/world/australasia/art-or-abuse-fury-over-image-girl-862068.html.

Media, Family Safe. *Pornography statistics* 2009. Accessed November 1 2009. http://www.familysafemedia.com/pornography_statistics.html.

Quayle, Ethel. "The COPINE project," *Irish Probation Journal* 5 (2008):65–83.

Quayle, Ethel, and Max Taylor. *Viewing child pornography on the internet: Understanding the offence, managing the offender, helping victims.* Dorset: Russell House Publishing, 2005

R v. Oliver and others. EWCA Crim 2766 (Court of Criminal Appeal Division 2002).

R v. Thompson. 2004. EWCA Crim 699.

Rogers, Marcus, and Sean Leshney. "Virtualization and digital investigations," In *Information Security Management Handbook*, edited by H. Tipton and M. Krause. New York: Auerbach, 2009.

Rogers, Marcus, and Kathryn Seigfried. "The future of computer forensics: A needs analysis survey," *Computers and Security* 23 (2004):12–16.

Rogers, Marcus. "DCSA: Digital crime scene analysis," In *Handbook of information security management*, edited by H. Tipton and M. Krause. Dunedin, FL: Auerbach, 2005.

Rogers, Marcus, and Kathryn Seigfried-Spellar. "Investigating online consumers of child Pornography," In *1st Annual ACM Northeast Digital Forensics Exchange.* John Jay College of Criminal Justice, City University of New York, New York, 2009.

Rogers, Marcus, Kate Seigfried, and Kirte Tidke. "Self-reported computer criminal behavior: A psychological analysis," *Digital Investigation* 3 (2006):116–120.

Schell, Bernadette, Miguel Martin, Patrick Hung, and Luis Rueda. "Cyber child pornography: A review paper of the social and legal issues and remedies — and a proposed technical solution," *Aggression and Violent Behavior* 12 (2007):45–63.

Seigfried-Spellar, Kathryn, Richard Lovely, and Marcus Rogers. *Personality assessment of self-reported Internet child pornography consumers using bandura's theory of reciprocal determinism.* Edited by K. Jaishankar, *Cyber Criminology.* Boca Raton, FL: CRC Press, 2010.

Skenazy, Lenore. "The myth of online predators." *The daily beast*, 2009 edited by L. Skenazy.

Slade, Robert M. *Software forensics : Collecting evidence from the scene of a digital crime.* New York: McGraw-Hill, 2004.

Stambaugh, Hollis, David S. Beaupre, David J. Icove, Richard Baker, Wayne Cassaday, and Wayne P. Williams. *Electronic crime needs assessment for state and local law enforcement.* Washington D.C.: National Institute of Justice, 2001.

Taylor, Max. "The nature and dimensions of child pornography on the Internet." In *US/EU International Conference, Combating Child Pornography on the Internet.* Vienna, Austria, 1999.

Taylor, Max, Gemma Holland, and Ethel Quayle, E. "Typology of paedophile picture collections." *The Police Journal* 74 (2001):97–107.

Taylor, Max, and Ethel Quayle. *Child pornography an Internet crime.* New York: Routledge, 2003.

U.S.S.C. 2009. *U.S. Sentencing Guidelines Manual* § 2G2.2.

Wolak, Janis, David Finkelhor, and Kimberley Mitchell. *Child pornography possessors arrested in Internet-related crimes: Findings from the national online victimization study.* Washington D.C.: National Center for Missing and Exploited Children, 2005. Accessed November 11, 2009. http://www.missingkids.com/en_US/publications/NC144.pdf.

Wolak, Janis, David Finkelhor, Kimberley Mitchell, and Michele Ybarra. "Online predators and the victims: Myth, realities and implications for prevention and treatment." *American Psychologist* 63 (2008):111–128.

Wolak, Janis, David Finkelhor, and Kimberly Mitchell. *Trends in the arrests of "online predators."* Durham, NH: Crimes Against Children Research Center, 2009. Accessed November 9, 2009. http://unh.edu/ccrc/pdf/N-JOV2_methodology_report.pdf.

6

Examining Cyberstalking and Bullying: Causes, Context, and Control

Catherine Marcum

In the early 1960s, J.C.R. Licklider of the Massachusetts Institute of Technology created the idea of an electronic global communication system (Licklider and Clark 1962, as cited in Leiner et al. 2003). His "Galactic Network" idea entailed an internationally connected set of computers that allowed for easy accessibility to information. His idea developed into what we now know as the Internet. This intercontinental information highway has enabled people of all ages, especially youth, to drastically expand their social circles and improve their ability to communicate with friends and family (Roberts, Foehr, Rideout, and Brodie 1999; Rosenbaum, Altman, Brodie, Flournoy, Blendon, and Benson 2000). Besides communication and socialization, users are able to participate easily in other activities, such as research, shopping, and online gaming.

Unfortunately, individuals are often unable to participate in online activities without the annoyance of uninvited communication and harassment from other online users. Illegal activities occurring with the Internet as the location of these crimes are becoming more and more prevalent for users. While online victimization can range from identity theft to child pornography, two of the more prevalent classifications of cybercrime are cyberbullying and cyberstalking. These crimes are also mirrored in the physical world, but due to the complexity of the Internet, are often more difficult to define and prosecute when they occur online.

This chapter will attempt to clarify issues related to cyberbullying and cyberstalking, as well as legislative and legal challenges that have arisen because of these complex crimes. First, cyberbullying and cyberstalking will be separately defined, as well as explored, in regard to behaviors of offenders and victims. Legislation and prevention techniques for each type of victimization will also be discussed. Finally, the effect of prosecution of these behaviors will be discussed in regard to the free speech rights of youth and adults.

Cyberbullying

Bullying in the physical world is defined as intentional, aggressive behavior that involves an imbalance of power (Nansel et al. 2001, 2094); therefore, cyberbullying is intentional, aggressive behavior that is performed through electronic means (Hinduja and Patchin 2008, 129; Reeckman and Cannard 2009, 41). Cyberbullying can take place in various forms of computer-mediated communication (CMCs), such as in instant messaging, email, or a chat room. Additionally, text messages are becoming a common method for cyberbullying as more young people use cellular telephones. For example, repetitive and harassing text messages can be sent continuously to a recipient.

Perhaps one of the most sensational examples of cyberbullying is the story of Megan Meier. Megan was a young teenager who faced the same developmental and emotional challenges experienced by most adolescent females. She befriended another teenager named Josh via her MySpace account, but after several weeks, the messages from Josh became hostile and demeaning. Megan became confused by Josh's aggressions and became devastated when he told her the world would be a better place without her. Sadly, Megan committed suicide as a result of these conversations and was completely unaware of the true identity of Josh. Her parents later discovered that Josh was actually the middle-aged mother of a former friend of Megan, Lori Drew. Drew was convicted in federal court of three counts of "accessing a computer without authorization via interstate commerce to obtain information to inflict emotional distress," but the conviction was later overturned based on the terms of use of MySpace. However, prosecutors and parents considered the case a victory as it paved the way for the criminalization of cyberbullying (Beckstrom 2008, 283).

Cyberbullying can occur in several forms of electronic communication (Hinduja and Patchin 2008, 129). The forms of cyberbullying are listed and defined as the following:

- Harassment in the cyber form entails repetitive messages, generally offensive to the recipient (Kowalski, Limber, and Agatston 2008, 47);
- Outing and trickery refers to the unintended sharing of personal information with others (Beckstrom 2008, 290);

- Flaming occurs in a public setting, such as a chat room or discussion board, and is a brief exchange of insults between two or more parties (Adams 2007; Bauman 2007; Willard 2006);
- Denigration involves posting information about another that is disparaging and untrue; and
- Exclusion/ostracism is the perception of feeling in or out (Kowalski et al. 2008, 48–49).

According to Wolak, Mitchell and Finkelhor (2007), while physical bullying occurs over multiple incidents, cyberbullying generally does not involve repeated aggression. However, the threats or offensive behavior performed online may only involve a single post, but that post could be passed on to many recipients. This challenges the notion that repetition is missing from cyberbullying, as the information could be posted in multiple places online. For example, YouTube is a website where anyone can post anything to be viewed by all other online users. This website has made homemade viral videos, such as the Star Wars kid and the Chocolate Rain singer, extremely popular. However, if someone takes a home video (whether it be on a video camera, digital camera, or cellular telephone) of another person performing an embarrassing act and posts it on YouTube without his or her permission, it can be viewed by thousands of online users. Moreover, the website link could also be emailed to thousands of other online users, continuing the cycle.

Cyberbullying can be both direct and indirect. Direct cyberbullying involves messages sent specifically to the victim, such as insults, demeaning words, or threats. On the other hand, indirect cyberbullying (also known as cyberbullying by proxy) occurs when the perpetrators poses as the victim by hacking into his or her account and sending out hateful and inappropriate messages (Aftab 2006). For example, sending harassing emails to a friend from your sister's email account and signing the emails with your sister's name instead of your own would be indirect cyberbullying. Further, a study of youth cyberbullying by Sbarbaro and Smith (2011) indicated that there is a significant relationship between grade level and victimization; in other words, as youth get older, there is a higher likelihood of victimization.

There is a disagreement among some researchers regarding the age group that can be cyberbullied. According to Aftab (2006), the term "cyberbullying" only occurs between minors. If an adult becomes involved in the exchange, the behavior is then termed cyber harassment or cyberstalking. However, Kowalski et al. (2008, 44) disagree with that assertion and believe that adults can be victims of cyberbullying as well. For instance, there have been instances of students superimposing teachers' heads on nude bodies or harassing teachers online.

Persons who participate in cyberbullying generally exhibit one or more of the same characteristics. For example, they have a temper and are easily frustrated. Second, they may have dominant personalities and relate to others in aggressive ways (proactively and reactively). They may also show little compassion for victims of bullying (Camodeca and Goossens 2005, 186–197). This lack of empathy by offenders presents a concern for school administrators, as this form of victimization can cause physical, psychological, and emotional harm to its victims (Hinduja and Satchin 2007, 89). Finally, Wang et al. (2009) found that African-Americans were more likely to perpetrate cyberbullying. At the same time, Hispanics were found to be the most likely race to report cyberbullying victimization (Wang et al., 2009).

There have been several notable studies performed regarding the prevalence of cyberbullying and the overall findings have been consistent. In a study of Internet behavior of high school seniors, Marcum (2009, 356) found that approximately 31% of the respondents had experienced some form of harassment online. The National Children's Home study (NCH 2002) found that almost 30% of youth (ages 11 to 19 years old) polled had been cyberbullied in some form, while O'Connell (2004, 4) found that 20% of children aged 9–16 were harassed specifically in chat rooms. Moreover, Patchin and Hinduja (2006, 148) found that among their respondents under the age of 18, 30% reported being a victim of cyberbullying and 11% confessed to perpetrating cyberbullying.

Findings regarding the separation of the sexes are not consistent, as males and females are shown to experience harassment differently depending on the study. Marcum (2010) found that 35.2% of male college freshmen had experienced some form of cyberbullying, compared to 16.0% of female college freshmen. Conversely, the National Children's Home (NCH 2002) found that females were more likely to be cyberbullied via text messaging compared to males (21% vs. 12%); however, females (3%) and males (5%) were quite comparable in regard to victimization via email (Holt and Bossler 2009; Marcum 2010).

Males and females also display aggression and perpetrate harassment in different ways. Males generally engage in more direct aggression, such as physical violence, while females use indirect forms of aggression, such as gossiping or spreading false rumors (Bjorkqvist, Lagerspetz, and Osterman 1992, 51); therefore, females should participate more in cyberbullying as offenders compared to males. As support for this assumption, a study of middle school students by Kowalski and Limber (2006, as cited in Kowalski et al. 2008, 78) found that 13% of females and 9% of males had perpetrated cyberbullying.

Cyberbullying can have varying effects on the victim and perpetrator, often mirroring reactions to physical bullying. Victims of cyberbullying can exhibit feelings of depression, stress, anxiety, and suicidal thoughts (Ybarra and Mitchell 2004, 1308). Kowalski et al. (2008) argue that the effects of cyberbullying can even be worse than physical altercations as the bullying messages can continue to reappear on the Internet in multiple places. Targets of cyberbullying often do not report incidences of abuse as they are afraid of losing the mediums where the bullying is occurring (cellular telephones and the Internet) as they are valued commodities (Campbell 2005; Li 2006). There has even been an assertion that social networking websites cause a "suicide contagion effect" (Zayas 2006), a term that indicates individuals who are contemplating suicide are more likely to act if they see others have published their suicide on social networking websites.

Conversely, perpetrators of cyberbullying often feel vindicated, pleased, and proud of their behavior (Kowalski and Witte 2006). By abusing someone else and feeling dominant, they feel compensated for wrongs done to them at one time. Patchin and Hinduja (2011) found that offenders of cyberbullying are often fueled by various forms of strain, as well as peer aggression. Moreover, in a separate study, Hinduja and Patchin (2008, 1) found that computer proficiency and time spent online were both positively related to committing the offense of cyberbullying.

Prevention of Cyberbullying

Other than formal legislation, there are steps that can be taken to prevent cyberbullying. For example, there are tips parents can use to protect their children while using the Internet. Kowalski et al. (2008, 113–114) held focus groups with high school students and obtained the following suggestions:

- Set age-appropriate guidelines;
- Communicate about appropriate ways to deal with conflict;
- Monitor use of the Internet;
- Supervise, but do not violate, privacy;
- Watch for warning signs;
- Do not punish the victim for the online offender's behavior; and
- Educate yourself.

Furthermore, organizations such as NetSmartz (www.netsmartz.org) and i-SAFE (www.isafe.org) provide resources for parents to educate themselves of the dangers online and how to be prepared for their children.

There are also steps that educators can take to better prepare themselves for incidences of cyberbullying in their schools. First, educators need to be given a definition of cyberbullying and instructed on how to assess potential problems in the classroom and with students. This can be accomplished through regular staff training. As the Internet changes by the second, it is imperative to keep abreast of new technology and its functioning. Next, educators should spend class time covering cyberbullying, proper and safe Internet use, as well as encouraging students to report incidences they encounter. Finally, educators not only teach children, but also parents. While there are steps parents should take to educate themselves, they are not always motivated to be proactive; therefore, teachers should send home literature to parents instructing them on what to watch for during Internet use (Kowalski et al. 2008, 128–138).

Parents also should inform teenagers that Internet communication is not fleeting, but permanent. For instance, Twitter is archiving all tweets from March 2006 to present, including mean tweets (Holladay 2010, 46). Records of bullying online will be much easier to recover and use as evidence in judicial procedures, if necessary.

Cyberstalking

The term "stalking" is defined as behavior that involves one individual repeatedly intruding on another in a manner that produces fear or distress (McEwan, Mullen, MacKenzie, and Ogloff 2009, 1469). There is a blurred line between the difference, if any, of harassment and stalking, as harassment is also categorized as behavior that annoys or distresses the victim. Often, the level of stress, fear and disturbance is considered when determining if a person is being harassed or stalked (Turmanis and Brown 2006, 184). However, according to Sinclair and Frieze (2000, 23), it is not possible to make a clear distinction between what behaviors should be labeled as harassment or stalking, and therefore it is beneficial to refer to the terms interchangeably.

Typical methods of physical stalking involve consistent, unwanted monitoring of a person, arriving at homes or workplaces uninvited, and participating in intimidating behavior. Much like the term "cyberbullying," the term "cyberstalking" refers to stalking in an electronic format. While cyberstalking can occur in a multitude of ways (much like stalking in the physical sense), methods include, but are not limited to, the following: gathering personal information to threaten or intimidate the victim; unwanted, repetitive emailing or instant messaging; sending hostile messages or threats; and impersonation of another person (Sheridan and Grant 2007, 627). Although Bocij (2004, 78) found that cyberstalking is experienced slightly more by females than males, it is still an issue for both sexes. Furthermore, Sheridan and Grant (2007) asserted that cyberstalking is perpetrated less by ex-intimate partners and more by acquaintances or strangers.

Multiple studies have indicated that Internet users of a wide age range have reported being victimized by a cyberstalker. In regard to the younger adolescent population (17 years and younger) a direct example comes from evidence derived from the Youth Internet Safety Survey, a nationally representative study (sponsored by the National Center for Missing and Exploited Children) of 1,501 adolescents, 10 to 17 years old, who participated in regular use of the Internet. The two administrations of the Youth Internet Safety Survey (the first [YISS-1] occurred between August 1999 and February 2000 and the second [YISS-2] between March and June 2005) showed an increase in Internet victimization between the two time periods. First, the proportion of youth who reported online harassment grew from 6% to 9%. A larger amount percentage of youth received unwanted sexual solicitation compared to the first survey (13% in 2001 versus 19% in 2006) (Mitchell, Finkelhor, and Wolak 2003; Wolak, Mitchell and Finkelhor 2006).

Although adolescent populations often fall prey to cyberstalking, adults are also experiencing various forms of cyberstalking. Fisher, Cullen, and Turner (2000) questioned approximately 4,500 female undergraduates and found that 13.1% had reported cyberstalking in some form. Alexy, Burgess, Baker, and Smoyak (2005) and Finn (2004) both found that 5–10% of male and female undergraduates reported cyberstalking online, generally in email form, and offline. Moreover, Spitzberg and Hoobler (2002) utilized the Cyber-Obsessional Pursuit scale to measure stalking and harassment online. Eighteen percent of respondents confirmed that someone had obsessively communicated with them in a sexually harassing way, while 3% had been threatened by them. While there is a limited amount of literature utilizing theory to explain online victimization, especially between sexes, Holt and Bossler (2009) found support for Routine Activity Theory as an explanation for this form of victimization. They found that females were more likely to be victimized due to their target suitability and hypothesized that this may be a result of their communication patterns online, which allow them to be easily identified as women (Holt and Bossler 2009).

Since the concept of cyberstalking is fairly new, there is a division amongst researchers about whether it truly is a social problem (Bocij and McFarlane 2002, 204). Some theorists believe that cyberstalking is a gateway to physical stalking. Lee (1998) stated that "electronic stalking often leads to, or is accompanied by, physical stalking, and explicitly or implicitly threatens physical stalking" (p. 407). Furthermore, McGrath and Casey (2002, 85) affirm that the anonymous availability of the Internet can turn a low-risk victim to a high-risk victim. As the Internet allows for masked or changed identity, the opportunities for deception are increased and offenders can better depersonalize their victims (Bocij and McFarlane 2003, 204).

Motivators of cyberstalking can vary for each offender. However, according to Bocji (2004, 92–106), they can be grouped into two categories: technological and social factors. Technological factors, such as easier access to technology and the ability to hide one's identity, allow for easier deceptive practices online. For example, many social networking websites do not validate the identity of their users, so it is easy to create false identities online. Social factors, such as disinhibition (based on the anonymity available online) and the perception of power and control, can increase the likelihood of the stalking behaviors. Furthermore, difficulty policing this behavior online increases the ability for a person to participate in the behavior, as well as become victims of it. An example of this can also be found in Holt and Bossler's (2009) study of college students and online victimization. Utilizing Routine Activity Theory to examine the behavior, they found a positive relationship between students who reported involvement in computer-based deviance and their likelihood of victimization. In other words, involvement in deviant and/or illegal behaviors online as an offender increased the likelihood that the student would also become a victim.

There is also some dispute of its uniqueness in comparison to offline stalking. Bocij (2004, 21–29) argued that the following fallacies about cyberstalking confirm it is a unique form of deviant behavior compared to offline stalking:

- Cyberstalking is an extension of offline stalking;
- Cyberstalkers are "obsessional";
- Cyberstalkers know their victims;
- Cyberstalkers cause less harm than offline stalkers;
- Cyberstalkers seldom use stalking-by-proxy;
- Cyberstalkers do not make "credible threats"; and
- Cyberstalkers share the same motivations as offline stalkers.

Bocij (2004, 21–29) disproves these fallacies by providing empirical research, as well as confirmation by Congress, that affirms the uniqueness of this deviant behavior and the potential danger that results from it. Moreover, the reactions victims experience from cyberstalking can mimic those of offline stalking and be just as serious (Bocij 2004, 66).

Bocij (2004, 66) asserted that victims of cyberstalking can be categorized into three groups based on their computer literacy: novice, intermediate, or expert. He reported that while novice users were more likely to receive threats, expert users were more likely to experience sophisticated attacks on their hardware and software. Despite the type of cyberstalking, the reaction of the victim can include: powerlessness, shame, feelings of isolation, anxiety/depression, and substance abuse (Ashcroft 2001, 24; Blaauw et al. 2002, 50). Furthermore, Pathe (2002, 48) asserted that friends and relatives of stalking victims may also become secondary victims, as the stalker may use them as a tool to control the primary target.

Prevention of Cyberstalking

According to the organization Working to Halt Online Abuse (W.H.O.A), there are several steps a person can take to decrease the likelihood of experiencing cyberstalking (Bureau of Justice Assistance 2009). For instance, it is suggested that a person use a free email account, such as Hotmail or Yahoo!, along with a gender neutral email address. Secondly, do not give out email addresses or personal information to people not known or trusted. Marcum (2009) found that people who provide personal information to online contacts are more likely to be victimized compared to those who keep personal information private. Therefore, release of personal information to strangers or people met online can be risky behavior. Finally, and most importantly, do not trust new online friends or acquaintances. Other sources also recommend installing a virus scanner on personal computers, as well as refusing file attachments from unknown sources to cut back on viruses and Trojans (Bocij et al. 2002, 628). Hinduja and Patchin (2007) also recommend installation of protective software, but warn that technically-savvy individuals are always finding ways around these measures and that they are not surefire means of protection.

Most large businesses have security specialists who control cyber security issues. However, there are steps smaller organizations can take to protect themselves. For instance, they can implement an acceptable use policy for all employees, as well as place controls on employee computers with regard to browsing and email use. Performing regular software audits is also a good way to make sure illegal content is not being stored on company computers (Blacharksi 2000; Lee 2001).

Emergence of Legislation

As mentioned previously, the issue of bullying and stalking in the electronic realm is a fairly new concept. As a result, few attempts at preventing and prosecuting the problem through legislation have been made. While states and the federal government recognize these forms of online victimization as a true problem, many technical issues, as well as constitutional issues, are present. While the constitutional problems will be addressed in the next section, this section will provide information on the current state of legislation that has been implemented to fight cyberbullying and cyberstalking.

The issue of bullying has increasingly become of concern in the public school system, especially since the shootings at Columbine High School. By the year 2000, over half the states in America had passed anti-bullying legislation. Along with other school shootings and publicized incidents, there has been widespread media coverage addressing the issue of bullying. As Internet use has become more prevalent (especially by adolescents), the concept of electronic harassment and stalking has placed school officials in a realm of uncertainty about how to control this behavior without infringing on constitutional rights.

Currently, approximately ten states have enacted some form of legislation requiring schools to create preventative cyberbullying policies, and other states are considering amendments to their current legislation. Generally, these states have extended their definition of bullying to include those of the electronic and physical form. Arkansas (Act 115 2007) defines bullying as "... intentional harassment, intimidation, humiliation, ridicule, defamation, or threat or incitement of violence by a student against another student or public school employee by written, verbal, electronic or physical act ..."

When referring to bullying that occurs at "school," the majority of states have extended that term to various locations related to school. For example, Iowa law asserts that policies against bullying will be enforced in the school building, on the outside property, and at any school function at any location. Furthermore, South Carolina asserted that "school" also includes any school-related vehicle or the school bus stop (Kowalski et al. 2008, 163).

With regard to cyberstalking, Alaska, California, Oklahoma, and Wyoming have added electronic communication to their anti-stalking laws. Furthermore, in 2000, the federal government passed the Violence Against Women Act, which made cyberstalking a part of the federal interstate stalking statute (National Center for Victims of Crime 2003).

There have also been international efforts to prosecute cyberbullying and cyberstalking. For example, Singapore law is currently in the process of amending its stalking statutes to include those made in electronic arenas (Chik 2008, 13). The United Kingdom passed the Malicious Communications Act of 2003, which allows for up to six months of imprisonment for a person participating in obscene or menacing communication online (Gillespie 2006, 125). Due to the innovation of this piece of legislation, cyberbullying and cyberstalking can now be prosecuted in Britain, Ireland, Scotland, and Wales.

Addressing Free Speech Issues

As cyberbullying and cyberstalking has become more prevalent among adolescents, the issue of censorship and free speech rights for students is often scrutinized. While the First Amendment guarantees the right to freedom of speech, there are always exceptions to the rule, especially when it involves infringing on the rights of others. The United States Supreme Court has examined these exceptions in a few notable cases.

The United States Supreme Court first considered these rights with the case *Tinker v. Des Moines School District* (393 U.S. 403, 507 (1969)). Students were demonstrating their opposition of the Vietnam War and wore armbands to school as a form of protest. The school enacted a policy to discipline any of the students who wore the armbands, and the lawsuit ensued as students insisted their right to free speech was violated through the restriction of their clothing. Under *Tinker*, the Court ruled that student speech may be censored if it causes a substantial disruption or invades the rights of other students. *Tinker* has recently been applied regarding off-campus cyberspeech by students. In cases such as *J.S. ex rel. H.S. v. Bethlehem Area School District* (807 A.2d 847, 850–51 (Pa. 2002)) and *Layshock v. Hermitage School District* (412 F.Supp. 2d 502, 504 (W.D. PA. 2006)), the Court ruled that certain types of cyber speech caused a substantial disruption on campus, affecting both staff and students, and was justifiably removed.

Thirty years after *Tinker*, the Supreme Court again weighed on the issue of student speech with the case *Bethel School District No. 403 v. Fraser* (478 U.S. 675 (1986)). Fraser, a student, nominated a fellow student for an office and delivered a speech that included explicit, sexual language. Shortly thereafter, Fraser was suspended for his language and his name was removed from the list of graduation speakers. The Supreme Court veered away from *Tinker* and stated that students are entitled to the same First Amendment protections as adults and that if the student was attempting to make a political point, offensive language was allowed. However, the Court did state that it is up to the discretion of school boards to determine what is offensive and prohibited in the school arena.

Lastly, *Hazelwood School District v. Kuhlmeier* (484 U.S. 260 (1988)) examined restrictions placed on student speech by school administration. The administration deleted portions of a school newspaper they believed to be inappropriate, without the students' approval. The Supreme Court supported the decision of the administration and stated that the First Amendment rights were not violated, as the newspaper was funded by the school district and part of school curriculum.

There are other standards that have been used as an alternative to the *Tinker* "substantial disruption test." Some courts use the "true threat" doctrine, as applied in *Watts v. United States* (394 U.S. 705 (1969)), in which threats made inside or outside the classroom are not constitutionally protected if designated a true threat. This "true threat" doctrine was applied via the "reasonable recipient" or "reasonable speaker" standard (as ruled in the Eighth and Ninth Circuit respectively), in which an objective person could interpret the communication as a true threat of intent to harm or assault (Beckstrom 2008, 306–308).

In summary, the Supreme Court has stated that there are certain circumstances in which school personnel can intervene on student speech without violating their First Amendment rights. First, according to *Watts v. United States* (1969), true threats are not protected. Furthermore, according to *Rogers v. United States* (1975), even statements that are intended to be threatening but not carried out are considered true threats. Additionally, according to the previously mentioned *Bethel School District* case, speech that is lewd, vulgar, and profane can be regulated at the very least if it is used on school grounds (Kowalski et al. 2008, 171).

There are other types of speech not protected by the First Amendment. Speech that is school sponsored, such as newspapers or theatrical productions, are subject to school intervention. Also, as was defined in *Tinker*, speech that disrupts the rights of others can be censored. Furthermore, although it is difficult to address the censorship of off-campus speech, the *Tinker* standard often applies if it involves "disruption of classwork, substantial disorder, or invasion of others' rights" (Kowalski et al. 2008, 172). For example, in *Coy v. Board of Education of the North Canton City Schools* (2002) and *J.S. v. Bethlehem Area School District* (2001), the Court ruled that although the websites were created off-campus by students, the access on school property and derogatory effect it had on students and teachers indicated it was not constitutionally protected speech.

Conclusion

Daily use of the Internet is a customary behavior for many Americans, whether for socialization, research, or various other activities. Though the idea of the Internet was not conceived until 1962 (Leiner et al. 2003) and just became a familiar facet of businesses and homes in the early 1990s (Sanger et al. 2004), this new commodity of communication has become a mainstay in American homes. Due to its easy accessibility and availability, the frequency of Internet use has increased in all age groups; however, Internet use by adolescents has had the largest increase compared to any other age group (Addison 2001).

Today's adolescents grew up using the Internet and are extremely familiar with the opportunities available online. Youth and younger adults are especially involved in online socialization with various methods of computer-mediated communication (CMC), such as email, chat rooms, instant messaging, and social networking websites. Not only are they using the Internet to socialize, they are also spending more time online (Nie and Erbring 2000; United States Department of Commerce 2002). Unfortunately, while the use of CMCs can produce positive interaction and enjoyable relationships for users, people spending extensive amounts of time online are also placing themselves at risk for victimization. Cyberbullying and cyberstalking are two main ways people can be victimized.

There needs to be a continued effort to research cyberbullying and cyberstalking so that credibility is given to these crimes as true threats of victimization for Internet users. Explanatory studies that provide better insight into the behaviors that increase these forms of victimization would be extremely beneficial, especially for younger Internet users who may engage in more risky online behaviors. Furthermore, these studies can help shape safety programs and policies to ensure a safer Internet experience for users. Another gap in the literature is research examining the effectiveness of legislation currently in place to prosecute cyberbullying and cyberstalking. First, studies investigating the amount of effort used to prosecute these crimes compared to bullying and stalking in the physical world would be beneficial. Secondly, the actual effectiveness of these pieces of legislation in regard to a deterrent factor for offenders should be explored as well.

While everyone is entitled to certain rights under the First Amendment regarding free speech, this does not give us the right to victimize others. There are certain things we can do to protect ourselves while online, such as using protective software and protecting personal information. However, the most important step to take in this process is to educate ourselves and others of the dangers online and what can be done to decrease the likelihood of victimization.

References

Alexy, Eileen M., Ann W. Burgess, Timothy Baker, and Shirley A. Smoyak. "Perceptions of cyberstalking among college students," *Brief Treatment and Crisis Intervention* 5 (2005): 279–289.

Ashcroft, John. *Stalking and domestic violence.* NCJ 186157. Washington, DC: U.S. Department of Justice, 2011.

Beckstrom, Darryn C. "State legislation mandating school cyberbullying policies and the potential threat to students' free speech rights," *Vermont Law
Review* 33 (2008): 283–321.

Bethel School District No. 403 v. Fraser, 478 U.S. 675 (1986).

Blacharski, Dan. "Emerging technology: Create order with a strong security
policy." *S.l.: Network Magazine*, 2001, Accessed May 15, 2010. http://www.
networkmagazine.com/shared/ article/showArticle.jhtml?articleId=8702862

Blauuw, Eric, Frans W. Winkel, Ella Arensman, Lorraine Sheridan, and Adri-
enne Freeve. 2002. *"The toll of stalking:* The relationship between features
of stalking and psychopathology of victims," *Journal of Interpersonal Violence* 17 (2002): 50–63.

Bocij, Paul. *Cyberstalking: Harassment in the Internet age and how to protect
your family.* Westport, CT: Praeger Publishers, 2004.

Bocij, Paul, and Leroy McFarlane. "Online harassment: Towards a definition
of cyberstalking," *Prison Service Journal* 39 (2002): 31–38.

Bocij, Paul, and Leroy McFarlane. "Cyberstalking: The technology of hate,"
Police Journal 76 (2003): 204–221.

Bureau of Justice Assistance. *2008 Internet crime report.* Department of Justice: Office of Justice Programs. Washington DC, 2009.

Chik, Warren. "Harassment through the digital medium: A cross-jurisdictional
comparative analysis on the law of cyberstalking." *Journal of International
Law & Technology* 3 (2008): 13–44.

Coy v. Board of Education of the North Canton City Schools, 205 F Supp. 2d 791
(2002).

Finn, Jerry. "A survey of online harassment at a university camps," *Journal of
Interpersonal Violence* 19 (2004): 468–483.

Fisher, Bonnie, Francis Cullen, and Michael G. Turner. *The sexual victimization of college women.* National Institute of Justice Publication No. NCJ
182369. Washington: Department of Justice, 2000

Gillespie, Alisdair. "Cyberbullying and harassment of teenagers: The legal response," *Journal of Social Welfare and Family Law* 28 (2006): 123–136.

Hazelwood School District v. Kuhlmeier, 484 U.S. 260, (1988).

Hinduja, Sameer, and Justin Patchin. "Offline consequences of online victimization: School violence and delinquency," *Journal of School Violence* 6
(2007): 89–112.

Hinduja, Sameer, and Justin Patchin. "Cyberbullying: An exploratory analysis of factors related to offending and victimization," *Deviant Behavior 29*
(2008): 1–29.

Holladay, Jennifer. "Cyberbullying: The stakes have never been higher for students—or schools," *Teaching Tolerance* 38 (2010): 42–46.

Holt, Thomas, and Adam Bossler. "Examining the applicability of Lifestyle-Routine Activities Theory for cybercrime victimization," *Deviant Behavior* 30 (2009): 1–25.

J.S. ex rel. H.S. v. Bethlehem Area School District, 807 A.2d 847, 850–51, (Pa. 2002).

Kowalski, Robin M., and James C. Witte. *Youth Internet Survey*, 2006. Available: http://www.camss.clemson.edu/KowalskiSurvey/servelet/Page1.

Kowalski, Robin M., Susan P. Limber, and Patricia W. Agatston. *Cyberbullying: Bullying in the digital age.* Maldon, MA: Blackwell Publishing, 2008.

Layshock v. Hermitage School District, 412 F.Supp. 2d 502, 504 (W.D. PA. 2006).

Lee, Doris. *Developing effective information systems security policies.* Bethesda, MD: SANS Institute, 2001. Accessed January 1, 2011. http://www.sans.org/rr/policy/effective.php.

Lee, Rebecca. Romantic and electronic stalking in a college context. *William and Mary Journal of Women and the Law* 4 (1998): 373–466.

Leiner, Barry M., Vinton G. Cerf, David D. Clark, Robert E. Kahn, Leonard Kleinrock, Daniel C. Lynch, Jon Postel, Larry G. Roberts, and Stephen Wolff. "A Brief History of the Internet." *Internet Society* (2003). Accessed June 7, 2007. http://www.isoc.org/internet/history/brief.shtml.

Marcum, Catherine D. "Identifying potential factors of adolescent online victimization in high school seniors," *International Journal of Cyber Criminology* 2 (2009): 346–367.

Marcum, Catherine D. "Assessing sex experiences of online victimization: An examination of adolescent online behaviors utilizing Routine Activity Theory," *Criminal Justice Review,* 35 (2010): 412–437.

McEwan, Troy, Paul Mullen, Richard MacKenzie, and James Ogloff. "Violence in stalking situations," *Psychological Medicine* 39 (2009): 1469–1478.

McGrath, Michael G., and Egohan Casey. "Forensic psychiatry and the Internet: Practical perspectives on sexual predators and obsessional harassers in cyberspace," *Journal of the American Academy of Psychiatry and the Law* 30 (2002): 81–94.

Mitchell, Kimberly, David Finkelhor, and Janice Wolak. "The exposure of youth to unwanted sexual material on the Internet: A national survey of risk, impact and prevention," *Youth & Society* 34 (2003): 3300–3358.

Nansel, Tonja R., Mary Overpeck, Ramani S. Pilla, W. June Ruan, Bruce Simmons-Morton, and Peter Scheidt. "Bullying behavior among U.S. youth: Prevalence and association with psychosocial adjustment," *Journal of the American Medical Association* 285 (2001): 2094–2100.

National Center for Victims of Crime. 2003. *Cyberstalking.* Accessed June 15, 2010. http://www.victimbar.org/ncvc/main.aspx?dbName=DocumentViewer&DocumentID=32458.

Nie, Norman, and Lutz Erbring. *Internet and Society: A Preliminary Report.* Stanford: Stanford Institute for the Quantitative Study of Society, 2000.

O'Connell, Rachel, Joanna Price, and Charlotte Barrow. *Cyberstalking, abusive cyber sex, and online grooming.* Centre for Cyberspace Research, Preston, 2004.

Patchin, Justin, and Sameer Hinduja. "Bullies move beyond the schoolyard: A preliminary look at cyberbullying," *Youth Violence and Juvenile Justice* 4 (2006): 148–169.

Patchin, Justin, and Sameer Hinduja. "Traditional and nontraditional bullying among youth: A test of General Strain Theory," *Youth and Society* 43 (2011): 727–751.

Pathe, Michele. *Surviving stalking.* Cambridge: Cambridge University Press, 2002.

Reekman, Barbara, and Laine Cannard. "Cyberbullying: A TAFE perspective," *Youth Studies Australia* 28 (2009): 41–49.

Roberts, Donald F., Ulla G. Foehr, Victoria J. Rideout, and Mollyann Brodie. *Kids and media @ the new millennium: A comprehensive analysis of children's media.* The Henry J. Kaiser Family Foundation, 1999.

Rogers v. United States, 422 U.S. 35 (1975).

Rosenbaum, Michele J., Drew Altman, Mollyann Brodie, Rebecca Flournoy, Robert J. Blendon, and John Benson. 2000. NPR/Kaiser/Kennedy school kids and technology survey. Accessed June 21, 2008. http://www.npr.org/ programs/ specials/pool/technology/technology.kids.html.

Sanger, Dixie, Amie Long, Mitzi Ritzman, Keri Stofer, and Candy Davis. "Opinions of Female Juvenile Delinquents about their Interactions in Chat Rooms," *Journal of Correctional Education* 55 (2004): 120–131.

Sheridan, L, and T. Grant. "Is cyberstalking different?" *Psychology, Crime & Law* 13 (2007): 627–640.

Sinclair, H Colleen, and Irene Hanson Frieze. "Initial courtship behavior and stalking: How should we draw the line?" *Violence and Participants* 15 (2000): 23–40.

Spitzburg, Brian H., and Gregory Hoobler. "Cyberstalking and the technologies of interpersonal terrorism," *New Media & Society* 4 (2002): 71–92.

Tinker v. Des Moines School District, 393 U.S. 403, 507 (1969).

Turmanis, Simon A., and Robert I. Brown. "The stalking and harassment behavior scale: Measuring the incidence, nature, and severity of stalking and relational harassment and their psychological effects," *Psychology and Psychotherapy: Theory, Research and Practice* 79 (2006): 183–198.

United States Department of Commerce. Computer and Internet usage by Age and Disability Status: 2002. Washington, DC: United States Department of Commerce, 2002. Accessed June 9, 2009. http://www.census.gov/hhes/ www/ disability/sipp/disab02/ds02f6.pdf.

Wang, Jing, Ronald J. Iannotti, and Tonja R. Nansel. "Social bullying among adolescents in the United States; physical, verbal, relational and cyber," *Journal of Adolescent Health, 45* (2009): 368–375.

Watts v. United States, 394 U.S. 705 (1969).

Wolak, Janice, Kimberly Mitchell, and David Finkelhor. *Online victimization of children: Five years later.* Washington, DC: National Center for Missing & Exploited Children, 2006.

Zayas, Alexandra. Online death dialogues prompt suicide? *St. Petersburg Times,* 2006. Accessed April 20, 2007. http://www.sptimes.com/2006/08/27/Tampabay/_Online_death_dialogu.shtml.

7

The Internet as a Tool for Terrorists: Implications for Physical and Virtual Worlds

Marjie T. Britz

The lack of a universal, or even generalizable, definition of terrorism has complicated both academic and government inquiries into the phenomenon. Obfuscated by ideological, cultural, or political agendas, conceptualizations of terrorism or terrorist activities may be characterized as localized reactions to situational or historical cultural events. In the wake of the Terror Attacks of 9/11, a virtual plethora of discussions, publications, and legislation was evident in the United States, including, but not limited to, the passage of the *Uniting and Strengthening America by Providing Appropriate Tools Required to Intercept and Obstruct Terrorism Act of 2001*. Commonly known as the U.S.A. Patriot Act, the legislation was originally introduced by Representative Frank Sensenbrenner (R-Wisconsin) and incorporated provisions of two earlier anti-terrorism bills (Public Law 107-56). While the Act brought together disparate House committees (e.g. Education and the Workforce, Transportation and Infrastructure, Armed Services, Financial Services, International Relations, Energy and Commerce, and the Permanent Select Committee on Intelligence), it neither led to a universally accepted definition nor a greater understanding of the potentiality of the Internet as a terrorist tool. Even those that acknowledged the emerging threat associated with technology concentrated too heavily on the web as a mechanism of destruction. Such characterizations, originally deemed implausible or fantastical, presented scenarios equivalent to a cyber-apocalypse or a digital Pearl Harbor.

The globalization of commerce, information, and communications has created a technological house of cards. As those in legitimate society have increasingly employed the medium to conduct business, disseminate research findings, store sensitive information, and communicate with others, those in illegitimate society have increasingly exploited the vulnerabilities associated with such interconnectivity. For individuals, potential areas for victimization include: data theft, identity fraud, computer damage, and stalking and harassment. While the costs associated with such activity can be both financial and emotional, they are largely individualized. For corporations, threats include: disruption of commerce or communication, extortion, theft or destruction of intellectual property or trade secrets, loss of consumer confidence, and, theft or destruction of funds or commodities. The costs and prevalence of such victimization have significantly increased in recent years, with targeted companies experiencing an average loss of nearly $6 million a year (Ponemon Institute 2011). The consequences associated with cybercrime involving corporations are farther reaching than those resulting from crimes experienced by individuals, and an attack may significantly impact the lives and livelihoods of both consumers and employees. However, neither individual nor corporate cases reach the level of significance of those attacks that may be directed at a nation's security, infrastructure, or military.

Discussions of a "digital" or "electronic" Pearl Harbor began in earnest in 1998, when Richard A. Clarke, the National Security Council's Senior Director and National Coordinator for Security, Critical Infrastructure, and Counter-Terrorism, presented a fantastical scenario where multiple system failures occur in a single day.[1] These included: multiple computer failures at military bases across the world; a massive blackout in San Francisco; telephone outages across Miami and New York; and, widespread failure of personal pagers, airline reservation systems, and automatic teller machines. Such an occurrence, he stated, would be more catastrophic than Pearl Harbor. As such, he encouraged proactive measures to prepare for the "giant tsunami coming" (Madsen 1998).

The cataclysmic events portended by Clarke have not yet been realized, and both scholars and governments remain divided on the potentiality of a catastrophic disruption of communication, commerce, and government services and systems. By focusing almost exclusively on the Internet as a trigger for terrorist attacks, both traditional and contemporary definitions have obscured other, perhaps more insidious, uses of the Internet. That is not to suggest, however, that such conceptualizations should be entirely discounted. Recent

---

1. Although Clarke was not the first to use the term (e.g., Bowman 1995; Washington 1995), he is often credited with its origination. Since his remarks, the terms "digital" or "electronic" Pearl Harbor have become part of the verbiage associated with discussions of cyber-terrorism and cyber-warfare. There is little consensus in terms of the likelihood of such an event, but the discussion continues (see Britz 2009; Gable 2009).

events in Iran and Estonia have certainly demonstrated that the medium may be employed as a mechanism of attack, but operationalization of the term must also recognize the utility of the web as a facilitator. In fact, the interconnectivity of the web perfectly complements the amorphous structure and the media-centric nature of contemporary terrorist organizations, which most often use the medium for propaganda, recruitment, fund-raising, dissemination of information, and justification. In this regard, the Internet may be most appropriately characterized as a force multiplier and agility enabler that connects geographically disparate individuals and entities by affecting situational awareness. Thus, emergent definitions must include both recognition and discussion of the Internet as a multipurpose terrorist tool—one which is increasingly important in the Digital Age.

Defining Terrorism

While most contemporary scholars trace the term terrorism to the Latin *terrere* which is defined as *to arouse fear*, the modern etymology of the term is most commonly attributed to Robespierre's "The Terror," which immediately followed the French Revolution (Tsfati and Weimann 2002). However, the notion that the fear of a populace could result in political, ideological, or social change is more deeply rooted. In fact, the justification of attacks on noncombatants and institutionalized reactions to same may be as old as society itself (Britz 2009; Garrison 2003; Tsfati and Weimann 2002). While the parameters of this chapter preclude a comprehensive discussion of the history of such actions, it is sufficient and appropriate to recognize that terrorism, as both a notion and a reality, is neither a recent contrivance nor a novel field of academic inquiry or government scrutiny. At the same time, an examination of the extant literature reveals a marked absence of a singular definition which has been universally employed by either community. Rather, operationalization of the phenomenon tends to be localized and entirely dependent upon both the individual and social characteristics affecting the defining body. These include, but are not limited to: cultural norms, religious ideology, institutional history, political or organizational agenda, stability of government institutions, status of economic superstructure, situational placement or vulnerability, and historical stratification or marginalization.

Regardless of social, cultural, or political agenda, definitions of terrorism by government entities have traditionally required the demonstration of three common elements: 1) the use of violence against noncombatants, 2) political objectives, and, 3) the use of fear as a coercive tactic. For example,

- (1930)—*International Conferences for the Unification of Criminal Law* (3rd Conference, Brussels)—the intentional use of means capable of producing a common danger that represents an act of terrorism on the part of anyone making use of crimes against life, liberty or physical integrity of persons or directed against private or state property with the purpose of expressing or executing political or social ideas will be punished (Saul 2005, 59).
- (1931)—*International Conferences for the Unification of Criminal Law* (4th Conference, Paris)—whoever, for the purpose of terrorizing the population, uses against persons or property bombs, mines, incendiary or explosive devices or products, fire arms or other deadly or deleterious devices, or who provokes or attempts to provoke, spreads or attempts to spread an epidemic, a contagious disease or other disaster, or who interrupts or attempts to interrupt a public service or public utility will be punished (Saul 2005, 59).
- (1937)—*League of Nations Convention*—all criminal acts directed against a State and intended or calculated to create a state of terror in the minds of particular persons or a group of persons or the general public.
- (1991)—*Turkish Anti-Terrorism Act*—all kinds of activities attempted by a member or members of an organization for the purpose of changing the characteristics of the Republic which is stated in the constitution, and the political, jurisdictional, social, secular, economic system, destroying the territorial integrity of the state and the government and its people, weakening or ruining or invading the authority of the government, demolishing the rights and freedom, jeopardizing the existence of Turkish government and Republic, destroying the public order or peace and security (see Martin 2009).
- (1994)—*United Nations Resolution Language*—criminal acts intended or calculated to provoke a state of terror in the general public, a group of persons or particular persons for political purposes are in any circumstance unjustifiable, whatever the considerations of a political, philosophical, ideological, racial, ethnic, religious or other nature that may be invoked to justify them (see Martin 2009).
- (2007)—*United States Department of Defense*—the calculated use of unlawful violence or threat of unlawful violence to inculcate fear; intended to coerce or to intimidate governments or societies in the pursuit of goals that are generally political, religious, or ideological (see Martin 2009).
- (2011)—*United States Department of State*—the premeditated politically motivated violence perpetrated against non-combatant targets by subnational groups or clandestine agents, usually intended to influence an audience.

The lack of international consensus on cultural, religious, and expressive expectations has further complicated attempts at elucidation. Questions regarding the appropriate placement and treatment of "politically motivated" actions, delineation of state sponsored versus individual motivations, and legal clarification of sovereignty and extradition have rendered international consortium ineffectual (Britz 2009).

An analysis of the extant academic literature reveals a similar pattern of discord with a variety of scholars noting the impossibility of consensus (e.g. Altheide 2006; Reid and Chen 2006; Rice 2009; Ruby 2002; Merari 1993; Saul 2005; Schmid and Jongman 1988; Tsfati and Weimann 2002). At the same time, articulated commonalities suggest that a working definition of terrorism may best be approached as a compilation of characteristics. To wit, the following definitional elements were found: the presence of violence (83.5%); political (65%); fear or terror (51%); threats (47%); anticipated psychological reactions (41.5%); premeditation or system operation (32%); and, tactical, strategic, or combative methodology (30.5%) (Schmid and Jongman 1988). A synthesis of the academic and political entomologies reveals that traditional acts characterized as terrorism may be conceptualized as a sum of the following components:

- Violence
- The victimization of innocents
- Methodical or serial operations
- Advance planning
- Criminal character
- Absence of moral restraint
- Political, social, or ideological motivation
- Attempt to garner attention
- Performed for an audience
- Unpredictable and/or unexpected
- Intended to instill fear (Britz 2009)

However, it must be noted that across all landscapes fear and violence are necessary definitional elements, and ends and means are often used interchangeably, with academic definitions concentrating exclusively on the ends while government definitions further obfuscate the discussion by focusing entirely on the means employed (i.e., violence). Violence, for example, is often treated as both the ends and the means to both physical and hypothetical scenarios. Subsequently, government policies, legislative actions, and academic inquiry are founded upon approaches which unavoidably overlook the potentiality of technologically facilitated terrorist actions. Thus, dissection of traditional definitions of terrorism and other sorts of criminal behavior is not simply an intellectual exercise; rather, it is an essential component for the evolution of social constructions of reality which are not necessarily defined by situational characteristics.

Traditional Definitions of Cyberterrorism

Although discussions of "cyberterrorism" as a concept have exploded in recent years, a universal operationalization of the phenomenon has not.[2] Rather, the dissonance surrounding notions of traditional terrorism has been exacerbated by the introduction of new approaches, constructs, and theaters in a borderless, intangible environment. In fact, definitions are widely disparate and range from the general to the specific. The term has been used to include actions as varied as: attacks on information systems, incitement to violence, theft of data, and the planning of terrorist attacks (Foltz 2004). For the most part, however, definitions maintain foundational elements which require attacks on computer systems which result in physical violence. To wit, Denning's testimony before Congress stated:

> Cyberterrorism is the convergence of terrorism and cyberspace. It is generally understood to mean unlawful attacks and threats of attack against computers, networks, and the information stored therein when done to intimidate or coerce a government or its people in furtherance of political or social objectives. Further, to qualify as cyberterrorism, an attack should result in violence against persons or property, or at least cause enough harm to generate fear. Attacks that lead to death or bodily injury, explosions, plane crashes, water contamination, or severe economic loss would be examples. Serious attacks against critical infrastructures could be acts of cyberterrorism, depending on their impact. Attacks that disrupt nonessential services or that are mainly a costly nuisance would not (Denning 2000).

---

2. It must be noted that the operationalization of other technologically facilitated political or social action has been equally disparate. While space and time constraints preclude a comprehensive discussion of such here, it is sufficient to state that "hacktivism" may be defined as "the act of computer trespass to achieve or advance political causes" (Britz 2009); and "netwar" may be defined as "conflict (and crime) at societal levels where the protagonists rely on network forms of organization, and related doctrines, strategies, and technologies" (Ronfeldt and Martinez 1997). Neither may be considered "cyberterrorism," as the former involves peaceful, social resistance and the latter involves actions by government entities.

Similarly, Pollitt (1998) defined cyberterrorism as the "premeditated, politically motivated attack against information, computer systems, and data which result in violence against noncombatant targets by subnational groups." The identification of particular target populations necessarily precluded government entities as terrorist actors. As a result, Foltz (2004) concluded that:

> Cyberterrorism is an attack or threat of an attack, politically motivated, intended to: interfere with the political, social, or economic functioning of a group, organization, or country; or induce either physical violence or the unjust use of power; or in conjunction with a more traditional terrorist action.

Operationalizing Cyberterrorism as a Multipurpose Tool

While Foltz (2004) effectively synthesized traditional notions of cyberterrorism, it must be noted that neither fear nor violence should be preponderant in the conceptualization of cyberterrorism. In fact, both are equally important, worthy of discourse, and must be incorporated into emergent terminology or inquiry. For operationalization purposes, fear may be defined as a strong emotion caused by an awareness of vulnerability or an anticipation of danger. It is individually perceived and contingent upon situational characteristics. Violence, on the other hand, may be characterized as an intentional force which is exerted to inflict damage or abuse on living things or physical objects. While terrorists may use violence to affect fear within a population, their primary objective remains political, ideological, or social change. In fact, both concepts are necessarily dependent upon the cultural expectations and values of the selected audience.

Generally speaking, terrorism may be characterized as a theater—a stage in which the audience is far more important than the actors. While it was originally conceptualized that the invocation of fear was best achieved through displays of catastrophic physical destruction to human life, it must be recognized that the impact of such demonstrations are necessarily related to the particular target's prioritization and sensitization of same. It can be argued that in some societies, perception of situational or potential victimization may significantly lessen or even negate the impact of a particular event. In addition, cultural values or beliefs may heighten fear or perceptions of vulnerability in the aftermath of a terrorist incident which might otherwise be characterized as insignificant or having minimal impact on another society. Consequently, a violent act causing significant loss of life in one culture may result in an equivalent level of fear as a disruption in the communications or economic system of another. For example, the Russian cyberattacks in Estonia were particularly significant as the country has long been characterized as the European leader of web-based banking, commerce, and communication. Regardless of the mechanism of harm, actions taken to facilitate either physical or virtual attacks are appropriately designated as terrorism. Indeed, cyberterrorism may be conceptualized as a technological extension of traditional definitions of terrorism, which recognizes that fear and violence are neither interchangeable, nor inevitable, components.

Although the former director of the Central Intelligence Agency (CIA) articulated in 1996 the recognition that political or ideological extremists may use the Internet to communicate and facilitate attacks on both physical and virtual structures, government and academic entities have steadfastly refused to incorporate both into formal definitions of cyberterrorism (Conway 2010). Instead, conceptualizations and subsequent discussions have focused almost exclusively on the web as a mechanism of attack. While recent activities like the Russian cyberattacks and the Stuxnet worm have certainly demonstrated the capacity of the medium in this regard, an analysis of web usage by terrorists indicates that extremist organizations are more likely to use the Internet as a facilitator as opposed to a trigger (Kohlmann 2006; Rogan 2006). Such actions include, but are not limited to: propaganda, information dissemination, recruitment, training, communication, research and planning, criminal activities and money laundering, and, of course, mechanism of attack. Thus, "cyberterrorism" may be defined as:

> the premeditated, methodological, ideologically motivated dissemination of information, facilitation of communication, or, attack against physical targets, digital information, computer systems, and/or computer programs which is intended to cause social, financial, physical, or psychological harm to noncombatant targets and audiences for the purpose of affecting ideological, political, or social change; or any utilization of digital communication or information which facilitates such actions directly or indirectly (Britz, 2009, 40).

Propaganda, Information Dissemination, and Recruitment

Without question, the introduction of the Internet has both globalized and revolutionized communication systems, knowledge acquisition, and commercial enterprise. In addition, the increasing accessibility and availability of the medium represents a method of empowerment in class-based systems in which information and commerce are regulated by formal structures. Such interconnectivity and anonymity has also resulted in a virtual renaissance in which intellectual and ideological discourse has flourished. At the same time, it has created a forum in which extremists communicate, conduct research, and promote their agendas.

The propagandizing of ideologies and activities has long been recognized as fundamental to both the maximization of fear among the target audience and the longevity and growth of the organization itself. Throughout much of the second half of the twentieth century, the mechanisms for dissemination have included self-published documents, word of mouth, and homemade videos. Such methods required significant financial expenditures, and posed considerable risk of identification. However, increases in technology have minimized both. Ideologues and jihadists have embraced the medium as the primary platform to stage their campaign of terror—effectively using it to enhance perceptions of vulnerability and to promote their rhetoric to a global community. In fact, usage of the Internet has become a staple in jihadist training and formally championed by terrorist leaders. A statement posted on www.assam.com urged extremists to use the web to disseminate news and information about jihad, stating, "the more Web sites, the better it is for us. We must make the Internet our tool." (Weimann et al. 2008, 884) Ironically, al-Qaeda and other organizations are increasingly using American ISPs, and exploiting the protections afforded under both the First and Fourth Amendments to the Constitution of the United States (Ahituv 2008).

The utilization of the technological medium for recruitment and propaganda is not new among religious zealots or political extremists. Leaders of neo-Nazi and supremacist groups in the United States, like Tom Metzger, embraced the medium in the 1980s to recruit college-aged members (Grennan et al. 2005). Using generational images, humor, and content, the White Aryan Resistance (WAR) effectively broadened its appeal and increased membership rolls. In fact, the increase in American hate groups in the 1990s was directly related to the use of online recruitment and propaganda (Crilley 2001). Today, all active terrorist groups maintain organizational websites irrespective of their ideological orientation or physical location (Weimann et al. 2008). These groups include, by global region: *Asia*—al-Qaeda, Aum Shinrikyo, the Japanese Red Army (JRA), the Islamic Movement of Uzbekistan, and the Liberation Tigers of Tamil Eelam (LTTE); *Europe*—the Basque ETA movement and Armata Corsa (the Corsican Army); *Latin America*—Shining Path, Colombia National Liberation Army (ELN), and the Armed Revolutionary Forces of Colombia (FARC); *Middle East*—Hamas, Lebanese Hezbollah, the Popular

Front for the Liberation of Palestine (PLFP), the Kurdish Workers' Party (PKK), People's Mujahedin of Iran (PMOI), and Mujahedin-e-Khalq.

Many of the above listed groups maintain multiple sites and make them available in different languages. However, the prevalence or exact accounting of online terrorist/extremist sites does not lend itself to traditional empirical research for a variety of reasons. These reasons include, but are not limited to: technological portability, filter configurations, alternative spellings or designations, absence of translational context, etc. This is true of research on both domestic and international groups. Prevalence notwithstanding, the mechanisms employed and the messages communicated may be evaluated for both content and consistency. Terrorists use the Internet to propagandize their actions and ideologies to recruit new members, justify their actions, and to evoke fear within a specific population.

Similar to their physical counterparts, online terrorist sites construct a rationalization frame through which their aggressive tactics are made palatable to a broad audience. While justifications range from patriotism to divinity, all include the vilification of a particular group, and all demonstrate adaptability. Such bastardization characterizes the group's actions as self-defensive—a necessary byproduct in their campaign for universal principles and humanity. Thus, the insurgent becomes the purveyor of truth and justice, and the soldier or citizen becomes a representative of the malevolent warmongers. Ironically, these strategies often appeal to the very victims of their terrorist acts. To wit:

> This year, the Nobel Prize Committee in Sweden awarded the Peace Prize to Obama while he was in the White House for less than ten days before the nomination deadline. Ironically, the committee chose him among 205 candidates to win the prize—still less for any concrete accomplishments but for his inspirational words. It is a pity that he will now receive the prize after the announcement of the troop surge for Afghanistan. This year, USA launched vast military operations in Helmand in South Afghanistan. Ten thousand American troops and almost the same number of British troops participated in the operations named Sword and Panther's claws. They killed hundreds of innocent Afghans during the most trumpeted operations, the largest ever after the Vietnam War.
> As for the Afghans, they did not expect Obama, a Nobel peace prize winner, to flare up the war in the country. Nor would Alfred Nobel ever have agreed to give a peace prize to a person who is fanning the flames of war rather than spreading fraternity and peace ... It seems, the peace prize winner Obama is trying to implement the expansionist policy left to him as a legacy by W. Bush.

The aim of the Mujahedeen is to have a free and independent country and Islamic government which represents the aspirations of the
Afghan people ... But the so-called advocates of democracy and human
rights are not ready to give these natural rights to the Afghans ...
Washington turns down the constructive proposal of the leadership
of Mujahedeen who ... will ensure that the next government of the
Mujahedeen will not meddle in the internal affairs of other countries,
including the neighbors, if foreign troops pull out of Afghanistan ...
Thousands of innocent Afghans have been killed ... the invading Americans have focused ... their conduct ... war seem(s) more like ... a
cleansing campaign ... Those with free conscience living anywhere in
the world should come forward and defend their shared values of humanity which are being violated by an imperialist power insatiably
extending its tentacles over countries of the world.

This statement, issued by the Islamic Emirate of Afghanistan (i.e., the Taliban)
and posted on a variety of sites sympathetic to the group, clearly characterizes
the United States as an invading army. This statement and those similar in content have been published in a variety of venues, including, but not limited to:
official organizational websites (e.g., www.alemarah.info/english/), blog spots
(e.g., http://al-tawbah.blogspot.com; http://supporttaliban.blogspot.com), media
outlets (e.g., www.afghanvoice.com), social networking sites (e.g., www.face-
book.com; www.myspace.com), and community forums (e.g., www.scribd.com).
    Statements of justification are often accompanied by visual aids which fur-
ther the illusion of victimization. Depictions of dead children, destroyed villages, and weeping mothers are used to evoke a collective anger of the populace,
an element which is essential to organizational longevity and growth. In April
of 2004, anti-American extremists across the world were handed the equivalent of the golden ring when images from Abu Ghraib were aired on an American news program. Within hours, these images were posted on websites across
the world. These photos appeared to show the use of torture and humiliation
against Arabic prisoners. Without exception, the global community condemned
both the soldiers involved and the Bush administration, arguing that such
treatment was made more reprehensible due to the country's democratic foun-
dations. While all of the images provided fodder for terrorist organizations
across the globe, the images depicting piles of naked detainees and female soldiers with unclothed male inmates were used to demonstrate America's apathy to the cultural values and religious obligations of others. In fact, the photos
were used to portray the United States as inherently anti-Middle Eastern and
anti-Islamic. Thus, both political and religious terrorist organizations benefitted

from the widely available images. Political groups employed the visual aids to further the illusion of victimization, and religious groups used them to solidify their divination as the chosen ones.

As previously stated, propaganda is a necessary component of any terrorist organization for both longevity and growth. The contextual presentation of such information is necessarily related to the intention of the poster. Lines of justification or rationales are more essential for the recruitment and retention of members within political terrorist organizations. Downplaying the harm suffered by innocents and making their rhetoric and propaganda available in multiple languages appeals to many in the global community and increases the potential for cooperation between multinational individuals. Jihadists, on the other hand, openly embrace and promote the human suffering of noncombatants. Depicting themselves not as victims but as martyrs, such organizations glorify violence as divine ordination. Two of al-Qaeda's most visible leaders, Abu Musab al-Zarqawi and Khalid Sheikh Mohammed, successfully used the medium to transmit the videotaped beheadings of contractor Nick Berg and journalist Daniel Pearl (Gunaratna 2004; Heuston 2005). Both of these videos continue to have global implications outside the boundaries of the viewing audience and continue to be used for recruitment and to induce terror.

The terrorist capital which is expended in the production and promotion of the recorded assassinations of both Americans is relatively insignificant compared to the impact on the global audience. Both films, designed to incite religious fervor among believers, were similarly intended to create terror among those identified as the enemy. This type of propaganda tactic is more effective than traditional methods as both the gruesomeness and the accessibility of the images conjoin to create an environment in which the film eludes containment and the viewing itself becomes irrelevant. Indeed, the psychological and cultural weight afforded these depictions are far greater than those displayed in traditional venues, as they intrude upon those self-identified safe zones (i.e., private homes or areas shared with loved ones) (Heuston 2006). Thus, the Internet as a means for inciting fear cannot be overlooked, as it reinforces perceptions of vulnerability through self-propagation.

Videos and creative images have also been employed to enhance recruitment practices. While traditional practices still exist, the introduction of the Internet has enabled terrorists to extend their organizational reach to diverse populations and geographically distant locales. This is especially true as these groups target younger generations. Similar to Metzger's use of music and popular culture in the development of WAR, contemporary jihadists have developed assorted videos which use rap music to communicate extremist ideology. *Dirty Kuffar*, released on the Internet in 2004 by Sheikh Terra and the Soul

Salah Crew, was the first widely circulated video of this sort. The video opens with the Title, "Dirty Kuffar Murder Iraqi Civilian," prefacing what appears to be a CNN report of an American soldier bragging about killing an innocent Iraqi citizen. Although the majority of the rap is difficult to understand, clever editing and the superimposition of images clarify the meaning of the film. Various world leaders are vilified, and Vladimir Putin is characterized as George W. Bush's "lapdog." The power of the video cannot be overstated; the flow of images and the relationships inferred clearly justify the use of violence against infidels. Although jihad is encouraged against assorted nations, including Great Britain and Russia, the video focuses on the killing of Americans and ends with a listing of countries which they claim have been "Victims of U.S. Violence Since 1945."[3]

Since the release of *Dirty Kuffar*, "djihad" (i.e., digital jihad) has experienced exponential growth. While many of these videos may be viewed or downloaded from official terrorist sites, most have been uploaded to popular video sharing or social networking sites, like www.islamicvideos.net, www.YouTube.com, www.metacafe.com, www.MySpace.com, www.orkut.com, and www.Facebook.com. To further broaden their appeal, they are available in multiple languages and cultural contexts. By identifying unique social icons and historical tensions specific to a particular audience, propagandists can effectively target those social groups most predisposed to extremist ideology. A video of the song "By Any Means Necessary,"[4] by Sheikh Terra and Soul Salah Crew, targets young, black males in the United States. From the onset of the opening credits, it is apparent that the filmmakers wish to incite anger among this population by displaying images of racial hatred in the 1960s superimposed with the atrocities of Abu Graib. Unlike the messages in *Dirty Kuffar*, which include Shiekh Terra dancing with a gun, the presentation of images and the inference of relationships are more subtle. This approach is more palatable to Americans, as it enables them to perceive their actions as defensive and necessary as opposed to aggressive and hostile. Towards this end, a portion of Malcolm X's Grass Roots Speech, from 1963, prefaces the video:

> There's nothing in our book the Qur'an, as you call it Koran, that teaches us to suffer peacefully. Our religion teaches us to be intelli-

---

3. Copies of this video may be found on YouTube and GoogleVideos under the title *Dirty Kuffar*.

4. Copies of this video may also be found on YouTube and GoogleVideos under the title *By Any Means Necessary by Sheikh Terra*.

gent. Be peaceful, be courteous, obey the law, respect everyone, but
if someone puts his hand on you, send him to the cemetery (Malcolm
X, the Grass Roots speech, November 1963, Detroit).

Verbalizations throughout the video remain consistent with the specter of op-
pression and marginalization. This medium of communication is successful
in the indoctrination of individuals, as it breaks down psychological barriers
to involvement (O'Rourke 2007). A 2008 study revealed that the vast majority of individuals accessing this type of content are between the ages of 18 to
34 and are most likely to be located in either the United States or the United
Kingdom (Conway and McInerney 2008).

In August 2011, President Barack Obama, in a public White House statement, formally recognized the threat posed by the technological proliferation
of violent extremist propaganda. To wit:

> Radicalization that leads to violent extremism includes the diffusion
> of ideologies and narratives that feed on grievances, assign blame, and
> legitimize the use of violence against those deemed responsible. We must
> actively and aggressively counter the range of ideologies violent ex-
> tremist employ to radicalize and recruit individuals ... Towards this
> end, we will continue to closely monitor the important role the In-
> ternet and social networking sites play in advancing violent extrem-
> ist narratives. We protect our communities from a variety of online
> threats, such as sexual predators ... we are using a similar approach
> to thwart violent extremists (Obama 2011).

Summarily, the Internet is increasingly employed as the medium of choice
for terrorist propaganda, information dissemination, and recruitment. As
amorphous or fluid networks increasingly define contemporary terrorist groups,
the use of technology provides an ideal environment for the globalization of
extremist rhetoric. Logistical and financial impediments are minimized, and
propaganda and recruitment strategies can be easily modified to include par-
ticularized social icons and cultural boundaries. The explosion of social networking and video sharing sites has further proliferated terrorist propaganda
and all but negated the need for a formal organizational website. This is critical to their continued development, as official sites are often hacked or blocked
by ISP's at the government's request. For example, internet service providers
in the United Kingdom are required to "take down" jihadist sites, so that they
are no longer accessible (Goth 2008). While First Amendment considerations
preclude such government censorship in the United States, many ISPs in the
country voluntarily remove jihadist material. After the U.S. named al-Awlaki,

the mastermind behind the attempted Times Square bombing, "a specially designated global terrorist," both Google and YouTube took down hundreds of his propagandist videos. In fact, both sites denounce "hate speech" and "incitement to violence" in their community guidelines (i.e., www.youtube.com/t/community_guidelines and http://support.google.com/places/bin/answer.py?hl=en&answer=176519).

The Internet as a Medium of Communication

In addition to using the Internet to disseminate propaganda, terrorist organizations are increasingly using the web as a means of communication. Online dialogue is cheaper, international in scope, more widely accessible, and poses far less risk of discovery or interception than traditional methods. In fact, the global interconnectivity of the Internet has proven invaluable to extremists, as was evidenced when al-Qaeda members went into hiding in the wake of September 11. As Hamid Mir reported, laptops and Kalashnikovs were among the few possessions that individuals transported as they fled (Britz 2009). Ironically, the Taliban, who have traditionally eschewed such technology, are now embracing it as a means of communication (Giustozzi 2008).

As stated previously, terrorist organizations in the 21st century have evolved from hierarchical structures to less centralized, cell based networks. This amorphous approached more effectively insulates members from detection and protects the organization as a whole and is made plausible due to advancements in communication technology and the borderless nature of the Internet. In 2001, Krebs (2001a) used social network metrics to establish that all nineteen of the 9/11 hijackers were within two degrees of two terrorist suspects identified more than a year prior to the attacks. Much of their communications in the final stages of planning were facilitated through online chat rooms.[5]

In the days preceding his capture, Ramzi Binal-Shibh, the alleged 20th hijacker and former roommate of Mohammed Atta, granted an audio-taped interview to al-Jazeera. Throughout the interview, Binal-Shibh emphasized the importance of electronic communication and the decentralized nature of al-

---

5. Kreb's research on social networking may be found on his website, www.orgnet.com. In addition to his analysis on the hijackers of 9/11, Krebs has also used this approach to delineate relationships and networks of a variety of groups, including those in academia, politics, and sports.

Qaeda operations. He also revealed contents of online chats between himself and Atta in which Atta communicated:

> The first semester starts in three weeks. Nothing has changed. Every-thing is fine. There are good signs and encouraging ideas. Two high schools and two universities. Everything is going according to plan. This summer will surely be hot. I would like to talk to you about a few details. Nineteen certificates for private study and four exams. Re-gards to the professor. Goodbye (CNN 2002).

Discussing the utility of Internet communications, Binal-Shibh recognized the impossibility of monitoring all electronic exchanges and identifying all par-ticipants in a cell based conspiracy (CNN, 2002). Such weaknesses were fur-ther exploited by Younis Tsouli, a Pakistan-based terrorist who employed *Irhaby007* (i.e., Terrorist 007) as a screen name.

Arrested by Scotland Yard in 2007, Tsouli was responsible for the creation of a global virtual support network for terrorists in Bosnia, Denmark, Canada, and the United States. Towards this end, Tsouli used the terrorist web forum Muntada al-Ansar to: 1) propagate the terror induced by assorted videotaped be-headings, 2) claim responsibility for assorted attacks, 3) promote the mission and ideologies of al-Qaeda leader Abu Musab al-Zarqawi, 4) provide a secure mech-anism for online communication between operatives, and 5) disseminate train-ing videos. All of these methods were designed to facilitate situational awareness of Islamic extremists across the globe. As a propagandist, recruiter, and web-master, Tsouli effectively promoted the spread of violent jihad as evidenced by the convictions of two Atlanta men who were originally attracted to the ex-tremist rhetoric in their teens (FBI, 2009c). While both men, Ehsanul Sadequee and Syed Harris Ahmed, were arrested prior to the execution of a physical at-tack, their case illustrates the power of the Internet as a mechanism for com-puter mediated communication and information exchange. The decentralized, uncensored nature of the medium reaches across geographical boundaries and is creating a community of radical jihadists within American borders.

In October 2009, David Headley, a former drug trafficker and government informant, was arrested for conspiring to commit terrorist attacks in Denmark after the publication of cartoons offensive to many Muslims. A subsequent in-vestigation revealed that Headley had used online communications to further the extremism of Lashkar e Tayyiba (LeT), a Kashmiri separatist group who was responsible for the 2008 Mumbai terror attacks. Towards this end, Headley had conducted extensive surveillance and provided videos of various targeted locations in India, including the Nariman House, the Taj Mahal hotel, gov-ernment facilities, public transportation systems, and infrastructure facilities.

Prior to his arrest, Headley had communicated his commitment to radical Islam on various open boards, in chat rooms, and in electronic exchanges with friends. Such public posting is typically eschewed by operatives responsible for the collection and dissemination of mission-related information, as the effectiveness of the proposed operation is necessarily contingent upon the level of secrecy maintained. Indeed, terrorists often employ methods involving electronic dead drops, social networking sites, anonymizer software and sophisticated encryption to hinder detection of their pre-mission activities.

In late 2009, federal authorities continued to find evidence of the use of electronic dead drops in the furtherance of terrorist acts. On September 24, 2009, the Department of Justice reported that Najibullah Zazi, an American resident, was conspiring with others to detonate explosives in New York City. Towards this end, he had received bomb-making training in Pakistan, conducted extensive research on the Internet, and, purchased components necessary to produce TATP (Triacetone Triperoxide) and other peroxide-based explosives similar to those used to attack London's subway system. He communicated with other conspirators through the use of shared e-mail accounts, where he left documents in the "drafts" folder for retrieval by others. Both David Headley and the Madrid bombers also employed this technique, known as dead dropping. Theoretically, such methods facilitate asynchronous, anonymous communication and defeat electronic sniffers as the e-mails are never transmitted. Instead, co-conspirators use a single account and password to exchange information.[6] Terrorists further insulate themselves from surveillance and undercover operations through the use of encryption. In fact, ranking al-Qaeda members have been employing this technology for more than sixteen years. For example, Ramzi Yousef, the mastermind behind the 1993 World Trade Center bombings, employed encryption, as did the individuals who were responsible for the deaths of eighteen American soldiers in Somalia in the same year. Further examples of encrypted communications include, but are not limited to, the 1998 bombings in Africa and the attack on the U.S.S. *Cole* (Voors 2003). Such techniques can significantly hamper counter-terrorism efforts (Freeh 2001). As a result, federal authorities have petitioned the prohibition of sophisticated encryption software.[7] However, the practice continues unabated in both e-mail and social networking communications.

---

6. Confidential government sources indicate that such practices do not defeat electronic surveillance techniques as data is transmitted from a user (e.g. mbritz@hotmail.com) to a server account (e.g. Hotmail) irrespective of transmission to a third party.

7. While the debate between privacy advocates and the federal government continues, it must be noted that encryption is not an effective tool of concealment in cases where electronic surveillance software is employed.

As stated, the use of social networking sites as a mechanism for propaganda dissemination has been increasingly recognized by government authorities. However, the utility of this medium reaches far beyond the parameters of recruitment or sensationalization. In fact, popular sites like Yahoo!, MySpace, Second Life, *Orkut*, and Facebook provide for the use of invitation-only, online communities. While the majority of the resulting forums do not represent threats to national security, there exists a small minority which includes various groups comprised of terrorist sympathizers (Britz 2009). For example, there were at least 10 communities which advocated jihad against the United States (Denning 2009). Additional information available to identified members includes, but is not limited to: videos of terror attacks, photos of deceased American soldiers, recruitment solicitations, propaganda materials, and, most importantly in this discussion, secured means of communication.

The use of social networking sites by terrorists cannot be overstated. One of the first notable examples, *Orkut*, was originally established as an invitation-only social network and was popular among terrorist sympathizers and deviant subcultures. While it is still a favorite in both Brazil and India, searches for "al-Qaeda" and "global jihad" returned thousands of hits on both MySpace and Facebook. In December 2009, Howard University dental student Ramy Zamzam was arrested with four other Americans for suspected terrorist associations. Along with other terror suspects, Zamzam was a member of Facebook and had used the site to reach out to extremist groups in Pakistan. Such social networking sites provide extremists with a medium to identify and communicate with similarly inclined members. In the wake of his arrest, assorted Facebook groups and YouTube videos were posted which demonstrated their support.

Summarily, the Internet as a mode of communication has proven invaluable to contemporary terrorists. Online dialogue is cheaper, international in scope, more widely accessible, and poses far less risk than traditional methods. Like other netizens, radical jihadists increasingly rely on the technology for both social networking and communication. Websites, e-mail, chat rooms, and virtual message boards are all employed to recruit new members, propagandize actions, provide an electronic auditorium for organizational rhetoric, and secure their communications. Recent arrests indicate that utilization of the medium has proven successful in spreading radical jihad within the borders of the United States.

Training, Research, and Facilitation

The globalization of information has revolutionized the manner in which terrorists conduct both training and research. Like their predecessors, contemporary terrorists have demonstrated an ability to adopt training modules appropriate to both the resources available and the current technological landscape. While effective, methods of instruction for most of the 20th century were largely limited to jihadist encampments, training films, and text manuals. These approaches to training were expensive, and the impact of the subsequent attack was largely localized and small in scope. However, the globalization of communication, commerce, and information has provided an avenue for mass dissemination of rhetoric, propaganda, and instruction.

Just as corporations and organizations with legitimate goals have turned to web-based training to offset corporate downsizing and shrinking budgets, jihadists have maximized their available resources by employing the web and media enhancements to offer online tutorials to geographically distant participants. As such, web-based learning is presented in a variety of formats and languages. In keeping with the media-centric culture of contemporary society, much of this content is available in the form of AVI or MPEG files; however, textual communications, like checklists and outlines, are still available. Terrorist videos or documents cover topics ranging from tactical operations (e.g., bomb making, use of surface-to-air missiles, assembling a suicide vest, etc.) to research (e.g., data mining, public information sites, etc.) to hacking (e.g., social engineering, unauthorized access, Trojans, etc.) to facilitation (e.g., creation of fraudulent identification, transfer of funds, money laundering, etc.). Such materials and information are circulated by the same methods as those previously discussed, but the synergy created by the marriage of extremist social networking and video sharing websites has created a self-propagating phenomenon.

A solo search of YouTube.com revealed a significant number of videos devoted to "terrorist training" (n=3,340), "bomb making instructions" (n=743), "bomb making tutorials" (n=3,370), "make explosives" (n=13,600), and "how to make explosives at home" (n=840). A random viewing of each category reveals an assortment of news reports, spoofs, and, instructional videos. The sheer volume of material presented and the dynamic nature of the medium render empirical analysis impractical. Thus, evaluation of alternative avenues, government actions, and court transcripts is increasingly important. Such sources indicate that the popularity of such searches suggests an unprecedented interest in such material, but that official training videos are most often located on organizational websites. However, the greatest utility of the Internet in terms of training may be found in the information contained on seemingly innocuous sites, such as those that were used by a variety of the individuals previously mentioned. In addition, Mohamed Atta used both flight simulator software and computer games via the Internet to prepare for flight training (Hamilton 2004).

A solo Google search for "how do I make TATP" returned over 25,000 hits from a variety of sites. Of the first ten hits returned, at least four (i.e., globalsecurity.org, en.wikipedia.org, wiki.answers.com, and askville.amazon.com) of them gave detailed, easy-to-follow instructions. The same search on Bing returns over 17,000 hits. Of the first ten hits returned, three provided the same type of instructions, including two from en.wikipedia.org and one from scribd.com. A subsequent search for "how do I make cyanide" returned over two million hits on Google and 780,000 on Bing. Of the first 10 hits, detailed instructions were found on Google (5) and Bing (2). In addition, two of the first ten hits on Bing provided information on where to buy cyanide. In 2009, federal authorities revealed that Ali al-Marri had been conducting extensive research on the manufacturing of cyanide gas in an al-Qaeda plot to release the gas in dams, waterways, and tunnels in the United States (FBI 2009d). Additional evidence recovered from al-Marri's computer included anonymizer and wiping software programs. Finally, the government uncovered various fraudulent identities and credit card and social security numbers. Al-Marri played a pivotal support role in the Terror Attacks in NYC, and was actively involved in online communications with Khalid Sheikh Mohammed and other al-Qaeda leaders.

In addition to training and research, the Internet has also proven to be a critical component in pre-mission planning and coordination. For example, the al-Qaeda hijackers used the Internet to evaluate flight schedules and purchase at least nine of the plane tickets on 9/11. In December 2008, Ahmed Ansari, a conspirator in the Mumbai attacks, claimed that he had been shown satellite images of targeted locations, including the Taj Mahal hotel. Downloaded from Google Earth, these images were employed in the attacks that killed more than 160 people. An India High Court is considering whether Google has a responsibility to censor such information. Other countries have also expressed concern, asking the company to blur certain images. A search of Google Earth for satellite images indicated that such information was available without exception and without obfuscation. Additional information provided by the site included: surrounding areas, labels, topical maps, and driving directions. These include, but are not limited to: *Executive Residences*: U.S. White House (U.S.); Camp David (U.S.); 10 Downing Street (Great Britain); Great Kremlin Palace (Russia); The Lodge (Australia); and The Vatican. *Government Buildings*: U.S. Pentagon (U.S.). Northwood Headquarters (Great Britain). *Nuclear Facilities*: Paducah Gaseous Diffusion Plant (U.S.); Sandia National Laboratory (U.S.); and Siberian Chemical Combine (Russia).

Terrorist groups also use the Internet to commit criminal activities to further their mission and to supplement the funding they receive from organizational supporters. According to a recent report to Congress,

> cybercrime has now surpassed international drug trafficking as a terrorist financing enterprise. Internet Ponzi schemes, identity theft, counterfeiting, and other types of computer fraud have been shown to yield high profits under a shroud of anonymity ... terrorists and extremists.... May be increasingly collaborating with cybercriminals for the international movement of money and for the smuggling of arms and illegal drugs (Theohary and Rollins 2011).

In fact, money laundering, identity fraud, theft of proprietary data, narcotics trafficking and hacking are but a few of the activities employed by jihadists. Identity theft and the creation of fraudulent forms of identification have been noted in all acts of recent terrorist activity directed at the United States. For example, each of the suicide bombers involved in the Terror Attacks had established fraudulent identities. The documentation included, but was not limited to: stolen credit cards, fictitious or temporary addresses, passports, and driver's licenses. Identity theft is beneficial to these organizations in a variety of ways as it may grant them access to protected data, allow travel to and within a particular geographic location, and provide an environment free from government scrutiny. While there are a variety of ways to create fraudulent identification, much of this is done with information received from data mining or computer hacking, both of which are included in training curriculum (Hamilton 2004).

As an Attack Vector

Traditionally, both the academic and practitioner communities repudiated the notion that the Internet could be employed as a mechanism through which a terrorist act could be affected. Based on the premise that the measure of effectiveness was necessarily contingent upon catastrophic loss of life, a collective rejection effectively chilled any inquiry into the possibility, creating a level of apathy in both communities. It must be noted that such conceptualizations are inherently flawed as they are based on the assumption that fear and vulnerability are universally constructed. As stated previously, reactions to performances and events are defined by cultural values and expectations. In order to affect social change via a physical or cyber attack, terrorist groups must focus on those elements which define and sustain a given society.

While the Internet has become a conduit through which to globalize the impact of a geographically distant act, it can be argued that the impact of any given event is affected by both the cultural expectations and the normalcy of the image to the targeted audience. Thus, the inducement of fear in some areas may require a more substantial or extraordinary demonstration of loss than others. For example, the Sbarro restaurant bombing in Jerusalem[8] and the Beslan[9] massacre, both of which occurred in areas accustomed to terrorist incidents, were considered significant by observers primarily due to the selection of targets traditionally deemed off limits. In Jerusalem, the bombing occurred at a popular intersection where teenagers and families were known to congregate. In Beslan, the seizing of School Number One was particularly significant as it occurred on First September, a day of great celebration where families accompanied their children to school. Both incidents resulted in immediate government actions. In Jerusalem, Israeli authorities forced the closure of the PLO's east Jerusalem headquarters. In Russia, government reforms included the consolidation of power within the Kremlin. The swift reaction of both governments is similar to that of federal authorities in the United States. In each case, it can be argued that the reaction of formal government structures demonstrates the abnormality of the terrorist act.

Founded on capitalist principals, there are critical complex networks which both define and sustain the United States. These include: financial markets, commerce and capitalism, transportation, and communications. The selection of targets on 9/11 was based on knowledge of American culture and was both deliberate and methodical. The attacks on the World Trade Center were a deliberate attempt to strike at the foundation of the country. Targeting the Pentagon and the White House, al-Qaeda attempted to display the vulnerability of both our government and our military. It can be argued that the group chose unwisely due to their superficial understanding of American culture. The symbolism of their targets was not entirely understood or appreciated by the intended audience. In addition, the existence of alternate facilities for data, information, and computer equipment minimized the damage to financial markets, and the physical security of future targets has been improved.

While the attacks of 9/11 were not successful in creating and maintaining perceptions of vulnerability, it is possible that a major disruption of the financial market or a significant threat to quality of life could create a sense of unrest or fear within a capitalist population. Such occurrences could be pred-

---

8. Additional information regarding the Sbarro bombing and resulting government actions may be located at the Israel Ministry of Foreign Affairs, www.mfa.gov.il.

9. For additional information on the Beslan massacre, see Giduck (2005).

icated on a compromise of digital systems in two areas: physical infrastructure and critical data. Digital threats to the physical infrastructure would be those that involve systems essential to physical infrastructures. These would include power grids, water and sewer systems, dams, hospitals, communications, GPS, air traffic systems, etc. Critical data threats would be those that involved the compromise of critical databases including, but not limited to Social Security, Centers for Disease Control, Department of Defense, etc. (Britz 2009). In fact, the tight coupling and feedback loops which characterize the architecture of the Internet result in an unsound and unsecure infrastructure. While projections that the Internet will replace traditional physical attacks have not been realized, recent events across the globe suggest that concentrated and/or protracted cyberattacks may result in significant disruptions to communication and financial networks.

In April of 2007, websites across Estonia were crippled as a result of a coordinated distributed denial of service (DDoS) attack. The attacks, sparked by the relocation of a Soviet-era war memorial, were largely directed at government and financial sites. In a country that is 97% dependent on Internet banking, the unsophisticated attacks were extremely effective and were a clear indication that concentrated attacks on government and banking sites could be used to substantially disrupt a targeted population (Espiner 2008). Later attacks on other Soviet satellites, like those experienced by Lithuania, Georgia, and Kyrgyzstan, further demonstrated the viability, or perception thereof, of concerted cyberattacks against government and financial resources (Ashmore 2009). In fact, Russia, or Russian sympathizers, effectively used botnet armies as strategic multipliers throughout the 2008 Russian-Georgian war. Among the DDoS attacks that were launched against Georgian media and government sites, one commercial grade botnet effectively disabled communications between the government and its people. Initially, speculation blamed the Russian government for the attacks against the former Soviet satellites. However, the individual or institutional perpetrators have never been conclusively identified.

In June of 2010, reports surfaced that a highly sophisticated self-replicating worm program was targeting industrial processes computers across the globe. Appropriately characterized as a military-grade cyber missile, Stuxnet was the first known malware designed to effectuate the hijacking of programmable logic controllers (PLC) which are utilized by facilities ranging from industrial factories to electric power plants. By 2011, the work had infected more than 60,000 computers in Iran, India, Indonesia, China, Azerbaijan, Malaysia, South Korea, Finland, Germany, Australia, the United Kingdom, and the United States (Farwell and Rohozinski 2011). Post-infection analysis suggested that Iran was the primary focus of the attack, as the worm targeted Windows operating systems with specific configurations of PLC software such as those used in Iran's Bushehr nuclear power plant and Natanz uranium enrichment facility (Porteous 2010: Farwell et al. 2011). The complexity of the worm was immediately apparent in the one-two process of its design.

The first component of the Stuxnet worm attacked the nuclear centrifuges by manipulating PLC computer commands sent to the frequency converter drives. By alternating extreme speeds, the worm interfered with the normal operation of the industrial control process. Over time, such alterations would also cause the machine to combust or burst. Towards this end, Stuxnet deceived security by substituting prerecorded images of normal operations. This second component was essential as it concealed the fact that the centrifuges were sabotaging themselves. Although it remains unclear as to the extent of the damage caused to Iran's nuclear capabilities, it appears that the worm was originally introduced to a single USB port in Iran. (Such methods of infection are increasingly common on isolated networks lacking interconnectivity.)

Recent evidence indicates that the US government was responsible for the creation and implementation of this malware in the wild (Sanger 2012). In fact, it appears to have been developed under the Bush administration but activated and approved for use under President Obama. Thus, the role of nation states in cyberattacks confounds the investigation and prosecution of responsible parties. The first issue lies in the masking techniques involved that make it difficult to prove individual or state culpability. Such subterfuge is not simply a byproduct of an amalgam of technological sophistication and multiple contributors; rather, the ambiguity is deliberately cultivated as a means of self-preservation. The public posting of malware source codes and the subsequent alteration and evolution of programs serve to obfuscate the original etiology, and both states and individuals remain insulated behind the cloud. In the unlikely event that an individual state actor could be definitively linked to a particular attack against another, the lack of a universally accepted definition of cyberterrorism makes the next step in the progression of justice unclear. Theoretically, recourse of victimized states is likely to be dependent upon the justifiability of the actions undertaken by the accused nation. Unfortunately, the UN Charter is relatively ill-defined in this regard, and interpretations of proportional response to avoid collateral damage, which justify the right to wage war, are entirely subjective. In reality, reactions in the global community are likely to be mediated by the relative power of the states involved—a lesson learned by Estonia as their efforts to invoke collective self-defense under Article V of the North Atlantic Treaty was rejected (Farwell et al. 2011).

Conclusions

Historically, the conceptualization of terrorism by both ideologues and observers necessitated physical displays of catastrophic destruction. Firmly rooted in the belief that evidence of damage to physical structures and the loss of human life were intrinsically related to the measure of operational effectiveness, discussions of and reactions to ideologically and/or politically motivated attacks have almost exclusively concentrated on the corporeal vulnerability of potential targets. While incidents like the Russian cyberattacks and Stuxnet demonstrate the paramount importance of the protection of physical infrastructures, analytical, policy, and operational communities must recognize the potentiality of the Internet in the furtherance of political, religious, or ideological extremism. Such implications for web utilization include, but are not limited to: medium of communication; dissemination of information; propagandizing of ideology; platform for recruitment; environment for fundraising; and, mechanism of both cyber and physical attacks. As such, "cyberterrorism" should be defined as "the premeditated, methodological, ideologically motivated dissemination of information, facilitation of communication, or, attack against physical targets, digital information, computer systems, and/or computer programs which is intended to cause social, financial, physical, or psychological harm to noncombatant targets and audiences for the purpose of affecting ideological, political, or social change; or any utilization of digital communication or information which facilitates such actions directly or indirectly" (Britz 2009, 40).

While the portended digital apocalypse has not been witnessed, evidence suggests that terrorist organizations are increasingly utilizing web-based technology to communicate, plan, propagandize, recruit, and finance their operations. Unfortunately, traditional definitions of the phenomenon, relying exclusively on the web as a mechanism, obfuscated these activities. As a result, both private and public awareness of the potentiality of web facilitation must be reconsidered. Policymakers must develop legislation that addresses all of these areas and which specifically recognizes the globalization of financial and communications systems. It is anticipated that such recognition will result in significant modifications to investigative strategies and prosecutions. Opportunities for academic inquiry are boundless and will continue to grow in pace with technology. Some possible areas include: the evolution of organizational ideology and the social framing of online rhetoric, the level of indoctrination and/or individual commitment of online recruits, the nature and growth of grassroots organizations, the operational effectiveness of netcentric relative to physical cells, and the architecture of terror via social networking analysis.

References

Ahituv, Niv. "Old Threats, New Channels: the Internet as a tool for terrorists." NATO Workshop, Berlin (2008).

Altheide, David L. "Terrorism and the politics of fear." *Cultural Studies and Critical Methodologies 6* (2006): 415–439.

Anti-Defamation League (ADL) "Jihad Online: Islamic terrorists and the Internet," (2000): www.adl.org/internet.jihad_online.pdf.

Ashmore, William C. "Impact of alleged Russian cyber attacks." Monograph submitted to School of Advanced Military Studies, United States Army Command and General Staff College (2009).

Bardis, Panos D. "Violence: Theory and Quantification." In George A. Kourvetaris and Betty A. Dobratz, *Political Readings in Research and Theory* (pgs. 221–244), Amsterdam, New Holland: Transaction Books (1980).

Bergen, Peter. *The Osama bin Laden I know: An oral history of al Qaeda's leader.* New York: Free Press (2006).

Bowman, M.E. "Is International Law Ready for the Information Age?" *Fordham International Law Journal 19* (1995): 1935.

Brachman, Jarrett M. "High-tech terror: Al-Qaeda's use of new technology," *The Fletcher* Britz, Marjie T., *Computer Forensics and Cybercrime* (2nd edition). New Jersey: Prentice-Hall, (2009).

Britz, Marjie T. "A new paradigm of organized crime in the United States: Criminal syndicates, cyber-gangs, and the worldwide web," *Sociology Focus 2* (2008): 1750–1765.

Britz, Marjie T., *Computer Forensics and Cybercrime* (2nd Edition). New Jersey: Prentice-Hall, (2009).

Bunt, Gary. *Islam in the Digital Age: E-jihad, online fatwas and cyber Islamic environments.* London: Pluto Books. (2003).

Chiricos, Ted, Sarah Escholz, and Marc Gertz. "Crime, news and fear of crime: Toward an identification of audience effects," *Social Problems 44* (1997): 342–357.

Choo, Kim-Kwang Raymond and Russell G. Smith. "Criminal exploitation of online systems by organised crime groups."*Asian Criminology 3* (2008): 37–59.

Claburn, Thomas. "DOD says cyber attacks may mean war." *InformationWeek* (2011). Retrieved on 24 January 2012 from www.informationweek.com.

Collin, Barry. "Future of cyberterrorism: The physical and virtual worlds converge," *Crime and Justice International 13* (1997): 15–18.

Conner, Maura and Lisa McInerney. "Jihadi video and auto-radicalisation: Evidence from an exploratory YouTube study." *Lecture Notes in Computer Science 5376* (2008): 108–118.

CNN, "Al-Jazeera offers accounts of 9/11 planning," (September 12, 2002): http://archives.cnn.com/2002/WORLD/meast/09/12/alqaeda.911.claim/index.html.

Crilley, Kathy. "Information warfare: New battlefields, terrorists, propaganda and the Internet," *Aslib Proceedings: New Information Proceedings 53*:7 (2001): 250–264.

Dahlberg, Lincoln. "Rethinking the fragmentation of the cyberpublic: From consensus to contestation." *New Media & Society 9* (2007).

Davis, Joshua. "Hackers take down the most wired country in Europe." *Wired15* (2009)

Denning, Dorothy E. (2000). Cyberterrorism. Testimony before the Special Oversight Panel on Terrorism Committee on Armed Services U.S. House of Representatives, May 23, 2000. Retrieved from www.cs.georgetown.edu/~denning/infosec/cyberterror.html on 11 November 2011.

Denning, Dorothy E. "Terror's web: How the Internet is transforming terrorism." In Y. Jewkes and M. Yar's, *Handbook on Internet Crime* (eds.). Willan Publishing (2009).

Denning, Dorothy E. "Information technology and security." In Michael E. Brown (ed.) *Grave New World: Security Challenges in the Twenty-First Century*: 91–112. Washington, D.C.: Georgetown University Press (2003).

Department of Defense. "Department of Defense Cyberspace Policy Report." *A Report to Congress Pursuant to the National Defense Authorization Act for Fiscal Year 2011, Section 934.* November 2011.

Espiner, Tom. "How Estonia's attacks shook the world." ZDNet Australia, (2 May 2008): http://www.zdnet.com.au/insight/security/soa/How-Estonia-s-attacks-shook-the-world/0,139023764,339288625,00.htm.

Espiner, Tom. "Cyberattack caused multiple-city power failure," ZDNet Australia, (22 January 2008). http://www.zdnet.com.au/news/security/soa/Cyberattack-caused-multiple-city-power-failure/0,130061744,339285286,00.htm.

Farwell, James P. and Rafal Rohozinski. "Stuxnet and the future of cyber war." *Survival 53* (2011): 23–40.

Federal Bureau of Investigation. "NajibullahZazi indicted for conspiracy to use explosives against person or property in the United States." Department of Justice Press Release, (September 24, 2009a): http://newyork.fbi.gov/dojpressrel/pressrel09/nyfo092409.htm.

Federal Bureau of Investigation. "Two men charged in connection with alleged roles in foreign terror plot that focused on targets in Denmark," Department of Justice Press Release, (October 27, 2009b).

Federal Bureau of Investigation. "The path to terror: The jihadists of Georgia," Department of Justice Headline Archives, (December 15, 2009c): http://www.fbi.gov/page2/dec09/jihadists_121509.html.

Federal Bureau of Investigation. "Ali Al-Marri pleads guilty to conspiracy to provide material support to al Qaeda," Department of Justice Press Release, (April 30, 2009d).

Fellman, Philip Vos and Roxana Wright. "Modeling Terrorist Networks: Complex systems at the mid-range." Joint Complexity Conference, London School of Economics, September 16–18, 2003.

Foltz, C. Bryan. (2004). "Cyberterrorism, computer crime, and reality," *Information Management & Computer Security, 12* (2004): 154–166.

Freeh, Louis J. "Testimony of Louis J. Freeh, Director, FBI, Before the United States Senate, Committees on Appropriations, Armed Services, and Select Committee on Intelligence."- Threat of Terrorism to the United States, May 10, 2001.

Gable, Kelly. "Cyber-apocalypse now: Securing the Internet against cyberterrorism and using universal jurisdiction as a deterrent." (August 14, 2009). Available at SSRN: http://ssrn.com/abstract=1452803.

Ganor, Boaz. "Defining terrorism: Is one man's terrorist another man's freedom fighter?" *Police Practice and Research 3* (2002): 287–304.

Garrett, R. Kelly. "Protest in an information society: A review of literature on social movements and new ICTs." *Information, Communication and Society 9* (2006): 202–224.

Garrison, Arthur H. "Terrorism: The nature of its history," *Criminal Justice Studies 16* (2003): 39–52.

Giacomello, Giampiero. "Bangs for the buck: A cost-benefit analysis of cyberterrorism," *Studies in Conflict & Terrorism 27* (2004): 387–408.

Giduck, John. *Terror at Beslan: A Russian tragedy with lessons for America's schools.* USA: Archangel Press. (2005).

Giroux, Henry A. *Beyond the Spectacle of Terrorism: Global uncertainty and the challenge of the new media.* Paradigm Publishers, 2006.

Giustozzi, Antonio. *Koran, Kalashnikov and Latop: The neo-Taliban insurgency in Afghanistan.* New York: Columbia University Press. (2008).

Goth, Greg. "Terror on the Internet: A complex issue, and getting harder." *IEEE Distributed Systems Online 9* (March, 2008).

Grennan, Sean and Marjie T. Britz. *Organized Crime: A worldwide perspective.* New Jersey: Prentice-Hall, 2005.

Gunaratna, Rohan. "Abu Musab Al Zarqawi: A new generation terrorist leader," IDSS Commentaries. (July 5, 2004). Available at: http://dr.ntu.edu.sg/bitstream/handle/10220/4048/RSIS-COMMENT_212.pdf?sequence=1.

Hamilton, Lee. *The 9/11 Commission Report: Final report of the National Commission on Terrorist Attacks upon the United States.* Washington, D.C. :National Commission on Terrorist Attacks upon the United States (2004).

Heuston, Sean. "Weapons of mass instruction: Terrorism, propaganda film, politics, and us," *Studies in Popular Culture 27* (2005): 59–73.

Hoffman, Bruce. "Al Qaeda, trends in terrorism, and future potentialities: An assessment," *Studies in Conflict and Terrorism 26* (2003): 429–442.

Hoffman, Bruce. "Rethinking terrorism and counterterrorism since 9/11". *Studies in Conflict and Terrorism 25* (2002): 301–316.

Ito, Harumi and Darin Lee. "Assessing the impact of the September 11 terrorist attacks on U.S. airline demand," *Journal of Economics and Business 57* (2005): 75–95.

Kaplan, Eben. "Terrorists and the Internet." *Council on Foreign Relations.* (2009). http://www.cfr.org/publication/10005/.

Kohlman, Evan. "Expert report on the ~AQCORPO website."*Global Terror Alert,* (August, 2006). http://nefafoundation.org/miscellaneous/FeaturedDocs/ekirhaby0108.pdf.

Krebs, Valdis. "Connecting the dots: Tracking two identified terrorists."(2001a) http://www.orgnet.com/tnet.html.

Krebs, Valdis. "Uncloaking terrorist networks," First Monday (2001b). http://www.orgnet.com/hijackers.html.

Lewis, James. "Cyber terror: Missing in action," *Knowledge, Technology & Policy 16* (2003): 34–41.

Loza, Wagdy. "The psychology of extremism and terrorism: A Middle-Eastern perspective," *Aggression and Violent Behavior 12* (2007): 141–155.

Lynch, Marc. "Al-Qaeda's media strategies," The Institute of Communication Studies, Leeds: http://ics.leeds.ac.uk/papers/vp01.cfm?outfit=pmt&folder=1087&paper=2662.

Madsen, Wayne. "Critical Infrastructure Protection Gathering at the Supreme Court," *Computer Fraud and Security 9* (1998): 12–15.

Martin, C. Augustus. *Understanding terrorism: Challenges, perspectives, and issues, 3rd Edition.* Thousand Oaks, CA: SAGE (2009).

McAfee Labs. *Protecting your critical assets: Lessons learned from "Operation Aurora."* White Paper. (2010). Retrieved from www.macafee.com on 6 January 2012.

Merari, Ariel. "Terrorism as a strategy of insurgency," *Terrorism and Political Violence 5,* 4 (1993): 213–251.

Montalbano, Elizabeth. "Social networks link terrorists: A new breed of cyberterrorists are using online forums to recruit people who support Al-Qaeda, creating global networks of would-be terrorists," *PCWorld* (1 August

2009): http://www.pcworld.idg.com.au/article/272364/social_networks_link_terrorists.

Nacos, Brigette L., "The terrorist calculus behind 9-11: A model for future terrorism?," *Studies in Conflict and Terrorism 26* (2003): 1–16.

NEFA Foundation, "Taliban: 'Obama, following in Bush's steps," Statement of the Islamic Emirate of Afghanistan. 8 December 2009. http://www.nefafoundation.org/miscellaneous/nefaTaliObamaBush1209.pdf.

Obama, Barack. "Empowering local partners to prevent violent extremism in the United States." August 2011. Retrieved from www.whitehouse.gov on 29 January 2012.

O'Rourke, Simon. "Virtual radicalization: Challenges for police". *Proceedings of the 8th Australian Information Warfare and Security Conference.* Perth: Australia (2007): 29–35.

Pollitt, Mark M. "Cyberterrorism—fact or fancy?" *Computer Fraud & Security 2* (1998): 8–10.

Ponemon Institute. *Second annual cost of cyber crime study: Benchmark study of U.S. companies.* Sponsored by ArcSight and HP Company (2011).

Power, Richard. *Tangled Web: Tales of digital crime from the shadows of cyberspace.* Indianapolis, Indiana: Que, (2000).

Reid, Edna F., "Evolution of a body of knowledge: An analysis of terrorism research," *Information Processing and Management 33* (1997): 91–106.

Reid, Edna F. and Hsinchun Chen. "Mapping the contemporary terrorism research domain," *International Journal of Human-Computer Studies 65* (2006): 42–56.

Rice, Stephen K. "Emotions and terrorism research: A case for a social-psychological agenda," *Journal of Criminal Justice 37* (2009): 248–255.

Rogan, Hanna. "Jihadism Online—A study of how al-Qaida and radical Islamist groups use the Internet for terrorist purposes."Norwegian Defence Research Establishment. 2006.

Ronfeldt, David and Armando Martinez. "A comment on the Zapatista 'Netwar,'" In J. Arquilla and D. Ronfeldt (eds.) *In Athena's Camp: Preparing for Conflict in the Information Age.* California: RAND Corporation (1997).

Ruby, Charles S. "The definition of terrorism," *Analyses of Social Issues and Public Policy* (2002): 9–14.

Sanger, David E. *Confront and Conceal: Obama's secret wars and surprising use of American power.* New York: Crown Publishing (2012).

Saul, Ben. "Attempts to define 'terrorism' in international law," *Netherlands International Law Review L II* (2005): 57–83.

Schmid, Alex P. and Albert J. Jongman. *Political Terrorism.* Amsterdam: North Holland, Transaction Books. (1988).

Sheffer, Matthew J. "Awareness through agility: Teenagers as a model for terrorist development of situational awareness." (May, 2006). http://www.dtic.mil/cgibin/GetTRDoc?AD=ADA474177&Location=U2&doc=GetTRDoc.pdf.

Shelley, Louise I. and John T. Picarelli. "Methods not motives: implications of the convergence of international organized crime and terrorism," *Police Practice and Research 3* (2002): 305–318.

Stohl, Michael. "Old myths, new fantasies and the enduring realities of terrorism," *Critical Studies on Terrorism 1* (2008): 5–16.

Stohl, Michael. "Cyberterrorism: A clear and present danger, the sum of all fears, breaking point or patriot games." *Crime, Law & Social Change 46* (2007): 223–238.

Talbot, Brent J. "Stuxnet and after."*Journal of International Security Affairs 21* (2011).

Theohary, Catherine A. and John Rollins. "Terrorist use of the Internet: Information operations in cyberspace." *CRS Report for Congress R41674* (2011).

Tsafati, Yariv and Gabriel Weimann. "Www.terrorism.com: Terror on the internet," *Studies in Conflict and Terrorism 25* (2002): 317–322.

Turk, Robert J. "Cyber Incidents involving control systems,"—INL/EXT-05-00671: Idaho National Laboratory for the U.S. Department of Homeland Security, contract DE-AC07-05ID14517, (2005).

U.S. v. Zazi (2009), 09-CR-00663 (RJD), Memorandum of Law in Support of the Government's Motion for a Permanent Order of Detention.

United States Department of State. *Country Reports on Terrorism.* Washington D.C.: US Department of State, Office of the Coordinator for Counterterrorism. (2011).

Vijayan, Jaikumar. "Hackers evaluate Estonia attacks," *PC World* (4 August 2007).

Voors, Matthew Parker. "Encryption regulation in the wake of September 11, 2001: Must we protect national security at the expense of the economy?" *Federal Communications Law Journal 55* (2003):

Washington, Douglas Waller. "Onward Cyber Soldiers," *Time Magazine 146*:8 (1995). http://www.csm.ornl.gov/~dunigan/timemag.html.

Weimann, Gabriel. "Cyberterrorism: The sum of all fears?" *Studies in Conflict & Terrorism 28* (2005): 129–149.

Weimann, Gabriel and Katharina Von Knop. "Applying the notion of noise to countering online terrorism," *Studies in Conflict & Terrorism 23* (2009): 883–902.

Wilkinson, Paul, "The media and terrorism: A reassessment," *Terrorism and Political Violence 9*:2 (1997): 51–64.

Wilson, Clay. "Computer Attack and Cyberterrorism: Vulnerabilities and policy issues for Congress." *CRS Report for Congress* (2005).Retrieved on 23 December 2011 from www.opencrs.com.

X, Malcolm. *Malcolm X Speaks: Selected Speeches and Statements.* Chicago: Grove/ Atlantic. (1969).

Zulaika, Joseba and William A. Douglass. *Terror and Taboo: The Follies, Fables, and Faces of Terrorism.* New York: Routledge. (1996).

8

Industrial Control Systems and Cybercrime

Aunshul Rege

Critical infrastructures are socio-economic entities that are vital to the day-to-day functioning of a society. Some of these include transportation, banking and finance, telecommunications, emergency services, electricity, and water supply systems (Blane 2002; DHS 2008; Verton 2003). Over the years, these infrastructures have started relying on industrial control systems (ICS), which are computer systems that oversee operations, improve efficiency, and provide early warning of possible disaster situations (Blane 2002; Fogarty 2011; NCS 2004; Rossignol 2001). These systems range in their complexity; some can be relatively simple, monitoring environmental conditions of a small office building, or very intricate, monitoring all the activity in a nuclear power plant or the activity of a municipal water system (NCS 2004). Furthermore, ICS have embraced the continually changing face of technology to improve critical infrastructure monitoring, control, and operations.

This technological dependency, however, increases their online exposure and susceptibility to cybercrime. In 2005 alone, approximately 2,700 businesses detected 13 million incidents, suffered $288 million in monetary losses, and experienced 152,200 hours of system downtime (Rantala 2008). Indeed, these systems are attractive targets and incapacitating them could have detrimental effects on everyday operations, the economy, and national security.

Given the importance of these systems, it is not surprising that a considerable amount of research has been conducted in the ICS area. Research includes descriptive accounts of ICS (DPS Telecom 2011a; Ezell 1998; Luiijf 2008); ICS functionality (Scadasystems.net 201; Stouffer, Falco, and Scarfone 2011); ICS threats, vulnerabilities, consequences, and risks (Lemos 2000; Luiijf 2008; Nicholson 2008; Oman, Schweitzer, and Robert 2001; Poulsen 2003; SANS

2001); ICS disruption simulations (GAO 2003); and ICS cybercrime case studies (Kuvshinkova 2003; Morain 2001; NSTAC 2000; ZDNN 2001). This literature, while important, is limited to industry and security sectors or media accounts, and is, therefore, technical or sensationalized (respectively) in nature. Furthermore, the studies on critical infrastructure and cybercrime are found in isolation; this disconnect hinders a thorough understanding of critical infrastructure cyberattacks.

More importantly, existing ICS research has minimally addressed the *human* component in cybercrimes, such as the organization and operation of offenders, the factors that influence offender decision-making, and how the cybercrime process is carried out. The discipline of criminology is thus highly beneficial as it offers yet another, important, perspective on the phenomenon of ICS cybercrimes. Despite the importance of these systems, criminological research is scarce. Some reasons for this paucity may be due to the lack of public disclosure and underreporting; the difficulty in accessing confidential and sensitive national security infrastructure data; and the methodological limitations in researching the ICS attackers, their modus operandi, and their organizational dynamics.

This chapter reviews the abundant technical literature, media cases, and the brief criminological research in the ICS area. First, the ICS literature is reviewed, which provides information on ICS components, their functions, and inter-relationships that can be targeted by cybercriminals. Second, the literature on ICS vulnerabilities is examined, which offers insight into system design or architecture flaws that make them suitable targets. Third, the literature on ICS threats is reviewed, which identifies the assortment of cybercriminals that may target these systems. Next, six case studies of ICS cyberattacks are listed to illustrate the varying nature and intensity of attack strategies and cybercriminal skills. Finally, the case is made for expanding criminological research inquiry using alternate methodologies, applying the rational choice perspective and situational crime prevention principles, employing simulation studies and agent based modeling, and exploring the physical-cyber relationships in ICS cybercrimes.

Industrial Control Systems

Industrial Control Systems (ICS) gained prevalence in the 1960s, when the need to monitor and regulate remote infrastructure equipment and processes increased (DPS Telecom 2011a). Early ICS required human operators to make decisions and were therefore very expensive to maintain; these systems are more automated today and hence cost-efficient (DPS Telecom 2011a). "ICS" is a general term, which covers an assortment of control systems, including Distributed Control Systems (DCS), Programmable Logic Controllers (PLC), and Supervisory Control and Data Acquisition (SCADA) systems.

SCADA systems are highly distributed systems, which are used to control geographically dispersed assets, often scattered over vast distances, where centralized data acquisition and control are critical to system operation (Stouffer et al. 2011). SCADA systems are designed to collect field data and transfer it to a central computer facility. This data is displayed graphically or textually to the plant operator, who can then monitor or control an entire system from the centralized location in real time (Stouffer et al. 2011). SCADA systems thus control *and* monitor plant operations and processes. A DCS is responsible for controlling production systems within the same geographic locations for industries (Stouffer et al. 2011). There is often confusion over the differences between SCADA and DCS. SCADA systems, as the acronym implies, includes data acquisition *and* control, while DCS is purely control oriented (DPS Telecom 2011b). Before the introduction of computer networks, a SCADA system was the top-level controller for lower-level systems, as it was impractical for SCADA to control every minute aspect of a system (DPS Telecom 2011b). Here, DCS did most of the lower level detail work and reported back to, and took orders from, the SCADA system (DPS Telecom 2011b). With the growth of fast computer systems, however, SCADA and DCS have blurred together into a single monitoring and control system (DPS Telecom 2011b).

PLCs are control systems that are typically used throughout SCADA and DCS systems to provide local management of processes (Stouffer et al. 2011). Data acquisition starts at the PLC level, which includes equipment status reports and meter readings, which are then communicated to the SCADA system (Scadasystems.net 2011). Based on the data collected from the stations, automated or operator-driven supervisory commands are sent back to the PLCs, which in turn control local operations such as opening and closing valves and breakers, collecting data from sensor systems, and monitoring the local environment for alarm conditions (Stouffer et al. 2011).

Consider the utilities industry, where ICS encompass data transfers between SCADA systems and PLCs. Here, PLCs are connected directly to geographically scattered field devices, such as reservoir level meters, water flow meters, temperature transmitters, and power consumption meters (NCS 2004). This information is relayed back to SCADA systems, enabling facility operators to determine utilities systems performance. Based on this data, operators can send commands back to the PLCs that, for instance, change the set points for temperature settings, open or close valves that regulate water flow, and enable alarm conditions, such as loss of flow and high temperature (NCS 2004).

Most ICS in use today were developed years before public and private networks or the internet were commonplace in business operations. These systems were designed to meet performance, reliability, safety, and flexibility requirements (Stouffer et al. 2011). They were physically isolated from outside networks and based on proprietary software, hardware, and communication protocols that included basic error identification and correction capabilities, but lacked the secure communication capabilities needed in today's interconnected systems (Stouffer et al. 2011). Information and communication technologies started making their way into ICS designs in the late 1990s, exposing them to new types of threats and significantly increasing their vulnerability (Stouffer et al. 2011). The US critical infrastructure is highly interconnected and mutually dependent through a host of technologies; an incident in one infrastructure can directly, or indirectly, impact other infrastructures through cascading and escalating failures (Stouffer et al. 2011).

While this literature identifies the different types of ICS and their uses in critical infrastructure, it does not shed light on their vulnerabilities. As such, the next section examines the types of vulnerabilities that are present in ICS and how they can be exploited by cybercriminals to conduct their attacks.

Industrial Control System Vulnerabilities

ICS were designed and implemented in an era when network trespass and data manipulation were not relevant. Information security was not built into these systems because there was "no public information on how SCADA worked, ... no connections to the [internet], ... the environment was assumed to be hacker-free, [and that the systems operated in] totally controlled and closed secure environments" (Luiijf 2008, 11; Nicholson 2008; Stamp et al. 2003).

Today, ICS use cost-cutting technology and non-proprietary software, which offers convenience and efficiency; these advancements have also resulted in several built-in vulnerabilities that increase the likelihood of ICS cybercrimes. Several overlapping definitions of vulnerabilities are found in the literature. Vulnerabilities are any weaknesses that can be exploited by an adversary to gain access to an asset (Byres and Hoffman 2004). Vulnerabilities have also been defined as any characteristics pertaining to the installation, system, asset, application, or its dependencies that could result in loss of functionality when subjected to a threat (Robles et al. 2008). The Department of Homeland Security's Risk Lexicon (DHS 2010) defines vulnerability as "a physical feature or operational attribute that renders an entity, asset, system, network, or geographic area open to exploitation or susceptible to a given hazard." The National Institute of Standards and Technology (NIST) Guide to Industrial Control Systems Security categorizes ICS vulnerabilities into three groups: Policy and Procedure, Platform, and Network categories. There is no pecking order of vulnerabilities with regards to the likelihood of occurrence or severity of impact (Stouffer et al. 2011).

Policy and procedure vulnerabilities are often introduced into ICS because of incomplete, inappropriate, or nonexistent security policy documentation. This documentation identifies safe user practices, such as regular password updates, and network connection requirements (Stouffer et al. 2011). The lack or paucity of security audits is also problematic as this process typically determines the adequacy of system controls and ensures compliance standards are met (Stouffer et al. 2011). To make matters worse, ICS information, such as proprietary protocols, reports, and specifications, are made available online by industry and ICS vendors to facilitate employee education and enable third-party manufacturers to build compatible accessories (GAO 2003; Luiijf 2008; Stouffer et al. 2011). Furthermore, SCADA tutorials are easily available online as downloadable white papers, YouTube videos, and 'ask SCADA experts' websites (DPS Telecom 2011a; YouTube 2009; Zintro 2011). Thus, the internet serves as an extensive knowledge base documenting system blueprints, tutorials, expert advice, and vulnerability details which cybercriminals can use to research their targets and design corresponding attack techniques.

The next type of vulnerability occurs due to flaws, misconfigurations, or poor maintenance of ICS platforms (Stouffer et al. 2011). Platform vulnerabilities can be configuration-based (patches implemented without exhaustive testing), hardware-based (insecure remote access), software-based (buffer overflow), and malware-based (malware protection software not installed, not current, or implemented without exhaustive testing) (Stouffer et al. 2011). ICS also utilize user-friendly browser applications that can be easily understood and employed by anyone, and thus little technical expertise is required to operate these systems (Luiijf 2008). Furthermore, organizations are transitioning from proprietary systems to less expensive, standardized technologies, such as commercial-off-the-shelf (COTS) SCADA systems and software. COTS software, however, has publicly known design errors and bugs which can be easily exploited using tools that are widely available online (Luiijf 2008; Stouffer et al. 2011).

A third source of ICS vulnerabilities occur from flaws, misconfigurations, or poor administration of ICS networks and their connections with other networks (Jordan and Taylor 1998; Stouffer et al. 2011). ICS are remotely accessible to plant operators for maintenance and to corporations for assistance with business decisions (Luiijf 2008; Stouffer et al. 2011). This integration of ICS networks with remote and corporate networks increases ICS accessibility to both legitimate and illegitimate users (Stouffer et al. 2011). Another problem is that unencrypted and/or static passwords are often used in ICS environments, which are assumed to be secure (Luiijf 2008; Nicholson 2008). Adversaries with password cracking software can easily gain access via remote connections and obtain administrator access without supervision (Luiijf 2008; Stouffer et al. 2011). Finally, technical protection is often lacking, with **virus** scans rarely being performed and security patches not being installed regularly and rigorously. Insufficient quality control for SCADA software, poor or improper usage of **firewalls**, lack of individual authentication and poor **intrusion detection systems** collectively increase the likelihood of ICS cybercrimes (Luiijf 2008; Nicholson 2008).

These three types of vulnerabilities can be abused individually but are more likely to be exploited in combination. Cybercriminals get the necessary access and information, while facing little resistance. Different types of cybercriminals may use these vulnerabilities in different ways. It is, therefore, important to identify the types of attackers that pose a threat to ICS, as well as their expertise and modus operandi.

Industrial Control System Threats

There are several definitions of threats found in the literature, which share common components. Threat is defined as any indication, circumstance, or event with the potential to cause the loss of, or damage to an asset (Byres and Hoffman 2004; Moteff 2005). Threat is also defined as the intent and capability to adversely affect (cause harm or damage to) the system by changing its state and function (Haimes 2006). The DHS Risk Lexicon (2010) defines threat as a natural or man-made occurrence, individual, entity, or action that has or indicates the potential to harm life, information, operations, the environment, and/or property.

Nine threat sources may attack critical infrastructures. First, *leisure cybercriminals* break into networks for thrill, challenge, curiosity, or bragging rights in the cybercriminal community (Holt and Kilger, 2012a; Krone 2005; Weaver et al. 2003). These attackers do not have to be technically knowledgeable; they can now download pre-written attack scripts to target ICS, thereby increasing the possible pool of attackers (McAfee 2005; Souffer et al. 2011). Second, *industrial spies* seek to acquire intellectual property, personnel files, or monitor proprietary activities through covert and illegitimate methods (Holt and Kilger 2012a; Stouffer et al. 2011; Taylor et al. 2010; Williams 2006). Third, *foreign intelligence services*, or *nation-states*, are developing information warfare doctrines, programs, and capabilities, which can disrupt ICS supply and communication functionalities in several infrastructures (Holt and Kilger 2012a; Stouffer et al. 2011). Fourth, *terrorists* seek to disrupt, debilitate, or exploit critical infrastructures to threaten national security, cause mass casualties, weaken the U.S. economy, and damage public morale and confidence (Stouffer et al. 2011; Weaver et al. 2003).

Fifth, *disgruntled insiders* possess ICS knowledge and unrestricted access to cause system damage or steal sensitive information; they may be current or past employees, contractors, or business partners (Datz 2004; Shaw and Stock 2011; Moore et al. 2011; Shaw and Stock 2011; Stouffer et al. 2011). Sixth, *criminal groups* attack ICS for monetary gain and use spam, phishing, and malware to conduct their attacks; they hire or develop cybercriminal talent to target ICS (Krone 2005; McAfee 2005; McMullan and Rege 2007).

Phishers are the seventh threat source to ICS. These are individual or small groups of cybercriminals that execute online schemes, via spam, spyware, and malware, to steal ICS operators' identities or ICS information for monetary gain (Stouffer et al. 2011). Eighth, *spammers* are cybercriminals that distribute unsolicited e-mail with hidden or false information to sell ICS-related products, conduct phishing schemes, or distribute spyware and malware (Stouffer et al. 2011). Finally, *spyware authors* are individuals or organizations with malicious intent that carry out attacks against users by producing and disseminating spyware to gather specific intelligence data and assets from ICS vendors, which is then used to design tailor-made cyber-attacks (Stouffer et al. 2011).

Table 1 summarizes the preceding technical discussion of ICS components, threats, and vulnerabilities. There is, however, limited publicly-available information on ICS cybercrime consequences. As such, a review of a few, well-known critical infrastructure cybercrimes are offered next to capture not only the consequences, but also the different threat agents and their attack techniques.

Critical Infrastructure Cybercrime Cases

Several publicly known critical infrastructure cybercrime cases have been documented in both technical literature and media cases. These cases cannot be covered extensively here, and as such this section discusses six cybercrime events to demonstrate that ICS cybercrimes can occur across different critical infrastructures: transportation, sewage, power, finance, and communication infrastruc-

Table 1. Summary of Industrial Control Systems, Vulnerabilities and Threats

Item	Details
Types	
Supervisory Control and Data Acquisition (SCADA)	Control geographically dispersed assets from centralized location
Programmable Logic Controllers (PLC)	Provide local management of processes based on SCADA commands
Vulnerabilities	
Policy and Procedure	Incomplete, inappropriate, or nonexistent security policy documentation
Platform	Flaws, misconfigurations, or poor maintenance of configuration, hardware, software and anti-malware elements
Network	Remote access, poor password practices, poor authentication, inadequate intrusion detection
Threats	
Leisure Cybercriminals	Thrill, challenge, curiosity, or bragging rights
Industrial Spies	Acquire intellectual property, personnel files, or monitor proprietary activities
Foreign Intelligence Services	Develop programs to disrupt ICS supply and communications
Terrorists	Threaten national security, cause mass casualties, weaken the U.S. economy, damage public morale and confidence
Disgruntled Insiders	Possess ICS knowledge and unrestricted access to cause damage or steal sensitive information
Criminal Groups	Hire or develop cybercriminal talent to target ICS for monetary gain
Phishers	Use spam and malware to steal ICS information and operators' identities
Spammers	Distribute unsolicited e-mail with hidden or false information to sell ICS-related products
Spyware Authors	Produce and disseminate spyware to gather specific intelligence data and assets from ICS vendors

tures. These cases offer preliminary insights into the history of ICS cyberattacks and the range of cybercriminal skills, techniques, and organization.

Oil and Gas Infrastructure

One of the earliest documented cyber attacks occurred during the Cold War, when US President Reagan approved a SCADA attack on the Russian pipeline system in Siberia. To automate the operation of valves, compressors, and storage facilities on such a large scale, the Russians needed sophisticated ICS software (Crowell 2010). They approached the United States for the necessary automation software but were turned down, and so sought to steal the necessary code from a Canadian firm. US Intelligence, however, was tipped off of the impending theft, and in cooperation with the Canadian firm, **modified** the software before it was stolen (*The Economist* 2010, Crowell 2010). The pipeline software, which ran the pumps, turbines, and valves, was reprogrammed to go haywire and "reset pump seeds and valve settings to produce pressures far beyond those acceptable to pipeline jolts and welds," resulting in a large blast in Siberia (Cornish et al. 2010; The Economist 2010). This attack was an indirect effort to disrupt Russia's technological capabilities and military industrial base; it was specifically designed to tamper with Russia's gas supply system, harm the Russian economy, and decrease its gas revenues from the West, which ultimately undermined its power (Cornish et al. 2010).

Transportation Infrastructure

In March 1997, a teenager hacked into the Worcester, Massachusetts, airport, resulting in the shutdown of communication services at the airport's Federal Aviation Administration Tower, fire department, airport security, weather service, and several private airfreight companies for over six hours (Lewis 2004; Taylor et al. 2010). Furthermore, the main radio transmitter and the circuitry activating runway lights were disabled. The hacker changed the system identification to "Jester," demonstrating his actions were driven by thrill (Rindskopf 1998). This attack caused flight delays and cancellations and major financial losses to the airport and numerous airlines. He received two years' probation, during which he could not access any computers or digital networks, paid restitution to the phone company, and forfeited all computer equipment used in the attack (Lewis 2004).

Another transportation sector cybercrime was the 2008 Polish tram system hack. A juvenile hacked into the tram system, using it like a "giant train set" (Baker 2008, 1). He visited tram depots to study the trams and tracks thoroughly and then built a remote control device to manipulate the trams and tracks and change signals (Baker 2008). While this attack did not result in any deaths, it did cause serious harm: four vehicles were derailed, others made emergency stops, and 12 people were injured (Baker 2008). The boy faced charges of endangering public safety in juvenile court.

Sewage Infrastructure

In 2000, the sewage system in Queensland, Australia, was hacked by Vitek Boden. He was a former temporary contractor with the company that installed a local computerized sewage system. Boden was angered after being denied a permanent job. He used his credentials to remotely access the sewage system and send commands to disrupt approximately 140 sewage pumping stations (Crawford 2006; Lewis 2004; Stamp et al. 2003; Verton 2003). This attack released up to one million liters of raw sewage into public parks, creeks, and a hotel, severely polluting the environment and killing numerous marine life (Lewis 2004; Verton 2003). Boden was found guilty on 30 charges of computer hacking, theft, and causing environmental damage; he was sentenced to two years in jail and fined 13,000AUD for his crime (Crawford 2006; Lewis 2004).

Finance and Communication Infrastructure

On April 26, 2007, Estonia suffered a massive cyberattack, resulting from anger over the relocation of a World War II statue. The country experienced approximately 128 unique crippling **Distributed Denial of Service (DDoS)** attacks. A DDoS attack occurs when several compromised computers attack a targeted system by flooding it with data. The target uses up all of its resources to manage this data, which forces it to shut down, thereby denying service to legitimate users. The Estonian DDoS attack disrupted the country's prime minister website functionality, financial transactions, telephone communications, and media transmissions (Davis 2007; Evron 2008). The cyberattacks ranged in duration, with some lasting for less than an hour and others for over 10 hours (Brenner 2007; Davis 2007; Evron 2008). Online Russian discussion boards had detailed instructions on cyberattack preparation, target selection, and response strategies to Estonia's defense, indicating that these attacks were organized and adaptive (Evron 2008). A conglomeration of several tactics were used, such as **website defacements**, using pre-written programs to overwhelm Estonian web servers, and herding **botnet armies**. Botnets comprise numerous malware-infected computers that are remotely controlled by a cybercriminal unbeknownst to their legitimate users. The computers used in the attacks were located in the USA, Brazil, Canada, Egypt, Peru, and Vietnam, which made tracing the attack source problematic (Brenner 2007; Davis 2007).

Power Infrastructure

The notorious Stuxnet **worm** first appeared in July 2010 and targeted PLCs made by Siemens, which were used in Iran's Bushehr nuclear facility (BBC 2011). The worm only activated when it detected the presence of a specific configuration of controllers, running a particular set of processes that only existed in a centrifuge plant (Broad, Markoff and Williams 2011). The worm was a "dual warhead" as it had two major components (Broad et al. 2011, 5). The first was designed to lie dormant for long periods, then sped up the machines to "send Iran's nuclear centrifuges spinning wildly out of control," leading to their eventual destruction (Broad et al. 2011, 2). The second component, the "man in the middle," was a computer program that secretly recorded normal plant operations, then played those readings back to plant operators, "like a pre-recorded security tape in a bank heist," to make it appear that everything was operating normally, when in fact, the "centrifuges were actually tearing themselves apart" (Broad et al. 2011, 2). This program appears to have been created as part of top secret program by the US government titled "Operation Olympic Games" (Sanger 2012). The code was actually ordered for use in the field under President Obama, but developed under then-President Bush. As a result, Stuxnet appears to be a nation-state driven attack in the same fashion as the Regan-ordered attack against Russia discussed earlier, rather than a random attack by sophisticated cybercriminals.

Table 2 summarizes the cases discussed above. These cases demonstrate the broad spectrum of critical infrastructure that has been targeted by cybercriminals, and provides insight into the attack vectors and the attackers, their organizational dynamics and modus operandi. Thus, different types of critical infrastructures relying on ICS are equally likely to be targeted using an assortment of techniques that range in their technical sophistication, planning, and duration.

The Brief Criminological Industrial Control System Cybercrime Research

The above discussion demonstrates that there is no shortage of ICS research in the technical domain, nor is there paucity in media accounts of critical infrastructure attacks. However, both these domains have shortcomings. The technical studies on infrastructure cybercrime are found in isolation, which

Table 2. Summary of Industrial Control System Cybercrime Incidents

Infrastructure	Year	Target	Technique	Damage	Organizational Dynamics
Oil & Gas	1982	Serbia Pipeline	Modification	Disruption of operations of valves, compressors, and storage facilities	Associates
Transportation	1997	Massachusetts Airport Polish Tram System	Modification	Flight delays, Communication Delays	Loner
Sewage	2000	Queensland Sewage System	Exploitation	Environmental Pollution	Loner
Finance and Communication	2007	Estonia	Modification; DDoS	Disruption of website functionality, financial transactions, phone communications, media transmission	Network
Transportation	2008	Polish Tram System	Modification	Vehicle Derailment, Passenger Injuries	Loner
Power	2011	Iran's Bushehr Nuclear Facility	Worm	Disruption of operations of nuclear centrifuges	Network

does not offer a thorough understanding of ICS cyberattack techniques, frequency, duration, intensity, and patterns. While technical research is undoubtedly crucial, it primarily focuses on ICS vulnerabilities and prevention measures from the industry's perspective and is, therefore, limited in scope. Media accounts of infrastructure cyberattacks are sensationalized, skewed, and result in myth-based thinking (Dubois 2002; Finckenauer 2010). Furthermore, they lack scholarly rigor and are descriptive in nature.

The criminological discipline has just started addressing critical infrastructure cybercrimes, focusing on the type of attackers, their organizational characteristics, the nature and properties of cyberattacks, and industry executive perception studies of infrastructure cybercrimes. First, criminological research on critical infrastructure cybercrimes involves cybercriminal taxonomies. Vatis (2002) offers a typology of critical infrastructure cybercriminals, which includes disgruntled insiders, criminal groups, virus writers, foreign intelligence services, state-sponsored cybercriminals, terrorists, and recreational hackers. Similarly, Cornish et al. (2010) focus on cyber warfare and identify four cyber threat domains: state-sponsored cyber-attacks, ideological and political extremism, serious organized crime, and lower-level/individual crime. This typology parallels those identified in the technical domains discussed above (Krone 2005; Stouffer et al. 2011; Weaver et al. 2003) as well as other general hacker taxonomies (Holt and Kilger 2012a; Jordan and Taylor 1998; Rogers 2005).

The second form of criminological research on ICS cybercrimes involves the organizational dynamics of attackers. Using documents from government agencies, security firms, media sites, and hacker forums, Rege-Patwardhan's (2009) research offers a cybercriminal organization taxonomy. Hackers often engage in solo operations; these loners use technology and automated techniques that enable them to bypass digital defenses, and hence operate alone. Loners vary with respect to their technical skills. Cybercriminals often work together and engage in a minimal division of labor. These alliances are transient in nature, allowing deviant associates to unite for specific crimes and disband upon their completion, once again becoming free agents to form new alliances. Some cybercrimes, however, are conducted by online crime networks with sophisticated organization, extensive group membership, elaborate divisions of labor, and networked group structure. Each player brings specific skill-sets to the operation, making the organization's expertise broad and diverse. Like associates, these organizations coalesce for the sole purpose of executing the attack, resulting in criminal organizations that are temporary, flexible, and networked. These organizational dynamics can also be found in McMullan and Rege's (2010) study on online gambling crimes and Rege's (2009) work on internet dating scams.

Third, criminological research on critical infrastructure cyberattacks also examine attack techniques. Some of these techniques include website defacements, **Domain Name Server (DNS) attacks**, DDoS attacks, viruses, worms, and **Trojan** horses, and **routing attacks** (Vatis 2002). Cybercriminals can also **exploit** bugs or loopholes in infrastructure programs, utilize their technical and programming skills to modify the actual infrastructure systems, and use **rootkits** and **toolkits** to conduct their attacks (Rege-Patwardhan 2009). These techniques have also been identified in the technical ICS research (Byres and Hoffman 2004; Luiijf 2008; Nicholson 2008; Souffer et al. 2011) and in criminological research addressing other cybercrimes (Holt and Kilger 2012a; Jordan and Taylor 1998). While certain techniques require greater expertise than others, the lack of technical knowledge does not imply attack failure. The techniques themselves vary with respect to their organizational dynamics. Some techniques are simpler in their organization, others require intricate preparation, scheduling, and sophistication, and some attacks are adaptive in nature (Rege-Patwardhan 2009). Finally, these criminal techniques can be used individually or in combination to create endless, unique, sophisticated, and damaging attack possibilities that are difficult to track (Rege-Patwardhan 2009; Vatis 2002).

More importantly, Rege-Patwardhan (2009) investigates the link between the organization of criminal techniques and the organization of criminals in cyberspace. The sophistication of criminal organization is not always directly proportional to the sophistication of criminal technique. Some loners conduct sophisticated attacks, while some associates and criminal organizations use simpler techniques (website defacements and toolkit-based attacks). Another important finding is that while cybercrimes involve digital attacks, traditional techniques are also used; this marriage of traditional/physical and technical tactics results in the successful execution of cybercrimes against critical infrastructures that can have more devastating impacts than when orchestrated in isolation (Rege-Patwardhan 2009; Vatis 2002).

Finally, industry perception studies offer an alternate perspective of ICS cybercrimes. Baker et al. (2010) survey 600 information technology and security executives from seven critical infrastructure sectors in 14 countries. These respondents are questioned about their practices, attitudes, and security policies, and the types of attacks they have faced. Executives fear that recession-driven cuts may affect their security practices and are concerned about how well-prepared critical infrastructure is to deal with large-scale attacks. Chinese executives report the highest rates of adoption of security measures, such as encryption and strong user authentication. Approximately 54 percent of the executives experience attacks from high-level adversaries, such as organized crime groups, terrorists, or nation states, as well as stealthy infiltration from large-scale spy rings. Roughly 59 percent believe that foreign governments are already involved in such cyber-attacks and infiltrations.

Baker et al. (2010) also identify the types of attacks faced by critical infrastructures. Nearly one-third of the respondents report suffering large-scale DDoS attacks multiple times per month, and two-thirds of these report that such attacks impact operations in some manner. However, DDoS attacks are not the most common type of attack; 89 percent experience attacks resulting from virus or malware infections. More than half experience DNS poisoning and **SQL injection attacks**.

Attacks against the utilities sector are aimed at SCADA systems roughly 55 percent of the time. Of the 600 respondents, only 143 have ICS responsibilities. Of these, China has the highest SCADA security measure adoption rate of 74 percent, followed by Australia and Brazil at 57 and 54 percent, respectively. The United States and Japan have rates of 50 percent each, with France, Russia, Germany, Saudi Arabia, Italy and Mexico in the 35 to 40 percent range. Adoption rates of these measures are lowest in India and Spain, at 29 percent each and the UK at 31 percent. Seventy-six percent of the 143 respondents have their networks connected to an IP network or the Internet, with nearly half of them knowing the risks involved with such online exposure. Ninety-two percent of the executives responsible for SCADA report monitoring them in some way, either using network behavior analysis tools (62 percent) or audit logs (59 percent). Thus, Baker et al. (2010) demonstrate that critical infrastructures, including ICS, are operating in a high-threat environment and face a number of risks.

Despite the importance of these systems, the criminological research on ICS cybercrimes is still in its infancy. One reason for this paucity of research may be due to the sensitive nature of the topic. Gaining access to information on cyberattacks against critical infrastructure faces several barriers, such as confidentiality and privacy issues, liability issues, access to classified national security information, and reservations about sharing information with the academic community. An equally important reason for the lack of research is methodological limitations. Data on the phenomenon of critical infrastructure cybercrimes are not easily available. Finding cybercriminals to interview or survey is nearly impossible because they belong to an underground culture that is unknown or inaccessible. Acquiring access to online deviance requires technical expertise and covert observation, which are difficult given the sensitive, national-security nature of the problem. Interviewing security experts and critical infrastructure personnel is equally challenging. The former are often hesitant to disclose confidential incident information, which may include up-to-date counter strategies, digital evidence and equipment, and the implementation of social control efforts. Industry representatives are reluctant to disclose incidents for fear of being perceived as vulnerable to such attacks, which, in turn, encourages further cybercrimes. Additionally, open knowledge of critical infrastructure attacks generates fear and uncertainty in the public.

Expanding the Criminological Lines of Inquiry

The limitations discussed above should not deter criminologists from research inquiry. Researchers can use existing criminological studies and schools of thought to study ICS cybercrimes from multiple perspectives. Using alternate modes of inquiry to study the same phenomenon of ICS cybercrimes may offer greater insights into the phenomenon of ICS cybercrimes.

Primary Data Collection

The criminological research discussed earlier is descriptive and rudimentary in nature. They rely on case studies and document analysis. Obtaining data on actual critical infrastructure cybercrime incidents is difficult, and accessing ICS attackers is problematic because they belong to an underground culture that is unknown, inaccessible, and geographically dispersed. However, future research can follow Baker et al.'s (2010) global study which surveyed information technology and security executives from various critical infrastructure sectors. Perception surveys can also be done using ICS vendors, infrastructure executives, and ethical hackers to identify how each domain views ICS threats, vulnerabilities, and consequences (TVCs). Vignettes detailing hypothetical critical infrastructure cyberattacks and mixed focus groups can also be used to get a more qualitative and in-depth understanding, stimulate alternate interpretations, and offer more in-depth information resulting from greater response clarity in group discussions (Holt and Kilger 2012b).

Interviews, vignettes, and mixed focus groups have already been successfully used in studying other cybercrimes, such as online child sexual abuse (Martellozzo, Nehring and Taylor 2010), youth victimization by online harassment (Moore, Guntupalli, and Lee 2010), online child pornography behavior (Seigfried, Lovely, and Rogers 2008), and identifying the risk propensity of hackers (Bachman 2010). These methods can be used in ICS cybercrime studies to explore offender decision-making, organizational dynamics, and the structural features, such as criminal roles, group dynamics, criminal expertise, and the characteristics of the offense and offender.

Offender Decision-Making, Crime Scripts, and Situational Crime Prevention

The rational choice perspective (RCP) views criminality as an outcome of the continual interaction between a criminal's desires and preferences and the opportunities and constraints to commit crime (Cornish and Clarke 2008). RCP therefore portrays offenders as active decision makers who perform a cost-benefit analysis of presenting crime opportunities; offenders are reasoning criminals who use cues from the potential crime environment in deciding whether to commit crimes and how best to commit them (Cornish and Clarke 2008). Crime scripts systematically partition the modus operandi of simple and complex crimes into discrete, standardized stages or units of action (Smith 2003). Thus, crime scripts identify every stage of the crime-commission process and the decisions and actions that are needed at each stage. Understanding offender crime scripts and the corresponding decision-making process are crucial in designing prevention measures using situational crime prevention (SCP) principles. These measures can impact the offender's cost-benefit analysis by increasing the effort required by the offender, increasing the risks of detection, reducing the rewards, removing excuses, and reducing provocations (Clarke 2008).

Crime scripts have been examined rudimentarily for cybercrimes such as online dating crimes (Rege 2009), cyberextortion (McMullan and Rege 2007), and cybercrimes at gambling websites (McMullan and Rege 2010). SCP has also been applied to cybercrimes, such as online frauds (Newman and Clarke 2003), cyberstalking (Reyns 2010), information systems security (Beebe and Rao 2005), and insider threats to systems security (Theoharidou et al. 2005). Using these studies as a guide, future research should use offender decision-making, crime scripts, and SCP to examine ICS cybercrimes. This school of thought can help identify a thorough set of factors that influence offender decision-making and examine whether these factors have a temporal sequence in crime scripts. For instance, one rudimentary crime script for critical infrastructure cyberattacks may involve five stages, such as preparation, entry, initiation, attack dynamics, and exit. It would be invaluable to determine how offenders make decisions at each of these stages in the crime script. Once this intricate working is understood, SCP principles can be used to implement appropriate ICS protection strategies at each stage of the crime script.

Furthermore, understanding the degree to which factors influencing offender decision-making vary across different infrastructure sectors can also be useful. This research can shed light on whether different infrastructures experience different types of attacks (frequency, duration, intensity) from different threat agents (terrorists, organized crime groups, nation states, individuals). This would improve our understanding of critical infrastructure attacks and offender decision-making, help develop an offender-technique profile matrix, and offer insight into the effective application of situational crime prevention principles. These future studies can move *beyond* existing technical research on infrastructure vulnerabilities, by including the human element in ICS cybercrimes

Simulation Studies and Agent Based Modeling

As noted earlier, access to "real-time" data or observing an ICS cybercrime unfold is problematic. This data can be useful in understanding the crime process. Simulation studies can provide a viable alternative for researchers to replicate environments that are hard to study. In fact, simulation studies have already been used in criminal justice research to simulate large scale drug-distribution networks (Dombey-Moore et al. 1994) and estimate the impacts of California's three strikes law on elderly prison populations (Auerhahn 2002). Following suit, ICS environments, their vulnerabilities, prevention measures, and accessibility points can be replicated (and modified) to examine how cybercrimes are executed in a variety of settings. Such studies can shed light on offender decision-making processes at each stage of the crime process.

Simulation studies can be supplemented by using agent-based-modeling (ABM) systems, which are modeled as a collection of autonomous decision-making entities (agents). ABM has also been used in criminological research to model civil violence (Epstein 2002), street robbery (Groff 2007), and crime simulations (Wang, Liu and Eck 2008). In ICS cybercrime research, for example, each agent can individually assess its situation and can make decisions accordingly. This interaction between simulated environments and agents can be extremely useful. By altering any single element (vulnerabilities, prevention measures, access points, agent decision rules), a rigorous analysis of numerous crime processes can be obtained.

Trend Analysis

Trend analysis is a form of comparative analysis that is often employed to identify current movements or trends in a particular area of interest. Trend analysis has been used in criminological research, some of which include domestic abuse (Roy 1982), sexual offenses (Veysey, Zgoba, and Dalessandro 2008), and relationships between alcohol and crime (Greenfeld 1998). The process of trend analysis for critical infrastructure cybercrimes can be conducted along six dimensions: criminal organization, division of labor, attack properties, alliances, communication, and physical elements. Comprehending how each of these dimensions has evolved over the years not only offers a more plausible and thorough picture of critical infrastructure cybercrimes, but also sheds light on the changing nature of these crimes, techniques, and threat agents.

Physical Components of Industrial Control System Cyberattacks

Exploring the physical and cyber relationships of crime is not new to criminological research. Studies exist about online dating scams (Rege 2009), cybercrimes at gambling sites (McMullan and Rege 2010), online child pornography (Marcum et al. 2010), deviant peer associations (Holt, Bossler and May 2011) and cybercrimes against critical infrastructures (Rege-Patwardhan 2009). The above cases suggest that ICS cybercrimes can have a physical component to them, either as **social engineering** strategies or when digital attacks are combined with physical attacks. Thus, understanding the physical-cyber relationship is also a useful and relevant research area.

Researching ICS cybercrimes is an important endeavor, as technologically-dependent societies are negatively affected by them. It is, therefore, imperative to understand cybercriminals and how they operate. As noted earlier, there is simply not enough data to study this area. Critical infrastructures cybercrimes are not reported frequently because they are a matter of national security, a public display of inadequate security measures, and likely to cause fear in the public and industry embarrassment. Furthermore, ICS cybercrimes are clandestine; they are not easy to access as they occur and oftentimes, the attacks go unnoticed. Finally, the topic is relatively new in the criminological discipline, which further hinders researchers in establishing rapport and access to the ICS industry and security sectors.

Initiating a discussion across multiple arenas, including the ethical hacking community, infrastructure industry, and criminal justice community, is crucial. Hackers share the same skill set as cybercriminals and therefore offer relevant insight into exploitable infrastructure vulnerabilities (Holt and Kilger 2012a). Industry experts have insider information on (undisclosed) infrastructure cybercrime, which sheds light on system weaknesses and cybercrime prevention measures. Offender decision-making, crime scripts, organizational dynamics, and modus operandi, however, are multi-faceted phenomena. Drawing on various criminological theories that account for these areas offers a more plausible take on critical infrastructure cybercrime. Thus, a collaborative effort is necessary to bring together a diverse set of people with different views, objectives, and knowledge to address a common problem. This collaborative approach expands existing studies, draws them together to make new points of contact, and enables "big picture" thinking about critical infrastructure ICS cybercrimes.

Glossary

Botnet armies: Computers that are compromised after hackers install malware that gives them complete control over the infected machine.

Domain Name Server (DNS) Attack: An attack where internet data traffic intended for one website is redirected to the cybercriminal's service. Neither the intended website nor the internet user who seeks to access it is aware of this redirection. This attack is also known as DNS Spoofing or DNS Cache Poisoning.

Distributed Denial of Service (DDoS) Attack: An attack created by amassing a botnet army to disrupt a targeted site's traffic band width capability and consume all disk space or CPU time. The site is thus overwhelmed with requests and is slowed down to a crawl, resulting in a DDoS attack.

Exploitation: Hackers study, note, and link software bugs and loopholes in order to achieve optimal exploitation of computer systems.

Firewall: Device that permits or denies network data transmissions based on preset rules. It protects networks from unauthorized access while allowing legitimate network traffic to pass.

Intrusion Detection System: Device that monitors network and system activities for malicious activity, identifies possible incidents, documents incident information in logs, and reports unauthorized access attempts.

Modification: Cybercriminals utilize their technical and programming skills to modify critical infrastructure/Industrial Control Systems.

Rootkits: Collections of computer programs that give hackers administrator-level, or "root," access to computer systems. Rootkits incorporate malware (malicious code), such as Trojans, worms, and viruses, which conceal their presence and activity from users and other system processes.

Routing Attacks: Routers, which ensure that information packets travel successfully from their source to destination, are also targeted, resulting in massive routing attacks.

Social engineering: A strategy used to trick individuals, such as ICS vendors and/or operators, into divulging sensitive information by obtaining their trust. These techniques can be both physical and digital in form.

SQL Injection Attacks: An attack that targets databases through web-based forms. Database programming code (SQL) is inserted into the online form input fields, which are thus injected into the database. This SQL code may change database content or dump the database content, such as customer credit card numbers, passwords, and social security numbers, to the attacker.

Toolkits: Collections of computer programs and/or user manuals that are designed by hackers and sold to technically challenged cybercriminals to commit cybercrimes.

Trojans: Programs that appear benign on the surface, but harbor malicious code within.

Virus: Malicious software spread through human actions, such as running an infected program or opening a malicious email attachment, which steals confidential information, blocks system resources, or tampers with system data.

Website Defacement: A website is maliciously altered by inserting or substituting provocative and offending data. Defacing the target's website exposes visitors to misleading, embarrassing, or revealing information that damages the target's security, functionality, productivity, and reputation.

Worms: Malicious software that replicates by spreading copies of itself through shared networks autonomously, without any human intervention.

References

Auerhahn, Kathleen. "Selective incapacitation, three strikes, and the problem of aging prison populations: Using simulation modeling to see the future," *Criminology and Public Policy*, 1 (2002), 353–388.

Bachman, Michael. "The Risk Propensity and Rationality of Computer Hackers," *International Journal of Cyber Criminology*, 4 (2010), 643–656.

Baker, Graeme. "Schoolboy hacks into city's tram system," *The Telegraph*, January 11, 2008. Accessed November 20, 2008. http://www.telegraph.co.uk/news/worldnews/1575293/Schoolboy-hacks-into-city's-tramsystem.html.

Baker, Stewart, Shaun Waterman, and George Ivanov. "In the Crossfire: Critical Infrastructures in the Age of Cyber War." *McAfee*, 2010. Accessed August 2012. http://www.mcafee.com/us/resources/reports/rp-in-crossfire-critical-infrastructure-cyber-war.pdf.

BBC (British Broadcasting Corporation). "US and Israel were behind Stuxnet claims Researcher." 2011. Accessed August 17, 2011. http://www.bbc.co.uk/news/technology-12633240.

Beebe, Nicole and Srinivasan Rao. "Using Situational Crime Prevention Theory to Explain the Effectiveness of Information Systems Security." Proceedings of the 2005 SoftWars Conference, Las Vegas, NV, Dec 2005.

Blane, John. V. *Cyberwarfare: Terror at a Click.* New York: Novinka Books, 2002.

Brenner, Bill. "Experts doubt Russian government launched DDoS attacks." *Search Security,* May 18, 2007. Accessed November 21, 2008. http://searchsecurity.techtarget.com/originalContent/0,281942,sid14_gci1255548,00.html.

Broad, William, John Markoff, and David E. Sanger. "Israeli Test on Worm Called Crucial in Iran Nuclear Delay."*The New York Times,* January 15, 2011. Accessed August 17, 2011. http://www.nytimes.com/2011/01/16/world/middleeast/16stuxnet.html.

Byres, Eric,and Dan Hoffman. "The Myths and Facts behind Cyber Security Risks for Industrial Control Systems" Paper presented at VDE 2004 Congress, VDE, Berlin, October 2004.

Clarke, Ronald. "Situational Crime Prevention." In *Environmental Criminology and Crime Analysis,* edited by Richard Wortley, and Lorraine Mazerolle, 178–194. Oregon: Willan Publishing, 2008.

Cornish, Derek, and Ronald Clarke. "The Rational Choice Perspective." In R. Wortley and L. Mazerolle. (Eds.), *Environmental Criminology and Crime Analysis* (pp. 21–47). Oregon: Willan Publishing, 2008.

Cornish, Paul, David Livingstone, Dave Clemente, and Claire Yorke. "On Cyber Warfare." *Chatham House.* Accessed January 5, 2012. http://www.chatham-house.org/sites/default/files/public/Research/International%20Security/r1110_cyberwarfare.pdf.

Crawford, Michael. "Utility hack led to security overhaul." *ComputerWorld,* February 16, 2006. Accessed November 20, 2008. http://www.computerworld.com/securitytopics/security/story/0,10801,108735,00.html.

Crowell, Richard. "War in the Information Age: A Primer for Cyberspace Operations in 21st Century Warfare." *U.S. Naval War College.* Accessed January 5, 2012. http://www.usnwc.edu/getattachment/01f666f2-40a6-4875-88a7-df65d53147d0/War-in-the-Information-Age-A-Primer-for-Cyberspace.

Datz, Todd. "Out of Control." *CSO Security and Risk,* August 2004. Accessed March 8, 2006. http://www.csoonline.com/read/080104/control.html.

Davis, Joshua. "Hackers take down the most wired country in Europe." *Wired Magazine,* August 21, 2007. Accessed November 21, 2008. http://www.wired.com/print/politics/security/magazine/15-09/ff_estoni.

DHS (Department of Homeland Security). "Infrastructure Taxonomy, Version 3: November 1, 2008." Infrastructure Information Collection Division (IICD). Office of Infrastructure Protection.

DHS. *Risk Steering Committee DHS Risk Lexicon—2010 Edition.* September 2010. Accessed August 1, 2011. http://www.dhs.gov/xlibrary/assets/dhs_risk_lexicon.pdf.

Dombey-Moore, Bonnie, Susan Resetar, and Michael Childress. *A system description of the cocaine trade.* Santa Monica, CA: Rand, 1994.

DPS Telecom. *SCADA Knowledge Base.* Fresno, CA: DPS Telecom 2011a. Accessed August 5, 2011. http://www.dpstele.com/dpsnews/techinfo/scada/scada_knowledge_base.php.

DPS Telecom. *DCS vs. SCADA in Modern Environments.* Fresno, CA: DPS Telecom 2011b Accessed August 9, 2011. http://www.dpstele.com/dpsnews/techinfo/scada/dcs_vs_scada.php.

Dubois, Judith. "Media Coverage of Organized Crime: Impact on Public Opinion?" Research & Evaluation Branch Community, Contract and Aboriginal Policing Services Directorate. Royal Canadian Mounted Police, 2002.

Epstein, Joshua. "Modeling Civil Violence: An Agent-Based Computational Approach," *Proceedings of the National Academy of Sciences of the United States of America,* 99 (2002), 7243–7250.

Evron, Gadi. "Battling Botnets and Online Mobs: Estonia's Defense Efforts during the Internet War." *Science & Technology,* Winter/Spring 2008: 121–126.

Ezell, Barry. "Risks of Cyber Attack to Supervisory Control and Data Acquisition for Water Supply." MSc diss., University of Virginia, 1998.

Falliere, Nicolas, Murchu, Liam., and Eric Chien. "W32.Stuxnet Dossier, Version 1.4." *Symantec,* February 2011. Accessed August 18, 2011. http://www.symantec.com/content/en/us/enterprise/media/security_response/whitepapers/w32_stuxnet_dossier.pdf.

Finckenauer, James. *Mafia and Organized Crime: A Beginner's Guide.* Oxford: Oneworld Publications, 2007.

Fogarty, Kevin. "U.S. power grid is a big, soft target for cyberattack, MIT study shows." *IT World,* December 5, 2011. Accessed December 7, 2011. http://www.itworld.com/security/230469/us-power-grid-big-soft-target-cyberattack-mit-study-shows.

Gabor, T. "Armed Robbery Overseas: Highlights of a Canadian Study." In: D. Challenger (ed.), *Armed Robbery.* Canberra, AU: Australian Institute of Criminology, 1988. (Seminar Proceedings No. 26.)

GAO (General Accounting Office). "Critical Infrastructure Protection: Challenges in Securing Control Systems." Washington DC: General Accounting Office, 2003. Accessed March 20, 2010. http://www.gao.gov/new.items/d04140t.pdf.

Greenfeld, Lawrence. *Alcohol and Crime: An Analysis of National Data on the Prevalence of Alcohol Involvement in Crime.* Washington, DC: Bureau of Justice Statistics, 1998.

Groff, Elizabeth. "Simulation for Theory Testing and Experimentation: An Example Using Routine Activity Theory and Street Robbery." Journal of Quantitative Criminology 23 (2007), 75–103.

Haimes, Yacov. "On the Definition of Vulnerabilities in Measuring Risks to In-frastructures."*Risk Analysis*, 26 (2006), 293–296.

Holt, Thomas, Adam Bossler, and David May. "Low Self-Control, Deviant Peer Associations, and Juvenile Cyberdeviance." *American Journal of Criminal Justice, Online First, June 2011*

Holt, Thomas and Max Kilger. "Know Your Enemy: The Social Dynamics of Hacking." The Honeynet Project, 2012a. Accessed June 10, 2012.https://honeynet.org/files/Holt%20and%20Kilger%20-%20KYE%20-%20The%20Social%20Dynamics%20of%20Hacking.pdf.

Holt, Thomas and Max Kilger. "Examining Willingness to Attack Critical In-frastructure On and Off-line," *Crime and Delinquency* 58 (2012b).

Jordan, Tim and Paul Taylor. "A Sociology of Hackers." *The Sociological Review*, 46 (1998),757–780.

Krone, Tony. "Hacking Motives." Australian Institute of Criminology. High tech crime brief no. 6 (2005).

Kuvshinkova, Svetlana. "SQL SLAMMER worm lessons learned for consideration by the electricity sector." My IT Forum, September 5, 2003.Accessed September 21, 2011. http://www.myitforum.com/articles/15/view.asp?id=5985.

Lemos, Robert. "Power play: Electric company hacked." *ZDNet*, December 15, 2000. Accessed September 20, 2011. http://www.zdnet.co.uk/news/emerging-tech/2000/12/15/power-play-electric-company-hacked-2083210/.

Lewis, James. "Cyber terror: Missing in action." In *Technology and Terrorism*, edited by David Clarke, 145–153. New Jersey: Transaction, 2004.

Luiijf, Eric. "SCADA Security Good Practices for the Drinking Water Sector." TNO: Netherlands Organization for Applied Scientific Research, 2008.

Marcum, Catherine, George Higgins, Tina Freiburger, and Melissa Ricketts. "Policing Possession of Child Pornography Online: Investigating the Training and Resources Dedicated to the Investigation of Cyber Crime," *International Journal of Police Science & Management*, 12 (2010), 516–525.

Martellozzo, Elena, Daniel Nehring, and Helen Taylor. "Online Child Sexual Abuse by Female Offenders: An Exploratory Study." *International Journal of Cyber Criminology*, 4 (2010), 592–609.

McAfee. *McAfee Virtual Criminology Report: North American Study into Organized Crime and the Internet*. San Francisco, CA: McAfee, 2005. Accessed October 20, 2005. http://www.mcafee.com/us/local_content/misc/mcafee_na_virtual_criminology_report.pdf.

McMullan, John, and Aunshul Rege. "Cyberextortion at Online Gambling Sites: Criminal Organization and Legal Challenges."*Gaming Law Review*, 11 (2007), 648–665.

McMullan, John and Aunshul Rege. "Online crime and internet gambling."*Journal of Gambling Issues*. Issue 24, July 2010.

Moore, Andrew, Dawn Cappelli, Thomas Caron, Eric Shaw, Derrick Spooner, and Randall Trzeciak. *A Preliminary Model of Insider Theft of Intellectual Property*. Pittsburg, PA: Computer Emergency Response Team 2011. Accessed June 10, 2012. http://www.cert.org/archive/pdf/11tn013.pdf.

Moore, Robert, Naga Tarun Guntupalli, and Tina Lee "Parental Regulation and Online Activities: Examining factors that influence a Youth's potential to become a Victim of Online Harassment." *International Journal of Cyber Criminology*, 4 (2010), 685–698.

Morain, Dan. "Hackers Victimize Cal-ISO." *Los Angeles Times*, June 9, 2001. Accessed August 18, 2011. http://articles.latimes.com/2001/jun/09/news/mn-8294.

Moteff, John. *Risk Management and Critical Infrastructure Protection: Assessing, Integrating, and Managing Threats, Vulnerabilities and Consequences*. CRS Report for Congress, Order Code RL32561, 2005.

NCS (National Communication System). *Supervisory Control and Data Acquisition (SCADA) Systems*. Washington DC: National Communication System, 2004. Accessed May 31, 2012. http://www.ncs.gov/library/tech_bulletins/2004/tib_04-1.pdf.

Newman, Graeme and Ronald Clarke. *Superhighway Robbery: Preventing e-commerce crime*. Oregon: Willan Publishing, 2003.

Nicholson, Rick. "Critical Infrastructure Cybersecurity: Survey Findings and Analysis." Energy Insights, an IDC company. White Paper sponsored by Secure Computing, November 2008.

NSTAC (National Security Telecommunications Advisory Committee). *Information Assurance Task Force: Electric Power Risk Assessment—Executive Summary*. Washington DC: National Security Telecommunications Advisory Committee, 2000. Accessed August 17, 2011. http://www.solarstorms.org/ElectricAssessment.html.

Oman, Paul, Edmund Schweitzer III, and Jeff Robert. "Safeguarding IEDS, Substations, and SCADA Systems Against Electronic Intrusions."*Schweitzer Engineering Laboratories* 2001. Accessed August 11, 2011. http://www2.selinc.com/techpprs/6118.pdf.

Poulsen, Kevin. "Slammer worm crashed Ohio nuke plant network." *Security Focus*, August 19, 2003. Accessed August 10, 2011. http://www.securityfocus.com/news/6767.

Rantala, Ramona. "Cybercrimes Against Businesses, 2005."*Bureau of Justice Statistics*, October 27, 2008. Accessed February 19, 2009. http://bjs.ojp.usdoj.gov/content/pub/pdf/cb05.pdf.

Rege, Aunshul. "What's Love Got to Do With It? Exploring Online Dating Scams and Identity Fraud."*International Journal of Cybercriminology*, 3 (2009), 494–512.

Rege-Patwardhan, Aunshul. "Cybercrimes against critical infrastructures: a study of online criminal organization and techniques."*Criminal Justice Studies*, 22 (2009), 261–271.

Reyns, Bradford. "A situational crime prevention approach to cyberstalking victimization: Preventive tactics for Internet users and online place managers."*Crime Prevention and Community Safety*, 12, (2010) 99–118.

Rindskopf, Amy. "Juvenile computer hacker cuts off FAA tower at regional airport: First federal charges brought against a juvenile for computer crime."*Department of Justice*, March 18, 1998. Accessed November 20, 2008. http://ncsi-net.ncsi.iisc.ernet.in/cyberspace/law/responsibility/cybercrime/www.usdoj.gov/criminal/cybercrime/juvenile.htm.

Robles, Rosslin, Min-kyu Choi, Eun-suk Cho, Seok-soo Kim, Gil-cheol Park, and Jang-Hee Lee. "Common Threats and Vulnerabilities of Critical Infrastructures." *International Journal of Control and Automation, 1* (2008), 17–22.

Rogers, Marcus. *The Development of a Meaningful Hacker Taxonomy: A Two Dimensional Approach.* Accessed January 23, 2007. https://www.cerias.purdue.edu/tools_and_resources/bibtex_archive/archive/2005-43.pdf.

Rossignol, Michael. "Critical Infrastructure Protection and Emergency Preparedness." *Government of Canada Publications*, June 2001. Accessed August 27, 2007. http://dsp-psd.pwgsc.gc.ca/Collection-R/LoPBdP/BP/prb017-e.htm.

Roy, Maria. *Abusive Partner—An Analysis of Domestic Battering.* New York: Van Nostrand Reinhold, 1982.

SANS (System Administration, Networking, and Security Institute). *Can Hackers Turn Your Lights Off? The Vulnerability of the US Power Grid to Electronic Attack.* Chicago, IL: SANS Institute, 2001. Accessed August 30, 2011. http://www.sans.org/reading_room/whitepapers/hackers/hackers-turn-lights-off-vulnerability-power-grid-electronic-attack_606.

Scadasystems.net. "SCADA systems." Accessed August 9, 2011. http://www.scadasystems.net/.

Seigfried, Kathryn, Richard Lovely, and Marcus Rogers. "Self-Reported Online Child Pornography Behavior: A Psychological Analysis." *International Journal of Cyber Criminology*, 2 (2008), 286–297.

Shaw, Eric and Harley Stock. "Behavioral Risk Indicators of Malicious Insider Theft of Intellectual Property: Misreading the Writing on the Wall." 2011. Accessed June 10, 2012. https://www4.symantec.com/mktginfo/

whitepaper/21220067_
GA_WP_Malicious_Insider_12_11_dai81510_cta56681.pdf.

Smith, Martha. "Introduction." *Crime Prevention Studies*, 16 (2003), 1–5.

Stamp, Jason, John Dillinger, William Young, and Jennifer DePoy. "Common Vulnerabilities in Critical Infrastructure Control Systems."*Energy.gov*, May 22, 2003. Accessed August 27, 2007. http://www.oe.netl.doe.gov/docs/prepare/vulnerabilities.pdf.

Stouffer, Keith, Joe Falco, and Karen Scarfone. "NIST Guide to Industrial Control Systems (ICS) Security."*National Institute of Standards and Technology*. Computer Security Division, Computer Security Resource Center, June 2011. Accessed August 5, 2011. http://csrc.nist.gov/publications/nistpubs/800-82/SP800-82-final.pdf.

Taylor, Robert, Eric Fritsch, John Liederbach, and Thomas Holt. *Digital Crime and Digital Terrorism, 2nd Edition*. NJ: Pearson Education, Inc, 2010.

The Economist. "Cyberwar: War in the Fifth Domain." *The Economist*, 2010. Accessed January 5, 2012. http://www.economist.com/node/16478792.

Theoharidoua, Marianthi, Spyros Kokolakisb, Maria Karydaa, and Evangelos Kiountouzis. "The insider threat to information systems and the effectiveness of ISO17799." *Computers & Security*, 24 (2005), 472–484.

Vatis, Michael. "Cyber Attacks: Protecting America's Security Against Digital Threats." Executive Session on Domestic Preparedness, 2002. Accessed January 20, 2012. http://belfercenter.ksg.harvard.edu/files/vam02.pdf.

Verton, Dan. *Black Ice: The Invisible Threat of Cyber-Terrorism*. CA: McGraw-Hill, 2003.

Veysey, Bonita, Kristen Zgoba, and Melissa Dalessandro. "Preliminary Step Towards Evaluating the Impact of Megan's Law: A Trend Analysis of Sexual Offenses in New Jersey from 1985 to 2005." *Justice Research and Policy*, 10 (2008), 1–18.

Wang, Xuguang, Lin Liu, and John Eck. "Crime Simulation Using GIS and Artificial Intelligent Agents." In J. E. Eck & L. Liu (Eds.), *Artificial Crime Analysis Systems: Using Computer Simulations and Geographic Information Systems* (pp. 209–224). Hershey, PA: IGI Global, 2008.

Weaver, Nicholas, Vern Paxson, Stuart Staniford, and Robert Cunningham. *A Taxonomy of Computer Worms*. International Computer Science Institute, 2003. Accessed March 8, 2006. http://www.icir.org/vern/papers/taxonomy.pdf.

Williams, Dan. "Israel holds couple in corporate espionage case." *Computer World*, January 31, 2006. Accessed March 8, 2006. http://www.computerworld.com/s/article/108225/Israel_holds_couple_in_corporate_espionage_case.

YouTube. "SCADA Tutorial."Accessed August 5, 2011. http://www.youtube.com/watch?v=tIU_wDVoEVE.

ZDNN. "Humans opened the door for power hack."*ZDNet,* November 7, 2001. Accessed August 18, 2011. http://www.zdnet.com/news/humans-opened-the-door-for-calif-power-hack/117607.

Zintro. *SCADA Experts—Find SCADA Consultants, Expert Witnesses & More.* Zintro, 2011. Accessed August 5, 2011. https://www.zintro.com/area/scada.

9

Examining State and Local Law Enforcement Perceptions of Computer Crime

Thomas J. Holt, Adam M. Bossler, and Sarah Fitzgerald

The impact of computer-mediated communications and the Internet on all facets of human life has been well documented across the social sciences (Jewkes and Sharp 2003; Mann and Sutton 1998; Quinn and Forsyth 2005). Not only have these technologies changed the way that business and personal communications take place, but they have radically altered the capacity of offenders to engage in a variety of crimes (see Brenner 2008; McQuade 2006; Wall 2007). Electronic communications and the Internet have augmented or facilitated most forms of illegal behavior, including prostitution (Holt and Blevins 2007; Sharpe and Earle 2003; Soothhill and Sanders 2005), pedophilia (Durkin 1997; Durkin and Bryant 1999; Holt, Blevins, and Burkert 2010; Quayle and Taylor 2002), fraud (Burns, Whitworth, and Thompson 2004; Holt and Graves 2007; Holt and Lampke 2010; Newman and Clarke 2003) and piracy (see Higgins 2005; Higgins, Fell, and Wilson 2007; Hinduja 2001, 2003).

The economic impact of computer crimes is also substantial, affecting individuals and corporations alike. Businesses reported average losses of $500,000 in 2008 due to financial fraud incidents (Computer Security Institute 2008), while individual consumers lost an average of $575 to various types of fraud in 2009 (Internet Crime Complaint Center 2010). The music and movie industries also claim to have lost billions due to intellectual property theft and digital piracy (Higgins 2005; Higgins et al. 2007; Hinduja 2001, 2003; Motion Picture Association of America 2007). Furthermore, there are significant emotional and psychological consequences for victims of cyberstalking (Finn 2004; Holt and Bossler 2009) and children affected by pornography and pedophilia (see Berson 2003; Durkin and Bryant 1999).

In addition, computer-based terror attacks against all manner of targets have become an increasingly important issue for local law enforcement agencies across the nation (Aeilts 2005; Brenner 2008; Stambaugh et al. 2001). Many key resources in the public and private sector are linked to and depend on computer technology to function, including electrical grids, nuclear power plants, water infrastructure, and financial systems (Aeilts 2005; Denning 2001; Taylor, Fritsch, Liederbach, and Holt 2010). As a consequence, local law enforcement agencies must recognize and collaborate with private sector partners to protect and secure threats to critical infrastructure (see Brenner 2008; Taylor et al. 2010). Thus, law enforcement must be prepared to investigate a diverse range of offenses and offenders.

There is, however, a significant gap in our knowledge of law enforcement agencies' awareness, preparation, and attitudes toward computer crimes. Statistics on computer crimes are rarely collected by law enforcement agencies or reported in outlets such as the Uniform Crime Report or National Crime Victimization Survey. There are several reasons for this lack of data, including victim confusion over appropriate reporting agencies, concern that the incident is not important enough to report, and victims' inability to recognize when crimes have occurred (see Holt 2003; Speer 2000). This lack of statistical information makes it is difficult to estimate the true prevalence of computer crimes and how local law enforcement has or can respond to it. The lack of data at the local level is particularly significant, as these law enforcement agencies serve as primary first responders at all crime scenes, and their knowledge and ability to properly initiate an investigation has a significant impact on the way that cases are handled and investigated (see Burns et al. 2004; Goodman 1997; Hinduja 2004; McQuade 2006; Senjo 2004; Stambaugh et al. 2001). Thus, it is critical that researchers consider local agencies' attitudes toward the severity, frequency, and importance of computer crime offenses in order to assess training and resource needs, as well as their overall ability to properly investigate these offenses (see Burns et al. 2004; Hinduja 2004; McQuade 2006; Senjo 2004; Stambaugh et al. 2001).

This study seeks to fill this gap in our knowledge in two ways. First, we use data collected from a sample of state and local law enforcement officers and agents to understand their departments' and agencies' staffing and training for computer crime investigations and the handling of digital evidence. Second, we consider their perceptions of computer crime, their severity relative to street crimes, and knowledge of basic technology terms. The findings give insight into the preparedness of state and local police agencies to handle computer crime and the ways that their attitudes toward these offenses may affect investigations and officer behavior. The implications of this research for policy and future investigation are also considered.

Policing Computer Crime

There have been relatively few studies documenting the capacity for state and local law enforcement to properly investigate computer crime. One of the main studies considering police responses to computer crime is the Electronic Crime Needs Assessment for State and Local Law Enforcement report, published by the National Institute of Justice, which utilized data collected from a sample of 126 individuals from 114 agencies in 1998 (Stambaugh et al. 2001). Before conducting this study, the researchers recognized the complex issues surrounding the measurement of computer-based offenses and the lack of a universal definition for computer crime. Thus, they worked in collaboration with state and local agencies to develop a definition of "electronic crime" that refers to:

> fraud, theft, forgery, child pornography or exploitation, stalking, traditional white-collar crimes, privacy violations, illegal drug transactions, espionage, computer intrusions, or any other offenses that occur in an electronic environment for the purpose of economic gain or with the intent to destroy or otherwise inflict harm on another person or institution (Stambaugh et al. 2001, 2).

A similarly broad definition of cyberterrorism was developed, recognizing any "premeditated, politically motivated attack against information systems, computer programs and data … to disrupt the political, social, or physical infrastructure of the target" (Stambaugh et al. 2001, 2). The wide range of offenses included in these definitions was meant to provide a frame of reference for respondents and some standard to assess computer-based crime.

Using these definitions, Stambaugh et al. (2001) found a significant increase in computer crimes reported to law enforcement. At the same time, the respondents suggested that a substantial proportion of offenses were not being reported to law enforcement. Computer crime cases were given low priority across most agencies, unless they were child pornography or pedophile cases. This may have been a consequence of unsuccessful prosecutions, as many agencies felt that management, officers, and prosecutors appeared to have little knowledge and resources to adequately carry out computer crime investigations and prosecutions. Furthermore, respondents indicated the need for assistance with tools and training to better investigate these crimes. In fact, only half of all agencies had a formal electronic crime unit, and less than one third belonged to an interagency crime task force (Stambaugh et al. 2001).

Based on these findings, Stambaugh et al. (2001) identified ten critical needs to improve the capability of local and state law enforcement agencies to combat computer crimes. Specifically, these needs included (Stambaugh et al. 2001, 31–36).

1) **Public Awareness:** The public and private sectors needed to be better educated on the growing threat of computer crimes to decrease the likelihood of victimization.
2) **Data and Reporting:** Statistics and data collection on computer crime were needed to better understand computer crime prevalence and trends.
3) **Uniform training and certification courses:** Justice system actors, including prosecutors and judges, needed better training and certifications to effectively deal with computer crimes at all levels of the system.
4) **Onsite management assistance for electronic crime units and task forces:** State and local law enforcement agencies needed to develop computer crime units, as well as collaborative task forces, to better investigate computer crime cases.
5) **Updated laws:** Continuously updated legislation against computer crimes was needed to effectively prosecute cutting edge criminal acts and those crimes that cross jurisdictional boundaries.
6) **Cooperation with the high-tech industry:** The need for greater collaboration and communication with private industry was needed to increase reports of criminal incidents and improve high-tech crime training for law enforcement.
7) **Special research and publications:** A guidebook with information on training and investigative resources was needed to improve communications between investigators, forensic experts, management, and practitioners to deal with computer crime.
8) **Management awareness and support:** Law enforcement management and administrators needed to recognize the severity of computer crime and better support the investigation of these offenses.
9) **Investigative and forensic tools:** Better technological resources were needed to improve the investigation of computer crime cases, including budget conscious equipment to engender forensic examinations.
10) **Structuring a computer crime unit:** Research was needed to explore the needs and staffing issues present in the development of computer crime and forensic investigation units to create a best practices guide for law enforcement agencies.

Although a number of years have passed since the publication of the Electronic Crime Needs Assessment study (Stambaugh et al. 2001), there has been no systematic exploration of the impact of its policy recommendations or the general awareness of computer crime in local police agencies. A limited number of studies have examined the preparedness of law enforcement to examine specific forms of cybercrime, such as fraud (Burns et al. 2004), or cybercrime in specific areas (Hinduja 2004; Senjo 2004).

Burns et al. (2004) assessed the preparedness of law local enforcement to investigate Internet fraud. They found that most of the individuals responsible for filling out the survey believed online fraud was a serious problem (76.5 percent), but that law enforcement agencies in general did not consider Internet fraud to be a significant societal problem (41.0 percent). Most of them did not believe that they had sufficient funds to address Internet fraud (only 15.3 percent believed they had the necessary resources). Almost half of the agencies did not even have a computer crime division (46.7 percent). In fact, they would prefer Internet fraud laws to be enforced by federal (93.0 percent) or state law enforcement (69.7 percent) rather than local law enforcement (52.1 percent).

Hinduja (2004) considered the needs and preparedness of local law enforcement agencies in Michigan to deal with computer crimes. His study found that approximately twenty percent of the agencies (n=275) reported that they had one or more individuals trained to investigate these cases. Most agencies (66 percent), however, investigated less than ten computer crime cases in the year 2000. Of the computer crimes reported, harassment was the most common offense, followed by child pornography, solicitation of minors, identity theft, e-commerce fraud, and forgery. Thirty-six percent, however, reported that computer crimes detract attention from traditional crimes (Hinduja 2004).

The findings from Hinduja's (2004) research suggest that there is a need for greater preparation among law enforcement agencies to deal with computer crime, especially since some officers perceive computer crime cases to be insignificant. There has been little empirical research on police officer perspectives regarding the severity of computer crime: whether they think it is fundamentally different from "traditional" crime; the ways that law enforcement agencies have changed in response; and what they think should be done about these offenses. Senjo (2004) conducted one of the few studies examining line officers' perceptions of computer crime. In his sample of officers in a Western state, he found that officers, particularly younger officers with less experience, viewed pedophilia as the most serious computer crime that is occurring (Senjo 2004). Furthermore, officers believed computer criminals to be older males rather than young offenders. The reported officer perspectives were somewhat inconsistent with the larger empirical literature on computer crime, suggesting that there may be a gap in law enforcement knowledge of computer crime (Senjo 2004).

Taken as a whole, there is a critical need for greater research on local law enforcement awareness and training to deal with computer crimes. Few researchers have considered how the significant needs identified by the Electronic Crime Needs Assessment study (Stambaugh et al. 2001) have been met or improved on in local law enforcement agencies. Considering that the primary responsibility of investigating new types of crime falls on local law enforcement, it is critical that we understand how prepared first responders are to deal with computer crime and their attitudes toward the severity, frequency, and importance of these offenses. Such information can provide key policy recommendations to improve the training and resources available for local law enforcement agencies and increase the capability of first responders to appropriately handle computer crime cases.

Data

The data for this study were collected through an electronic survey solicitation administered by the Federal Law Enforcement Training Center (FLETC). This solicitation was delivered via email to approximately ten thousand individuals in state and local law enforcement agencies across the country who attended training classes related to computer crime and digital forensic examination. The solicitation provided a detailed introduction to the study, the relationship between the researchers and FLETC, and included a hyperlink to the online survey instrument. This process solicited 437 responses, less than five percent of the overall total of solicitations. Despite utilizing multiple measures to validate and encourage participation, the low response rate may have been a consequence of limited availability on the part of the responding officers. Alternatively, the respondents may have had some concerns over providing information on behalf of their agency on issues of training and caseloads. Although only 370 responses are needed to generalize to a solicitation of 10,000 (Krejcie and Morgan 1970), the volunteer bias precludes strong conclusions and does limit overall generalizability. Given the paucity of research in this area (see Hinduja 2004; Senjo 2004; Stambaugh et al. 2001), however, this sample provided a needed exploratory investigation into the capacity of state and local agencies to deal with computer crime.

Findings

Respondents were asked a battery of questions concerning their agency, computer crime investigations, and perceptions of computer crime offenders and activity. The survey instrument utilized measures adapted from multiple studies related to computer crime awareness in police agencies (see Goodman 1997; Hinduja 2004; Senjo 2004) and the general public (Furnell 2002). Each item will be explored and discussed in detail, starting with basic descriptive characteristics of the sample.

Demographic Composition

Basic descriptive information about the agency the respondent worked for was collected in lieu of demographic information from the respondent to maintain anonymity. In terms of agency size, 75.7 percent of the agencies had one hundred or less police officers serving in their agency (see Table 1). This is in fact under-representing smaller agencies as 93.9 percent of agencies have ninety-nine officers or fewer (BJS 2007). Thus, our sample consists of a higher percentage of larger agencies, which are more likely to have computer crime units and address computer crime, than is found in American policing. The geographic location of agencies was also collected using five bounded regions: the Midwest, South, Pacific, Northeast, and Mountain. Of the agencies surveyed, 28.5 percent indicated being in the Midwest, 33 percent in the South, 10.6 percent in the Pacific, 19.8 percent in the Northeast, and 8.1 percent in the Mountain region (see Table 1).

Table 1. Size and Geographic Location of Law Enforcement Agencies

Region	Less Than 20	20 to 100	101 to 200	201 to 500	501 to 1000	1001 to 5000	More Than 5000	Total
Midwest	48	39	6	4	1	4	0	102
South	36	51	11	12	2	6	0	118
Pacific	15	10	7	1	2	2	1	38
Northeast	27	20	7	9	1	4	3	71
Mountain	11	14	3	1	0	0	0	29
Total	137	134	34	27	6	16	4	358

Data on the number of individuals residing within the agency's geographic boundaries were also collected. Eleven percent of the agencies reported having one million or more individuals residing in their jurisdiction. Twenty-seven percent of the agencies had 5,001 to 20,000 citizens and twenty-two percent had five thousand or fewer individuals residing within their jurisdictional boundaries.

In order to understand the extent to which officers within departments handle computer-related crime issues, respondents were asked how many part-time officers or investigators they had within their agencies who were assigned to handle digital evidence. Results indicate that 76 percent of agencies had no part-time officers or investigators assigned to deal with digital evidence. Of those agencies with part-time personnel, the largest reported category (17.1 percent) was three to seven officers total. There were more agencies reporting full-time digital evidence handlers, as 44.7 percent had between one and four investigators. This is a significant improvement over previous research indicating that there have been some changes to increase law enforcement staffing for computer crime (see Goodman 1997; Hinduja 2004). It is important to note, however, that 23 percent of all agencies indicated that they had no part or full-time officers who could properly work with digital evidence. Thus, there are still some staffing issues concerning digital evidence at the state and local level.

Additionally, respondents were asked to assess the number of part-time and full-time officers assigned to the investigation of online crimes. This term was used in lieu of computer crime to assess any and all investigations that take place via the Internet. The overwhelming majority of departments (83.6%) had no part-time officers assigned to these investigations. This may be a function of the expense and manpower needed, making it more difficult to staff such roles with part-time investigators. Overall, 46 percent reported having between one to three full-time officers assigned to online crimes. At the same time, it is important to note that 38.7 percent of all responding agencies had no part or full-time officers trained to investigate online crime. This is a sizeable proportion, suggesting that there is still a need to increase the staff to support computer crime investigations in state and local agencies.

Respondents were also asked to estimate the percentage of officers within their agency that had received various training related to computer crime. Specifically, respondents were asked what percentage of their officers had been trained in handling digital evidence. Of those surveyed, 79.3 percent indicated that 20 percent or fewer of their officers had been trained in the handling of digital evidence (see Table 2). In terms of officers trained in investigating online crimes, the majority (88.1 percent) of agencies indicated that 20 percent or fewer of their officers had received such training. In terms of the percent of officers within each agency that had been trained in the handling of digital evidence, the Mid-

Table 2. The Percentage of Officers Trained for
Digital Evidence and Computer Crime

Percentage of Officers	Digital Evidence (n-354)	Online Crime (n-345)
10	70.3	81.2
20	9.0	6.9
30–40	5.9	6.4
50–60	5.0	2.9
70–90	4.2 ·	0.9
100	5.6	1.7

west had the greatest percentage, with nine agencies within this region indicating that 100 percent of their officers are trained in handling digital evidence. This finding is in keeping with previous research (e.g., Hinduja 2004) and suggests that there are slight improvements taking place to change the investigative power of state and local agencies to deal with computer crime.

Investigations

Respondents were asked to indicate whether or not their agency actively investigated various forms of economic, sexual, and hacking-related computer crimes (see Table 3 for detail). The most common type of investigation conducted involved identity theft (79.2 percent), followed by fraud (71.9 percent) and online harassment (71.8 percent) (see Hinduja 2004 for similar finding on harassment). This is a distinct shift from previously identified investigative priorities, as sex offenses appeared to be the dominant crime reported to state and local agencies (Stambaugh et al. 2001). Such a change may be a reflection of the increasing use of the Internet for financial transactions and information, as well as improved awareness of this type of crime in the general population (see Burns et al. 2004; Holt and Lampke 2010). Child pornography and the solicitation of minors were also somewhat common as more than half of the responding agencies conduct such investigations. The least examined form of computer crime were hacking and computer intrusion cases. This results from both the difficulty in investigating these crimes as well as the cross-state and international dynamics of computer hacking, as offenders can reside anywhere in the country or world and victimize multiple machines in any location (see Brenner 2008; McQuade 2006; Taylor et al. 2010; Wall 2007). The

Table 3. Types of Computer Crimes Investigated by State and Local Agencies

	Yes	No
Identity theft (n=355)	79.2	20.8
Fraud (n=356)	71.9	28.1
Harassment (n=358)	71.8	28.2
Child porn (n=358)	61.7	38.3
Solicitation of children (n=358)	51.7	48.3
Sex crimes (n=357)	42.0	58.0
Hacking/intrusion (n=353)	32.0	68.0

jurisdictional issues that can arise make hacking investigations more likely to fall under federal law enforcement agency purview.

Respondents were also asked to identify how many cases their agency had dealt with in the last twelve months involving online crime and digital evidence, to give some insight into the prevalence of these issues in state and local agencies (see Table 4). With regard to digital evidence, 70 percent of the agencies had nineteen or fewer cases involving digital evidence within the last twelve months. 18.7 percent had no cases within the prior year that had digital evidence. Thus, there are relatively few cases being investigated with digital evidence by these agencies among first responders, in keeping with previous research. Respondents were also asked how many digital evidence cases were cleared by arrest in the past twelve months (results not shown). Of the agencies involved, 33.5 percent indicated zero arrests, while 25.9 percent said that there were one or two cases that resulted in an arrest. Only 5 percent of agencies indicated that they had made one hundred or more arrests from cases involving the handling of digital evidence. Thus, despite the use of digital forensic techniques, there appears to be a relatively small number of cases cleared by arrest at the local level.

Similar patterns were identified concerning cases involving some form of computer crime, such as computer hacking or sex offenses (see Table 9.4). Specifically, 75.2 percent reported they had nineteen or fewer online crime cases within the previous year, more than half of the agencies (57.2 percent) had five or fewer cases, and 27.9 percent stated they had zero. The number of computer crime cases cleared by arrest was much smaller than in the digital evidence category. Most agencies (65 percent) had less than two cases cleared by

Table 4. Number of Active Cases Involving
Digital Evidence or Computer Crime

	Digital Evidence		Online Crime	
Number of Cases	N	Percentage	N	Percentage
0 cases	67	18.7	96	27.9
1–2 cases	54	15.0	53	15.4
3–5 cases	67	18.7	48	13.9
6–19 cases	63	17.6	62	18.0
20–99 cases	49	13.7	58	16.9
100–800 cases	40	11.2	23	6.7
1000 or more cases	18	5.0	4	1.2
Total	358	100	344	100

arrest, which is sensible given the relative anonymity the Internet provides for offenders (see McQuade 2006; Wall 2007).

Attitudes toward Computer Crime

Respondents were also asked to indicate their level of agreement with various statements related to computer crime, including offender behaviors, victim impacts, and citizen awareness of this problem (see Table 5). One of the most significant points of agreement (98.1 percent) was in support of the statement, "Computer crime is a serious problem in American society." This suggests that officers recognize the seriousness of computer crime. Clearly, a part of this is due to the fact that most of them (92.8 percent) agreed with the following statement, "Computers allow individuals to feel less responsible for their actions, increasing the likelihood of crime." In addition, 82.1 percent believed that attacks on computer systems pose a threat equal to or greater than physical attacks. This indicates that law enforcement agencies are aware of the danger posed by acts of cyberterror, particularly in the post 9/11 world.

Most respondents, however, felt that individuals in their community did not recognize the risk that they face from these offenses. Only 15.1 percent agreed that, "Citizens in our community understand the risk of computer crime." This is surprising in light of the significant recognition of cybercrime as a problem among law enforcement agencies. Thus, there may be a discon-

Table 5. Officers' Reported Attitudes Toward Computer Crimes

Statement	Agree	Disagree
Computer crime is a serious problem in American society.	98.1	1.9
Computers allow individuals to feel less responsible for their actions increasing the likelihood of crime.	92.8	7.2
Budget constraints limit our ability to investigate computer crimes.	89.4	10.6
Attacks on computer systems pose a threat equal to or greater than physical attacks.	82.1	17.9
Computer crimes have a greater impact in corporate settings rather than in home settings.	69.9	30.1
The majority of computer crimes are perpetrated by individuals in their teens and twenties.	48.5	51.5
Computer crimes detract officers' attention from street crimes.	47.9	52.1
Computer criminals often reside in foreign countries rather than the US.	45.9	54.1
Computer crime occurs more frequently in businesses rather than among home users.	41.5	58.5
Convicted hackers should be allowed to work in computing jobs.	18.1	81.9
Citizens in our community understand the risk of computer crime.	15.1	84.9
Convicted hackers should be allowed to have a computer at home.	13.2	86.8

nect between law enforcement and citizens' perceptions of the severity of computer crime.

A majority of the respondents (89.4 percent) also believed that budget constraints limited their ability to investigate computer crimes (see Hinduja 2004; Stambaugh et al. 2001). Coupled with their beliefs that computer crime is a serious problem, this implied that these officers believed that more funding would lead to better investigations of computer crime. Almost half of the respondents (47.9 percent), however, responded that computer crimes detract officers' attention from street crimes, possibly implying that this issue has not improved since earlier studies and commentaries (Goodman 1997; Hinduja 2004; Stambaugh et al. 2001). Thus, budget constraints might be a strong factor in why local law enforcement does not focus more on computer crimes. Also, state and local law enforcement agencies' interest in investigating these crimes may not be as strong as their belief that it is a serious problem.

There were, however, some disagreements among the respondents as to the types of offenders who engage in computer crimes and who is more likely to be victimized. A little less than half of the respondents (45.9 percent) agreed that computer criminals often reside in foreign countries, indicating that half of the respondents believed that most of our computer crime problem is home-grown. Half of the respondents (48.5 percent) agreed that most computer criminals are in their teens and twenties. This is a shift from previous studies, which found greater support for the contention that computer criminals are older individuals (Furnell 2002; Senjo 2004). The research literature is mixed concerning these issues, as computer hackers are largely younger males (Brenner 2008; Jordan and Taylor 1998; Holt 2007), while there are few metrics on the demographic composition of pedophiles and online sex offenders (see Quayle and Taylor 2002). The relative split noted in this data may be a reflection of increasing awareness of the variation in offender characteristics. In addition, only 41.5 percent believed that businesses were more likely to be the victims of computer crime relative to home users. At the same time, almost 70 percent agreed that computer crime had a greater impact in corporate settings. Thus, the respondents believed that individuals were more likely to be victimized, but the consequences were greater for corporations (see also Furnell 2002).

Furthermore, the majority of the sample did not support the notion that convicted computer hackers should be allowed to work in computing jobs (81.9 percent) or have a computer in their homes (86.8 percent). This finding is similar to research on the general population's attitudes toward computer crime offending (see Furnell 2002). It is important to note, however, that reformed hackers play important roles in the computer security community, and can assist in the investigation of computer crimes (see Furnell 2002; Holt 2007; Taylor et al. 2010). These individuals could also facilitate training and assist state and local law enforcement in light of the dearth of officers and resources to investigate these crimes. Thus, local law enforcement agencies desire to restrict hackers' access to technology may actually be problematic given their capacity to assist policing agencies.

Perceptions of Computer Crime Offending

In order to assess how law enforcement agencies perceive computer crimes relative to terrestrial crimes, respondents were asked to rank the severity of a variety of offenses on a five-point scale from least serious (1) to most serious (5). The mean scores for each form of crime are presented in Table 6 and provide an interesting perspective on the perceived impact of both computer and real world crimes and the relationships between these offenses (see also Senjo 2004).

Table 6. Perceived Severity of Computer Crimes

Offense Type	Mean Severity	N
Stealing something worth less than $5 dollars	2.09	357
Using someone else's wireless connection	2.92	355
Unauthorized copying of media	2.97	358
Stealing something worth more than $50	3.19	357
Unauthorized copying of software	3.26	358
Purposely damaging or destroying property	3.50	358
Harassment over the Internet	3.68	358
Breaking into a vehicle or building to steal something	3.82	357
Viewing someone else's electronic data without permission	3.85	358
Hitting someone without any reason	3.88	358
Viruses and malicious software infection	4.20	358
Electronic theft of money from accounts	4.46	357
Selling hard drugs such as heroin, cocaine, or meth	4.49	358
Terrorist attacks against electronic targets (cyberterror)	4.59	359
Terrorist attacks against physical targets	4.84	356
Child pornography and sexual solicitation	4.86	358

The respondents considered stealing something worth less than five dollars to be the least serious crime of the crimes examined. In fact, they considered five different types of theft—stealing something worth less than five dollars; using someone else's Internet connection; media and software piracy; and stealing something more than fifty dollars—to be the least serious crimes overall. Thus, less serious forms of crime and relatively equal, regardless of whether they based in the physical or virtual world. Purposely damaging property was considered slightly more severe than the minor forms of theft, with harassment via the Internet considered the next severe. The respondents indicated that threats, although virtual with possibly no physical contact ever between victim and offender, are still considered more serious than real world property damage.

A similar clustering of severity was noted for breaking into a vehicle or building to steal something, viewing electronic data without permission, and hitting someone without any reason. The relationship between burglary and hacking has been proposed by a variety of scholars, and the appearance of this relationship suggests law enforcement agencies may share this point of view (see Wall 2001). In addition, it appears that the respondents equated serious forms of privacy violation (e.g., having electronic data viewed and having something stolen from a vehicle or building) to be equivalent of minor forms of violence. Malicious software infections, such as the spread of viruses, however, were ranked higher than these offenses. This is sensible given that malware can be used as an attack platform for various types of hacking and theft (Bossler and Holt 2009; Brenner 2008; Taylor et al. 2010), as well as damage computer systems and networks. This finding suggests state and local law enforcement agencies recognize the severity of more significant hacker-related computer crimes.

The mean scores for electronic theft of money and the sale of hard drugs were also relatively similar. Both offenses have a significant impact, though for very different reasons. The financial impact of electronic theft for victims can be quite substantial, and are complex offenses for law enforcement agencies to investigate and clear by arrest (see Internet Crime Complaint Center 2010; Newman and Clarke 2003). Drug sales, however, have significant negative consequences for drug abusers and the larger community, including increased rates of disorder, theft, prostitution, and lethal violence (see Harocopos and Hough 2005). These issues may drive the similar perceived impact of these offenses.

Finally, officers reported the following crime types as the most severe: child pornography and sexual solicitation and physical and cyber terrorist attacks. Though there are clear and significant threats posed by virtual and real world acts of terror, it is surprising that child offenses are perceived as having greater severity than terror attacks. The significant social stigma associated with child sex offenses (see Durkin 1997; Durkin and Bryant 1999; Holt et al. 2010) may, however, account of this ranking. Specifically, child victims can be easily taken advantage of, and coerced into acts due to their innocence and naïveté (Durkin 1997; Durkin and Bryant 1999). Regardless, these findings suggest that local law enforcement agencies perceive there to be significant overlap between virtual and terrestrial crimes.

In addition, the respondents were asked to indicate the frequency with which certain computer crimes take place, ranging from never (1) to very frequently

(6). The mean scores for the frequency of each offense are presented in Table 7. The high mean scores suggest that local agencies feel computer crimes occur with some regularity, with acts of cyber-terror performed least often (4.58). Electronic theft and viewing data without permission are also perceived to occur with some frequency, which may be a reflection of the increasing investigation of these offenses at the state and local level (see Burns et al. 2004). The perceived prevalence of harassment and malware infections may be a consequence of increasing media and research coverage which suggest these offenses are increasing yearly (see Bossler and Holt 2010; Finn 2004; Holt and Bossler 2009; Taylor et al. 2010).

Table 7. Perceived Frequency of Computer Crimes

Offense Type	Mean Frequency	N
Terrorist attacks against electronic targets (cyber-terror)	4.58	359
Viewing someone else's electronic data without permission	4.83	359
Electronic theft of money from accounts	4.96	358
Harassment over the Internet	5.10	358
Viruses and malicious software infection	5.11	359
Child pornography and sexual solicitation	5.35	359
Unauthorized copying of software	5.38	359
Unauthorized copying of media	5.54	359

Respondents ranked the most common forms of computer crime to be software and media piracy. Empirical research on digital piracy suggests this is a prevalent offense that cuts across race, age, and economic conditions (see Higgins 2005; Higgins, Fell, and Wilson 2007; Hinduja 2001, 2003; McQuade 2006; Wall 2007). Thus, state and local agencies appear to have a perspective on computer crime that conforms to the broader research literature on computer offending generally.

Respondents were also asked to assess the threat of cyberterror attacks posed by various countries on a scale from least serious (1) to most serious (5) (see Table 8). The countries selected for this inventory were based in part on reports from various media and research on national participation in computer crime and attacks against military and private targets (see Brenner 2008; Holt,

Table 8. Perceived Threat of Cyberterror Attacks from Multiple Nations

Country	Mean Frequency	N
Brazil	2.91	357
Egypt	3.22	353
Afghanistan	3.33	355
Romania	3.33	357
Japan	3.36	356
Iraq	3.45	356
Russia	3.74	356
Iran	3.92	356
China	4.32	359

Soles, and Leslie 2008; Taylor et al. 2010). Additionally, a number of Middle Eastern nations were included as controls since they have limited participation in actual cyber-attacks, but heavy participation in e-jihad as a means of recruitment and information sharing for terror groups (see Brenner 2008; Taylor et al. 2010).

Brazil was ranked the least threatening nation overall by respondents. This could be a reflection of a lack of knowledge about the hacking landscape in Brazil, or a more general consequence of the fact that Brazilian hackers regularly target South American financial institutions and customers rather than those in other nations (Taylor et al. 2010). Egypt, Afghanistan, Romania, Japan, and Iraq were all considered moderate threats. It appears that some of the countries in this group might be viewed as threats more because of the war on terrorism and law enforcement perceptions that these countries desire to attack the United States rather than their actual ability to strike critical infrastructure.

Russia was ranked as a high threat, but placed below Iran. Russian hackers have engaged in a variety of attacks against US financial institutions and critical infrastructure (see Holt et al. 2008; Honeynet Research Alliance 2003) as well as cyber-attacks against neighboring nations, such as Estonia and Georgia (Brenner 2008; Jaffe 2006; Landler and Markoff 2008). Few, if any, attacks have been attributed to Iran. Thus, this threat ranking appears to stem from regular reports about the nuclear threat posed by Iran and its posturing toward other nations around the world. Finally, China was ranked as the highest overall threat in keeping with multiple media reports of high level intrusions by Chinese hackers into sensitive networks in governments around the world (Holt et al. 2008; Taylor et al. 2010). Thus, local and state law enforcement agencies appear to share some perspectives on the broader landscape of cyberthreats, but also appear to assign too high of threats to countries based more on the desire to attack the United States than their ability to complete such an intrusion.

Awareness of Technology

To gain some perspective on state and local officers' knowledge of computer technology and offending, respondents were presented with various technology-specific terms and asked to identify whether they were familiar with the term, unsure of its meaning, or had never heard it before (see Table 9). The findings indicate that most respondents felt that they knew the meanings of many essential terms needed to understand both basic computing software and computer crimes. A majority of the officers reported knowledge of the terms spam,

Table 9. Knowledge of Terms Related to Computer
Technology and Computer Crime

Term	I have a good idea what this term means	Not really sure what this term means	I have never heard this term
Identity theft	98.6	1.1	0.3
Viruses	97.7	2.3	0.0
Spam	96.6	3.4	0.0
Firewall	95.5	4.5	0.0
Spyware	93.8	5.9	0.3
Cookies	89.8	8.8	1.4
Cyberstalking	85.2	13.7	1.1
Phishing	79.3	13.1	7.7
Adware	78.3	17.7	3.9
Podcasts	65.4	28.6	5.9
Carding	18.9	44.5	36.6

firewall, spyware, and cookies. This is sensible given that these terms are commonly used with regard to the Internet and computer security as a whole (Taylor et al. 2010; Wall 2007). There was, however, less recognition for the terms Adware and podcast. Thus, state and local agencies have a grasp of the basic terms that support web browsers and Internet use.

Respondents also appeared to be familiar with most terms related to either a type of computer crime or an attack tool. For example, identity theft, virus, and cyberstalking were identified by most respondents. The reported knowledge of identity theft and cyberstalking may be related to the prevalence of investigations at the local level and in media accounts. Phishing, where criminals attempt to obtain financial information from unwitting victims via email (James 2005), was identified by fewer officers (79 percent). The one item most respondents did not know was "carding," where individuals buy and sell stolen personal information for the purposes of fraud and theft (Holt and Lampke 2010; Honeynet Research Alliance 2003). This may be a consequence of the relatively recent emergence of this crime and that it is mostly investigated by federal agencies due to the international scope of these offenses. Regardless, these findings suggest that local policing officers have a strong awareness of computer crime terms and that their knowledge has increased over the last decade (Goodman 1997).

In addition, respondents appeared to have some recognition of terms related to cyber-terrorism (see Table 10). Many of the respondents knew the term "critical infrastructure," which is a positive finding given the prominence

Table 10. Knowledge of Terms Related to Computer
Technology and Computer Crime

Term	I have a good idea what this term means	Not really sure what this term means	I have never heard this term
People's Liberation Army	78.5	17.8	3.7
Critical Infrastructure	77.3	15.3	7.4
E-jihad	70.5	20.2	9.4
Information Warfare	47.6	40.8	11.5
Firesale	34.7	43.8	21.5

of this phrase in recent years related to physical terror attacks (see Taylor et al. 2010). Most respondents had also heard of the People's Liberation Army and the term "e-jihad." This is encouraging since these phrases are related to two distinct groups involvement in cyberterror. The People's Liberation Army, the name of the Chinese military, is responsible for several serious computer intrusions against Department of Defense computer networks, power grids, and other systems (Brenner 2008). E-jihad is a phrase related to the development of terror groups' usage of the internet for various activities, from recruitment to misinformation to attacks against different targets (see Brenner 2008; Taylor et al. 2010).

Knowledge of the term "information warfare" was much lower, with less than half of all respondents recognizing this word. The phrase "information warfare" is primarily used in the military community to represent any behavior involving the use of or gathering of information to gain advantage over another party (see Taylor et al. 2010). This can include acts of cyberterrorism or data theft, and comprises a significant potential overlap between law enforcement practices and military activity. The relative concentration of this term among military actors may, however, account for the lack of awareness in state and local law enforcement agencies. Finally, the term "firesale" was included as a control because it is not a phrase used in the academic or policing communities. Instead, this term is used in popular media to describe a cataclysmic series of cyberattacks. Since only 34.7 percent of respondents knew this term, it appears that the respondents have not been significantly swayed by media accounts of cyberterror attacks. Taken as a whole, the respondents appear to have some sound understanding of key phrases related to cyberterror as well as computer crime generally.

Discussion and Conclusions

Despite the increasing body of research on computer crime offending and victimization, few studies have considered the capacity of local law enforcement agencies to investigate and combat these crimes (see Burns et al. 2004; Hinduja 2004; McQuade 2006; Senjo 2004; Stambaugh et al. 2001; Taylor et al. 2010). This study attempted to address this issue through an examination of 437 state and local law enforcement agents and officers to understand their investigative capabilities and perspectives on computer crime. As a whole, the findings suggest that law enforcement agencies have shifted their investigative resources to become more actively involved in financial offenses than in the past (see Burns et al. 2004; Hinduja 2004; Senjo 2004; Stambaugh et al. 2001). While local agencies are still investigating sex offenses, there were more agencies suggesting they investigate economic-driven computer crimes. Such a finding is a positive indicator, given the tremendous economic impact of computer-based fraud for businesses and individuals alike (Internet Crime Complaint Center 2010; Newman and Clarke 2003; Wall 2007).

At the same time, the lack of agencies investigating computer hacking and intrusions is in keeping with previous research on policing (see Hinduja 2004; Stambaugh et al. 2001). This may, however, be a function of limited resources and jurisdictional issues that complicate reporting and proper exploration (Brenner 2008; Taylor et al. 2010; Wall 2007). Additionally, the relative paucity of cleared and active cases involving both computer crimes and digital evidence indicate that these offenses are relatively underexamined at the local level (see Hinduja 2004). This exploratory finding, however, demands greater research, and emphasizes the need for improved statistical reporting to better comprehend the problem of computer crime (Brenner 2008; Hinduja 2004; Holt 2003; Wall 2007).

The attitudinal results suggest that state and local law enforcement may have improved their situational awareness and preparation to deal with computer crime cases. Specifically, local agencies have an increased overall recognition of the serious threat computer crimes pose. Additionally, the mixed agreement surrounding victim impact indicates that police officers may understand that certain offenses, such as hacking or fraud, may have a greater impact for businesses, while stalking could impact individuals more heavily. Finally, the respondents' significant agreement with the need for increased funding to support the investigation suggests that there is a need for greater resource allocation to improve the local response to computer crimes (Hinduja 2004; Stambaugh et al. 2001).

The perceived severity of computer offending relative to street crimes also gives some valuable insights into the nature of computer crime investigation. The relatively low significance of minor theft and piracy suggests that these offenses may have minimal priority among law enforcement agencies. This could be a function of the lack of victims or the underreporting of these offenses, particularly piracy where there is no distinct or immediate individual affected (see Hinduja 2001). The relatively high severity of malware is also a positive finding, as malware can be used in a variety of ways by computer hackers and attackers to engage in different forms of crime (see Bossler and Holt 2009; Brenner 2008; Taylor et al. 2010). Additionally, the noted severity of both physical and computer-based terror attacks suggests that state and local agencies understand the need to reorient some of their priorities in order to act as first responders to serious incidents, particularly in the wake of the 9/11 attacks (see Brenner 2008). Finally, the extremely high placement of child pornography is in keeping with previous research (see Senjo 2004) and reflects the social concerns surrounding this type of offense (see Holt et al. 2010).

Additionally, the noted variation in knowledge of various computer technology and crime terms indicates that law enforcement officers have some awareness of the resources that undergird the Internet and web browsers. In addition, the recognition of the more prominent forms of computer crime, including spam, phishing, and cyberstalking, provides some support for an improved response to computer crime at the local level. The fact that most officers ranked Russia and China as the greatest threats toward US critical infrastructure is also instructive, as this idea has been promulgated in both research and popular media (see Brenner 2008; Denning 2001; Holt et al. 2008; McQuade 2006; Taylor et al. 2010; Wall 2007). Thus, local agencies appear to have some grounding in the threats and problems operating in virtual environments today.

Taken as a whole, this study indicates an improvement in state and local law enforcement responses and training to deal with various computer crimes. In the years following the recommendations made by the National Institute of Justice report (Stambaugh et al. 2001), it appears that there is greater recognition of the problem of computer crime among first responders. The preliminary and exploratory nature of these findings, due to the response rate, however, clearly requires replication to be verified and validated. We caution others not to make strong conclusions from our findings, but rather examine the trends found. In addition to increasing the size and representativeness of the sample, future researchers will want to compare and contrast line officers with little to no training in digital forensics and computer crime investigation with officers who have more extensive training. Finally, sampling managers within law enforcement agencies is needed to consider the acceptance and knowledge of individuals who control the economic and procedural dynamics within state and local agencies. Such research can provide critical information on the greater landscape of law enforcement and their ability to adapt and respond to the growing problem of computer crime in modern society.

References

Aeilts, Tony. "Defending against cybercrime and terrorism," *FBI Law Enforcement Bulletin* 74 (2005): 14–20.

Berson, Ilene R. "Grooming cybervictims: The psychosocial effects of online exploitation of youth," *Journal of School Violence* 2 (2003): 5–18.

Bossler, Adam M., and Thomas J. Holt. "On-line activities, guardianship, and malware infection: An examination of routine activities theory," *International Journal of Cyber Criminology* 3 (2009): 400–420.

Brenner, Susan W. *Cyberthreats: The Emerging Fault Lines of the Nation State.* New York: Oxford University Press, 2008.

Bureau of Justice Statistics. *Census of State and Local Law Enforcement Agencies, 2004.* Washington, DC: Government Printing Office, 2007.

Burns, Ronald G., Keith H. Whitworth, and Carol Y. Thompson. "Accessing law enforcement preparedness to address Internet fraud," *Journal of Criminal Justice* 32 (2004): 477–493.

Computer Security Institute. *Computer Crime and Security Survey, 2008.* Accessed June 3, 2009. http://www.cybercrime.gov/FBI2008.pdf.

Denning, Dorothy E. "Activism, hacktivism, and cyberterrorism: The Internet as a tool for influencing foreign policy." In *Networks and Netwars: The Future of Terror, Crime, and Militancy*, eds. John Arquilla and David F. Ronfeldt, 239–288. Santa Monica, CA: Rand 2001.

Durkin, Keith F. "Misuse of the Internet by pedophiles: Implications for law enforcement and probation practice," *Federal Probation* 61 (1997): 14–18.

Durkin, Keith F., and Clifton D. Bryant. "Propagandizing pederasty: A thematic analysis of the on-line exculpatory accounts of unrepentant pedophiles," *Deviant Behavior* 20 (1999): 103–127.

Finn, Jerry. "A survey of online harassment at a university campus," *Journal of Interpersonal Violence* 19 (2004): 468–483.

Furnell, Steven. *Cybercrime: Vandalizing the Information Society.* Boston: Addison-Wesley, 2002.

Goodman, Marc D. "Why the police don't care about computer crime," *Harvard Journal of Law and Technology* 10 (1997): 465–494.

Harocopos, Alex, and Mike Hough. "Drug dealing in open-air markets," *Problem-Oriented Guides for Police* No. 31. Washington D.C.: U.S. Department of Justice Office of Community Oriented Policing Services, 2005.

Higgins, George E. "Can low self-control help with the understanding of the software piracy problem?" *Deviant Behavior* 26 (2005): 1–24.

Higgins, George E., Brian D. Fell, and Abby L. Wilson. "Low self-control and social learning in understanding students' intentions to pirate movies in the United States," *Social Science Computer Review* 25 (2007): 339–357.

Hinduja, Sameer. "Correlates of Internet software piracy," *Journal of Contemporary Criminal Justice* 17 (2001): 369–382.

Hinduja, Sameer. "Trends and patterns among software pirates," *Ethics and Information Technology* 5 (2003): 49–61.

Hinduja, Sameer "Perceptions of local and state law enforcement concerning the role of computer crime investigative teams," *Policing: An International Journal of Police Strategies & Management* 27 (2004): 341–357.

Holt, Thomas J. "Examining a transnational problem: An analysis of computer crime victimization in eight countries from 1999 to 2001," *International Journal of Comparative and Applied Criminal Justice* 27 (2003): 199–220.

Holt, Thomas J. "Subcultural evolution? Examining the influence of on- and off-line experiences on deviant subcultures," *Deviant Behavior* 28 (2007): 171–198.

Holt, Thomas J., and Kristie R. Blevins. "Examining sex work from the client's perspective: Assessing johns using online data," *Deviant Behavior* 28 (2007): 333–354.

Holt, Thomas J., Kristie R. Blevins, and Natasha Burkert. "Considering the pedophile subculture on-line," *Sexual Abuse: Journal of Research and Treatment* 22 (2010): 3–24.

Holt, Thomas J., and Adam M. Bossler. "Examining the applicability of lifestyle-routine activities theory for cybercrime victimization," *Deviant Behavior* 30 (2009): 1–25.

Holt, Thomas J. and Danielle C. Graves. "A qualitative analysis of advanced fee fraud schemes," *The International Journal of Cyber-Criminology* 1 (2007): 137–154.

Holt, Thomas J. and Eric Lampke. "Exploring stolen data markets on-line: Products and market forces," *Criminal Justice Studies* 23 (2010): 33–50.

Holt, Thomas J., Joshua B. Soles, and Lyudmila Leslie. "Characterizing malware writers and computer attackers in their own words," Proceedings of the 2008 International Conference on Information Warfare and Security, Peter Kiewit Institute, University of Nebraska Omaha.

Honeynet Research Alliance. "Profile: Automated Credit Card Fraud," *Know Your Enemy Paper* series, 2003. Accessed July 20, 2008. http://www.honeynet.org/ papers/profiles/cc-fraud.pdf.

Internet Crime Complaint Center. *IC3 2009 Internet Crime Report.* Accessed March 24, 2010. http://www.ic3.gov/media/annualreport/2009_IC3Report.pdf.

Jaffe, Greg. "Gates Urges NATO Ministers To Defend Against Cyber Attacks," *The Wall Street Journal On-line.* June 15, 2006. Accessed July 19, 2007. http://online.wsj. com/article/SB118190166163536578.html?mod=googlenews_wsj.

James, Lance. *Phishing Exposed.* Rockland: Syngress, 2005.

Jewkes, Yvonne, and Keith Sharp. "Crime, deviance and the disembodied self: transcending the dangers of corporeality," In *Dot.cons: Crime, deviance and identity on the* Internet, ed. Yvonne Jewkes, 1–14. Portland, OR: Willan Publishing, 2003.

Jordan, Tim, and Paul Taylor. "A Sociology of Hackers," *The Sociological Review* 46 (1998): 757–80.

Krejcie, Robert V. and Daryle W. Morgan. "Determining sample size for research activities," *Educational and Psychological Measurement,* 30 (1970): 607–610.

Landler, Mark and John Markoff. "Digital Fears Emerge After Data Siege in Estonia," *The New York Times*, May 24, 2007. Accessed July 17, 2009. www.nytimes.com/2007/ 05/29/technology/29estonia.html.

Mann, David, and Mike Sutton. "Netcrime: More change in the organization of thieving," *British Journal of Criminology* 38 (1998): 201–229.

McQuade, Sam. "Technology-enabled crime, policing and security," *Journal of Technology Studies* 32 (2006): 32–42.

Motion Picture Association of America. *2005 Piracy fact sheet.* Accessed December 12, 2007. http://www.mpaa.org/researchStatistics.asp.

Newman, Grame, and Ronald Clarke. *Superhighway robbery: Preventing e-commerce crime.* Cullompton: Willan Press, 2003.

Quayle, Ethel, and Max Taylor. "Child pornography and the Internet: Perpetuating a cycle of abuse," *Deviant Behavior* 23 (2002): 331–361.

Quinn, James F., and Craig J. Forsyth. "Describing sexual behavior in the era of the internet: A typology for empirical research," *Deviant Behavior* 26 (2005): 191–207.

Senjo, Scott R. "An analysis of computer-related crime: Comparing police officer perceptions with empirical data," *Security Journal* 17 (2004): 55–71.

Sharp, Keith, and Sarah Earle. "Cyberpunters and cyberwhores: prostitution on the Internet." In *Dot Cons. Crime, Deviance and Identity on the Internet*, ed. Yvonne Jewkes, 36–52. Portland, OR: Willan Publishing, 2003.

Soothhill, Keith, and Teela Sanders. "The geographical mobility, preferences and pleasures of prolific punters: A demonstration study of the activities of prostitutes' clients," *Sociological Research On-Line* 10 (2005). Accessed October 10, 2005. http://www.socresonline.org.uk/10/1/soothill.html.

Speer, David L. "Redefining borders: The challenges of cybercrime," *Crime, Law, and Social Change* 34 (2000): 259–273.

Stambaugh, Hollis, David S. Beaupre, David J. Icove, Richard Baker, Wayne Cassady, and Wayne P. Williams. *Electronic crime needs assessment for state and local law enforcement.* Washington, DC: National Institute of Justice, 2001. NCJ 186276.

Taylor, Robert W., Eric J. Fritsch, John Liederbach, and Thomas J. Holt. *Digital Crime and Digital Terrorism, 2nd edition.* Upper Saddle River, NJ: Pearson Prentice Hall, 2010.

Wall, D. S. "Cybercrimes and the Internet," pp. 1–17 in *Crime and the Internet*, edited by D. S. Wall. New York: Routledge, 2001.

Wall, David S. *Cybercrime: The transformation of crime in the information age.* Cambridge: Polity Press, 2007.

Contributors

Dr. Michael Bachmann is an Assistant Professor in the Department of Criminal Justice at Texas Christian University. His research interests focus on the investigation of computer and high-tech crimes ranging from Internet piracy to cyber fraud and computer-focused crimes such as hacking and malicious code releases.

Brittany Smith-Bachmann is an Adjunct Professor in the Department of Criminal Justice at Texas Christian University.

Dr. Adam M. Bossler is an Associate Professor of Justice Studies at Georgia Southern University. He received his PhD in criminology and criminal justice from the University of Missouri-St. Louis. His research interests include testing criminological theories that have received little empirical testing, examining the application of traditional criminological theories to cybercrime offending and victimization, exploring law enforcement readiness for cybercrime, and evaluating policies and programs aimed at reducing youth violence.

Dr. Marjie T. Britz is a Professor of Criminal Justice at Clemson University. She holds a Bachelor's of Science in forensic science and police administration from Jacksonville State University and a Master's of Science and a Doctorate of philosophy in criminal justice from Michigan State University. She has published in the areas of computer crime, organized crime, and the police subculture. She has acted as a consultant to a variety of organizations and provided training to an assortment of law enforcement agencies. In addition, she has served on editorial and supervisory boards in both academic and practitioner venues. Her latest work on computer crime includes the second edition of *Computer Forensics and Cybercrime: An Introduction*. She is currently completing her latest manuscript on Italian organized crime in the United States and continuing her research on street gangs, cybergangs, terrorism, and transnational organized crime.

Dr. Heith Copes is an Associate Professor in the Department of Justice Sciences at the University of Alabama-Birmingham. His research interests include criminal decision-making as it relates to various types of illegal behavior, including drug distribution, automobile theft, and identity theft, and has been published in *Social Problems*, the *British Journal of Criminology*, and *Justice Quarterly*.

Sarah Fitzgerald is a PhD student in the School of Criminal Justice at Michigan State University. Her research interests include terrorism, qualitative research, and on-line crime.

Dr. Thomas J. Holt (Editor) is an Associate Professor in the School of Criminal Justice at Michigan State University specializing in computer crime, cybercrime, and technology. His research focuses on computer hacking, malware, and the role that technology and the Internet play in facilitating all manner of crime and deviance. Dr. Holt has been published in a variety of academic journals, including *Crime and Delinquency*, *Deviant Behavior*, and the *Journal of Criminal Justice*, and is a coauthor of the book *Digital Crime and Digital Terror*. He is the project lead for the Spartan Devils Honeynet Project, a joint project of Michigan State University, Arizona State University, and private industry, and a member of the editorial board of the *International Journal of Cyber Criminology*.

Dr. Kent R. Kerley is an Associate Professor in the Department of Justice Sciences at the University of Alabama-Birmingham. His primary research interests include corrections, religiosity, cybercrime, and intimate partner violence. His research has appeared in outlets such as *Justice Quarterly*, *Social Forces*, and *Social Problems*.

Dr. Pat Kinkade is an Associate Professor and Chair of the Department of Criminal Justice at Texas Christian University. He has published in a wide variety of criminological issues ranging from prison privatization and the death penalty to more eclectic areas of cultural criminology and fringe subgroups.

Dr. Catherine D. Marcum is an Assistant Professor in the Department of Government and Justice Studies at Appalachian State University. She has recently been published in the journals *Deviant Behavior, Criminal Justice Studies: A Critical Journal of Crime, Law, and Society, International Journal of Cyber Criminology*, and *Journal of Child Sexual Abuse*. Her research interests include cyber criminality, adolescent victimization, sexual offending and victimization, and corrections.

Dr. Johnny Nhan is an Assistant Professor in the Department of Criminal Justice at Texas Christian University. His research focuses on issues of cyber and high-tech crimes within the criminal justice and legal system.

Dr. Aunshul Rege is an Assistant Professor in the Department of Criminal Justice at Temple University. She recently completed her PhD in the School of Criminal Justice at Rutgers University. Her research interests include cybercrime and cybersecurity, with an emphasis on critical infrastructure, as well as environmental criminology and offender decision-making.

Dr. Marc Rogers is the director of the Cyber Forensics Program in the Department of Computer and Information Technology at Purdue University. He is a Professor, University Faculty Scholar, and Fellow—Center for Education and Research in Information Assurance and Security (CERIAS). Dr. Rogers is the International Chair of the Law, Compliance and Investigation Domain of the Common Body of Knowledge (CBK) committee, Chair of the Ethics Committee for the Digital and Multimedia Sciences section of the American Academy of Forensic Sciences, and Chair of the Certification and Test Committee-Digital Forensics Certification Board. He is the Editor-in-Chief of the *Journal of Digital Forensic Practice* and sits on the editorial board for several other professional journals. He is also a member of other various national and international committees focusing on digital forensic science and digital evidence. Dr. Rogers is the author of books, book chapters, and journal publications in the field of digital forensics and applied psychological analysis. His research interests include applied cyber forensics, psychological digital crime scene analysis, and cyber terrorism. He has authored several book chapters and articles in the area of computer forensics and forensic psychology.

Dr. Kathryn C. Seigfried-Spellar is an Assistant Professor in the Department of Criminal Justice at the University of Alabama. Her research interests include computer forensics, child pornography, pedophilia, and cybercrime profiling.

Sarah Turner is a Master's student in the Department of Justice Sciences at the University of Alabama-Birmingham.

Gary Warner is the Director of Research in Computer Forensics in the Department of Computer and Information Sciences at the University of Alabama-Birmingham. His research focuses on cybercrime investigation, phishing, malware, and cybercrimes generally.

Index

Advance Fee Fraud, 12, 84, 107
Al-Qaeda, 16, 167, 170, 173–178, 180
Anonymity, 5, 6, 82, 148, 167, 179, 225, 229
Australia, 124, 156, 178, 181, 185, 188, 200, 205

Bullying, 17, 21, 141–146, 148–150, 152–157

Canada, 10, 116, 119, 121, 174, 201, 216
Cell phone, 4, 15
Chat rooms, 70, 125, 144, 153, 156, 173, 175, 176
Child abuse, 24, 112, 114, 121, 129, 138, 206, 214, 243
Child pornography, 8, 14, 17, 22, 24, 109–141, 206, 209, 214, 216, 221, 223, 227, 232–234, 239, 243
    And the Krone Model, 122, 127, 128, 130
    And the Lanning Model, 122, 125, 127
    Law enforcement and, 4, 7, 9, 14, 16–18, 20, 25, 26, 58, 66, 69, 85, 106, 109, 111, 115, 125, 139, 140, 219–225, 230, 231, 233–243

New forms, 6
Technology and, 3–7, 11, 16, 17, 21, 30, 31, 34, 41, 46, 49, 61, 64, 68, 74, 75, 77–80, 107–110, 113, 120, 122–127, 136, 137, 146, 148, 154, 156, 167, 173, 176, 183–185, 191, 194, 195, 203, 204, 206, 214, 217, 220, 236, 237, 240, 241, 243
Children, 14, 15, 20, 26, 109–116, 119–121, 123, 125, 126, 130, 136–140, 144–147, 156, 157, 169, 180, 220, 228
China, 4, 66, 104, 181, 205, 235, 240
Computer hacker, 17, 34, 47, 54, 57, 216
Computer crime, 6, 7, 10, 11, 19, 21, 186, 216, 217, 219–243
Computer Viruses, 3, 7, 11
Combating Paedophile Information Networks in Europe (COPINE), 113
Council of Europe, 112
Credit card fraud, 12, 22, 109, 242
Critical Infrastructure, 160, 164, 191–192, 194, 196–198, 201–212
Cyberbullying, 21, 141–146, 150, 151, 153–156

Cybercrime, 6–11, 14–21, 25, 26, 54, 55, 57–59, 138, 141, 155, 160, 179, 184, 191–218, 223, 229, 240–243
    Typology of, 10, 11, 15, 16, 24, 85, 110, 124, 130, 138, 140, 203, 243
Cyberspace, 6–8, 14, 17, 20, 21, 23, 29, 49, 53, 54, 79, 107, 155, 156, 164, 185, 188, 189, 204, 212, 216
Cyberstalking, 18, 141–157, 207, 216, 219, 236, 237, 240
Cyberterror/Cyberterrorism, 8, 164–165, 220, 229, 234–235

Denial of Service attack, 9, 181, 200, 210
Digital evidence, 110, 138, 140, 183, 205, 220, 226–229, 239
Digital Pearl Harbor, 159, 160

Encryption, 10, 122, 127, 175, 189, 204
Evidence, 3, 5, 15, 110, 111, 120, 122, 127, 137, 138, 140, 146, 147, 175, 178, 182, 183, 185, 205, 220, 226–229, 239
Extremist, 18, 166, 168, 170–172, 174, 176, 177

Federal Bureau of Investigation, 7, 54, 77, 106, 185, 186
First Amendment, 151–153, 172
Forensics, 19, 127, 139, 140, 184, 240
Forum, 35, 167, 174, 214
Fraud, 4, 5, 8, 11, 12, 17, 19, 21, 22, 81–85, 104, 106–109, 160, 179, 187, 188, 216, 219, 221, 223, 227, 228, 237, 239, 241, 242
Free speech, 18, 34, 142, 151, 153, 154

Gender, 56, 87–90, 100, 149
Google, 73, 74, 82, 93, 106, 107, 173, 178

Hackers, 3, 5, 9, 11, 12, 17, 18, 22, 23, 29–36, 40, 41, 43–46, 49, 52–56, 58, 59, 67, 185, 189, 203, 206, 209–212, 214–216, 230, 231, 235, 236, 239, 242
    Ethics, 21, 76, 80, 241
    Illegal activities of, 141
    Motives of, 28, 48, 49, 189, 214
    Social organization, 6, 55, 76, 165
    Subculture, 17, 21, 29, 31, 38, 48, 52, 54, 55, 59, 70, 74, 242
    Typology, 7, 10, 11, 13, 15, 16, 24, 85, 110, 124, 127, 128, 130, 137, 138, 140, 203, 243
    White hat, 32, 33
Hamas, 167
Harassment, 15, 17, 18, 20, 141–144, 146, 147, 150, 154, 156, 160, 206, 215, 223, 227, 228, 232–234, 241
Hezbollah, 167
Honeynet Project, 214

Identity theft, 5, 6, 11, 12, 18, 83, 84, 109, 141, 160, 179, 223, 227, 228, 236, 237
Infrastructure (see also critical infrastructure), 8, 34, 43, 55, 159, 160, 174, 181, 187, 191, 192,

194, 197, 199–210, 212–217, 220, 221, 235, 237, 240
Innocent images, 113, 119
Instant Messaging, 15, 142, 146, 153
Intellectual Property, 24, 61, 62, 66, 73, 79, 160, 196, 198, 215, 216, 219
Internet, 3, 4, 6, 7, 11–16, 18–26, 28, 30, 35, 41, 43, 52, 54, 57, 59, 61, 62, 64–81, 83, 84, 86, 92, 104, 106–141, 144–148, 150, 152–156, 159–190, 194, 195, 203, 205, 210, 213–216, 219, 223, 226, 227, 229, 232–234, 237–243
Internet Crime Complaint Center, 12, 22, 83, 106, 107, 219, 233, 239, 242
Internet Service Providers, 72, 84, 86, 172
Investigation, 7, 10, 17, 19, 54, 77, 106, 110, 117, 121, 130, 139, 174, 182, 185, 186, 214, 220–222, 224, 226, 227, 231, 234, 239, 240

Law, 4, 7–9, 12, 14, 16–18, 20, 21, 24–26, 58, 61, 63, 66, 69, 71–73, 76, 80, 84, 85, 92, 106, 107, 109, 111, 112, 115, 117, 122, 125, 136–140, 150, 154–156, 159, 162, 172, 184, 188, 189, 208, 214, 216, 217, 219–243
Law enforcement, 4, 7, 9, 12, 14, 16–18, 20, 21, 25, 26, 58, 66, 69, 80, 84, 85, 92, 106, 107, 109, 111, 115, 117, 122, 125, 138–140, 219–243

Legislation, 8, 72, 73, 110, 142, 145, 149, 150, 153, 154, 159, 183, 222

Malicious code, 210, 211
Megan Meier, 142
MySpace, 142, 169, 171, 176

National Center for Missing and Exploited Children, 20, 26, 110, 139, 140, 147
Needs Assessment for State and Local Law Enforcement, 25, 140, 221, 243
Nigerian Email Scam (419 Scam), 20, 28, 100

Oliver Image Description Scale, 115, 116, 118

Passwords, 10, 196, 211
PATRIOT Act, 159
Internet and, 3, 4, 6, 11–16, 18–26, 28, 30, 35, 41, 52, 54, 57, 59, 61, 62, 64, 66–69, 72, 74–81, 83, 84, 86, 92, 104, 106, 108–116, 118, 120–122, 124–127, 131, 136–141, 145–148, 152–156, 159–161, 164, 166–170, 172–179, 181, 183–190, 194, 203, 213–216, 219, 226, 227, 232–234, 237, 239–243
Phishing, 12, 22, 24, 82, 85, 107, 108, 197, 236, 237, 240, 242
Piracy, 13, 17, 21–24, 61–80, 82, 219, 232, 234, 239, 241, 243

Police, 7, 9, 18, 70, 71, 140, 154, 186, 188, 189, 213, 214, 220, 221, 223, 225, 239, 241, 243

Pornography, 8, 13, 14, 17, 22, 24, 109–141, 206, 209, 214, 216, 220, 221, 223, 227, 232–234, 239, 243

Programmable Logic Controller, 5, 181, 193, 198

Prostitution, 14, 22, 24, 219, 233, 243

Risky online behavior, 149

Routine Activities Theory, 19, 63, 240

September 11, 19, 173, 185, 187, 189

Sex Trade, 14

Sex work, 21, 242

Situational Crime Prevention, 192, 206–207

Social Engineering, 84, 91, 177, 210

Social organization, 6, 55, 76, 165

Spam, 17, 26, 81–85, 88, 94, 105–108, 125, 128, 129, 197, 198, 236, 240

Stalking cyberstalking, 146–148, 150

Stuxnet, 5, 166, 181–183, 201,

Subculture, 17, 21, 29, 31, 38, 48, 52, 54, 55, 59, 70, 74, 242

Tamil Tigers, 167

Terrorism, 24, 25, 156, 159, 161–166, 183–190, 214, 217, 235, 240, 243

Testimony, 164, 185, 186

Theft, 5, 6, 8, 11–13, 18, 21, 62, 73, 83, 84, 107, 109, 141, 160, 164, 179, 199, 200, 215, 216, 219, 221, 223, 227, 228, 232–234, 236–239

TJX, 3, 19, 20, 24

United Kingdom, 104, 112, 121, 150, 172, 181

Violence, 15, 16, 18, 20, 116, 144, 150, 153–156, 161–166, 170–173, 184, 187, 189, 208, 213, 233, 240, 241

Virus, 9, 11, 149, 196, 203, 204, 211, 237

Wall, 3–7, 10–13, 15, 16, 21, 23, 25, 26, 57, 78, 81, 108, 216, 219, 227, 229, 233, 234, 237, 239, 240, 242, 243

Worms, 8, 11, 203, 210, 211, 217

Yahoo, 93, 149, 176

youth, 4, 18, 20, 22, 28, 53, 59, 138, 141–144, 147, 153, 155, 156, 206, 215, 240

YouTube, 143, 171, 173, 176, 177, 185, 195, 217